ALI

MUHAMMAD ALI

igloobooks

igloobooks

Published in 2014
by Igloo Books Ltd
Cottage Farm
Sywell
NN6 0BJ
www.igloobooks.com

Writen by Louise Spilsbury

SHE001 0714
2 4 6 8 10 9 7 5 3 1
ISBN 978-1-78440-324-9

Printed and manufactured in China

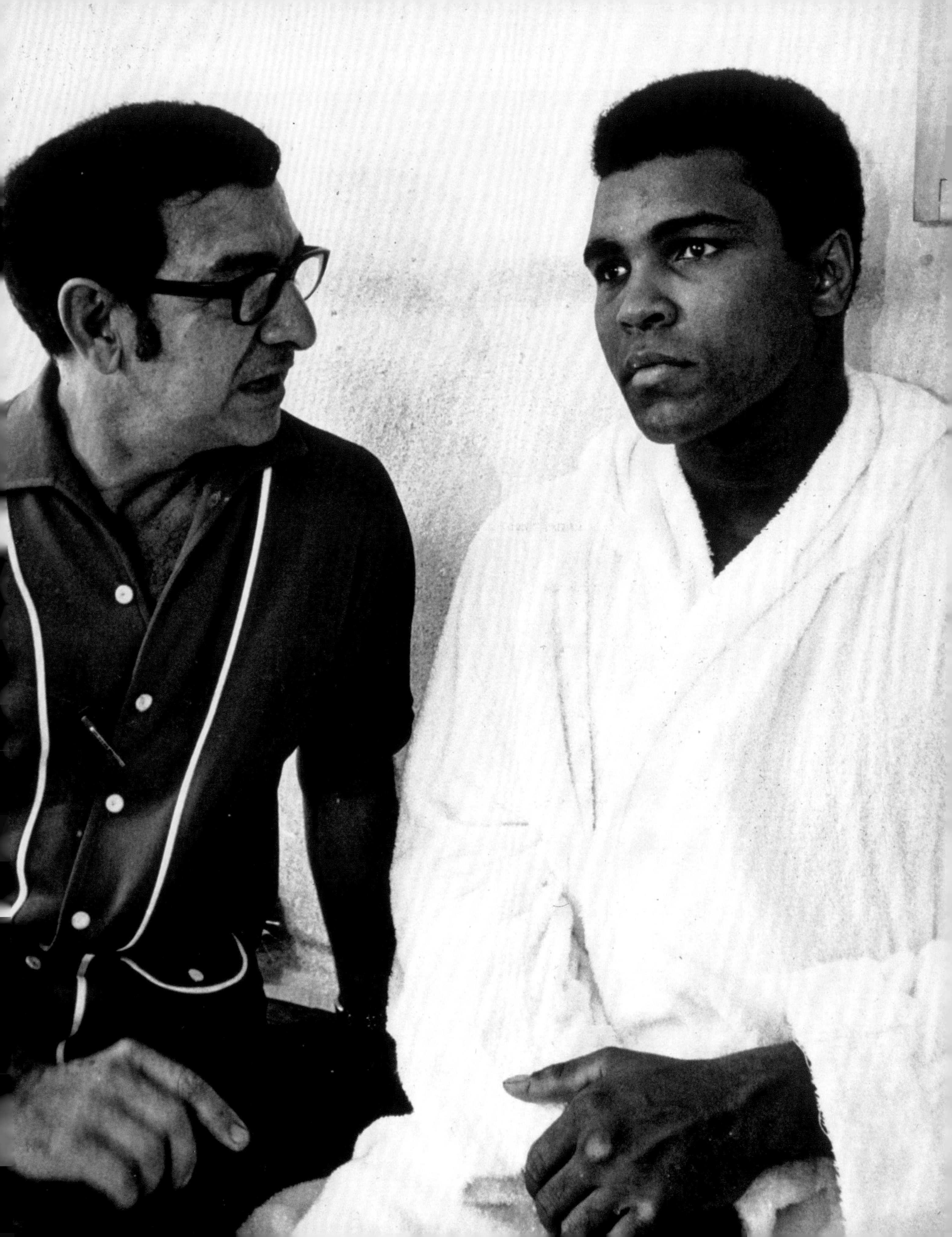

LISTON
ROUND

CONTENTS

MUHAMMAD ALI

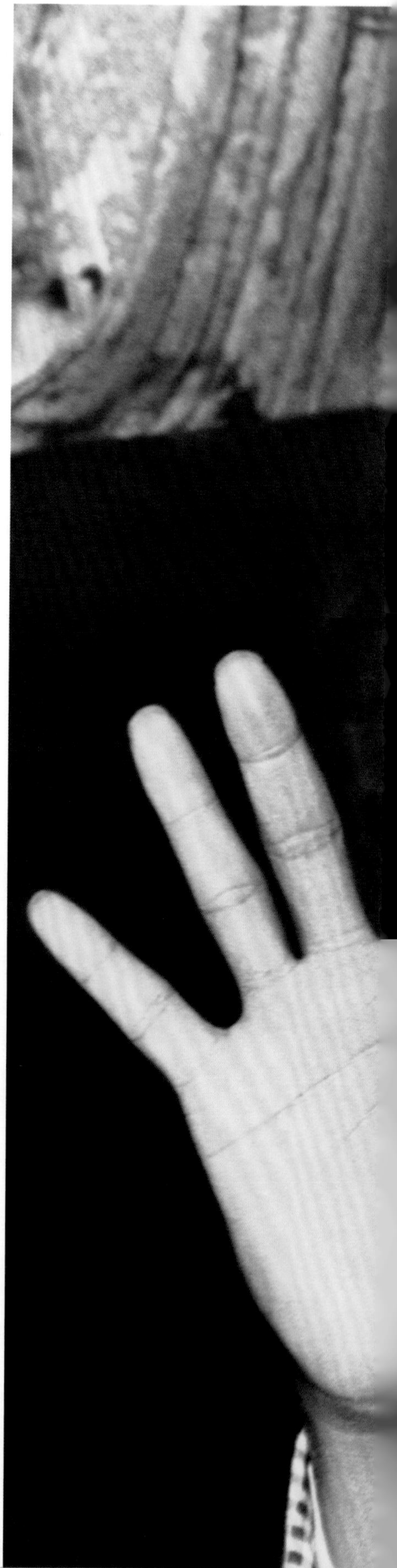

Muhammad Ali is probably the most famous boxer of all time and one of the most recognised athletes in the world. When he was still a skinny child with just one win under his belt, he started to boast about being the greatest, but he soon backed up his brash claims with ability, dedication and expertise, and proved them to be true. Ali was the first man to win the undisputed World Heavyweight boxing title three times and he beat more champions and top contenders than any other heavyweight champion in history.

At the height of his fame, Ali had it all. He was young, strong, handsome and charismatic. He enraged opponents and entertained fans with his arrogant proclamations and witty pre-match taunts. He lit up the ring with his quick reflexes, strong punches and unique fighting style: a style that went against many of the game's fundamental teachings. As well as being a sporting legend, Ali is almost as well-known for his actions outside the ring, as a thinker, poet and an artist.

The story of Muhammad Ali's long, successful life has all the drama, twists and turns of a movie script. His boxing career began with a chance encounter that would seem far-fetched if it weren't true. He wanted to be loved, but he never shied away from controversy. His conversion to Islam, his fights for civil rights, and his outspoken condemnation of and refusal to fight in the Vietnam War surrounded him with controversy for many years. Even after he retired from the ring, he stayed in the public eye through charitable work and humanitarian missions around the world. Muhammad Ali was and is simply a man no one could ignore.

"I am the greatest. I said that even before I knew I was."
Muhammad Ali

EARLY YEARS

Clay always called his mother "Mama Bird" because when he was young he said he thought she had a tiny, little bird nose. "I don't know why I thought that, because birds don't have noses, but from the moment I said it we all started calling her Mama Bird." Here he is seen fooling around with his mother in Pittsburgh, Pennsylvania, in 1963.

CASSIUS CLAY, JR

Muhammad Ali was born at 6:35 p.m. on 17 January 1942. At the first of many weigh-ins during his life, he was just 6 pounds, 7 ounces (2.92 kg). He was named Cassius Marcellus Clay, Jr., after his father, Cassius Marcellus Clay, Sr. His mother was Odessa Grady Clay. Two years after Cassius was born, his younger brother, Rudolph or Rudy (later Rahman Ali) joined the family.

All of Clay's four grandparents were free people, but his ancestors were slaves during the pre-Civil War era in the American South. Cassius Marcellus Clay, Sr. was named after Cassius Clay, the 19th century abolitionist who owned slaves but was also one of the first to set them free. Two of Cassius's paternal great-grandparents had been his slaves. His mother's paternal grandfather was Abe Grady, a white Irishman who emigrated to the United States soon after the Civil War and married a freed slave. Her maternal grandparents were a white man named Thomas Morehead and a slave.

Odessa was born in Kentucky, but moved to Louisville with her mother and siblings after her parents separated. Times were tough and she had to work to buy her own clothes so that she could go to school. She met Cassius's father when she was 16 years old. Cassius Marcellus Clay, Sr. was a muralist and painter, but earned a living painting billboards and signs. Odessa worked while the children were very young, as a house cleaner and a cook. The Clays weren't rich but they worked hard to bring up the boys in the best street they could afford. They lived at 3302 Grand Avenue, a small, four-roomed house in an all-black neighbourhood in Louisville, Kentucky. Clay remembered a mostly happy and loving home with his father always hugging and kissing him and Rudy, and his mother as a kind, gentle person.

Odessa Clay wipes down her son following a training bout in 1974. She was a calm, kind influence on him throughout her life.

CASSIUS AS A KID

As befits one of the world's great storytellers, there are many childhood tales about Clay. His mother started to call him 'GG' when he was a baby because that was the sound he made from his crib. When Clay became a Golden Gloves champion, he said of his first words, "You know what that meant? I was trying to say Golden Gloves." Odessa also used to tell people proudly that her eldest's first knockout punch was at six months old when he hit her and loosened two teeth so badly that she had to have them pulled out. Rudy remembered Clay asking his younger brother to throw rocks at him. However many rocks Rudy threw, he could never hit Clay. Even then Clay had some of the skills that would serve him so well in the ring, running left and right at speed, ducking, dodging, and weaving out of the way.

Odessa was a Baptist and Cash, as Clay Sr was known, was a Methodist but the boys always went to their mother's church. They never missed a morning of Sunday School and Clay remembered walking to church, knowing he looked handsome in his freshly ironed shirt and bow tie, and feeling proud of his pretty mother and handsome father. The Clays also instilled a sense of hard work in their boys. While Clay was at school, he worked at odd jobs to earn a few dollars a week and the boys used to accompany their father to work, where Cash taught them how to mix paint and lay out signs.

The Clays were a proud, contented family but not without problems. Cassius Clay Sr was arrested four times for reckless driving, twice for disorderly conduct and twice for assault. He had affairs and sometimes became violent when he was drunk. In fact, Odessa called the police three times when her husband turned nasty at home.

When Odessa Clay was taking her sons with her to church every Sunday, most churches, like this one, were segregated.

Postal Telegraph
HERE
WHITE
WAITING ROOM
5
4
3
2
CHATT

A DIVIDED CITY

Louisville was a quiet, peaceful city when Cassius Clay grew up in the 1950s and 1960s, but he became increasingly aware of the segregation around him. One of his first encounters with prejudice happened when he was very young, standing with his mother at a bus stop on a hot day. He was thirsty and when Odessa asked for a glass of water at a small diner nearby, the owner refused to help and closed the door in their faces.

Although he and Rudy didn't face real danger or violence in Louisville, as many people did in parts of the South, Clay was still shocked at being treated like a second-class citizen in the public realm, while being raised with pride and self-awareness at home. This was a time when laws known as Jim Crow Laws enforced segregation and made life difficult for African Americans. Louisville, like most cities, was a place where restaurants and swimming pools displayed signs that read 'Whites Only' and 'No Coloreds Allowed'. Black people had to go to separate schools, drink from separate water fountains and use separate restrooms. The boys never got into fights but white boys would call Clay and his brother 'nigger' and tell them to leave if they strayed into certain parts of town.

In spite of these challenges, Clay had a confidence and belief he was destined for great things from a young age. He remembers a time when, at about nine years old, he would wake up in the middle of the night and go outside to look at the stars and wait patiently for a message or a revelation from God. He never heard anything but never lost faith that a message would come.

In Clay's youth, segregation was a fact of life everywhere. There were separate waiting areas at bus stations (left) and separate entrances at theatres.

TURNING POINT

A message did come, but in the rather unlikely form of a local policeman named Joe Martin. In October 1954, when Cassius Clay was 12 years old, he and a friend cycled to the Louisville Home Show at Columbia Auditorium, mainly to sample the free food, popcorn and sweets on offer to visitors. When the boys had eaten their fill and were ready to leave, they discovered that Clay's bike had been stolen. Clay was furious and distraught – the bike was a new, red-and-white Schwinn that his parents had given him for Christmas. He was told to go and see a policeman, in the basement of the auditorium, who would fill out a police report for him.

Joe Martin was a Louisville cop who spent his spare time teaching boys to box for the city's recreation department in a gym, in the basement of the auditorium. When Clay burst in on Martin, the boy was crying and furious. He told Martin angrily that he was ready to search the whole state for whoever stole his bike and whip them soundly when he caught up with them. Martin asked if he knew how to fight. "No, but I'd fight them anyway," answered Clay. Martin replied, "Well, you better learn how to fight before you start challenging people that you're gonna whup," and gave Clay an application to join the gym, where boys could come and box every evening, Monday to Friday, from 6 p.m. to 8 p.m.

Call it chance or fate, this meeting was a turning point in Clay's life – everything changed when he entered the gym and started training. He began to learn the art and trade of boxing with a vengeance and would soon progress from a skinny kid with little talent into the greatest boxer that the world has ever known.

In this picture, taken at the gym in Louisville when he was just 12 years old, Clay looks young and vulnerable but his talent and training soon gave him the skills and confidence he needed to do more than strike the pose of a real boxer.

FROM AMATEUR TO OLYMPIAN

U.S.
U.S.A.

DETERMINATION AND DIET

A new boxing champion was born the first time Cassius Clay stepped into the gym. To make up for what he lacked in skill and experience, Clay had more than his share of determination and discipline. He began boxing with a vengeance. He spent all of his spare time training. He was the first one in the gym and the last to leave.

Clay trained six days a week and on school days he woke at four or five in the morning so that he could go running – what boxers call 'roadwork'. He was often seen racing city buses to school and was soon known by his peers as the kid who was obsessed with boxing. He took care about what he ate too, and over time, developed a special diet that included milk with two raw eggs in it for breakfast and a concoction of garlic and water that he drank throughout the day.

To go from skinny kid to Clay's strong boxing physique took relentless training and determination.

Joe Martin produced a popular local television show called 'Tomorrow's Champions' as part of the Columbia Gym's amateur programme. Boxing was important in Louisville and this Saturday afternoon show offered instant, local celebrity status to boxers. After just six weeks of training, Martin featured Clay on 'Tomorrow's Champions'. Thrilled at the prospect of being seen on television all over Kentucky, Clay trained even harder.

In his first ever televised bout, in 1954, he fought a local white boy named Ronny O'Keefe. Clay was only about 4 feet (1.2 m) tall and weighed just 89 pounds (40 kg), while O'Keefe was just a little older but bigger. The fight lasted three rounds of one minute each and Clay won by a split vote. From then on, Martin had him on the show each week. This was also the point at which Clay started bragging about being the greatest!

Clay's face shows the concentration and conviction he always had while training when he was young.

TOURNAMENTS AND TRAVEL

For the next few years, Clay continued to work and train hard, and to win the majority of the local fights. After 1958, he and other teenage boxers from the gym took part in boxing tournaments in different towns, including Indianapolis, Chicago and Toledo, staying in motels along the way. They were usually driven by Joe or his wife Christine Martin. Christine remembered young Clay as a very easy-going, polite boy who carried his Bible everywhere he went. She also recalled that in those days, the black kids were not allowed into restaurants, so she'd have to take their orders and get hamburgers for them to eat in the car.

By this time, Clay knew that he had a real talent for boxing and his dreams were going beyond earning enough to buy his parents a house and himself a fancy big car. Sometimes he would draw a picture of the back of a jacket with 'Cassius Clay, Golden Gloves Winner', or 'Cassius Clay, World Heavyweight Champ' written on it. Bob Surkein, an Amateur Athletic Union (AAU) referee and judge, recalled one tour in which Clay took all the sports sections from newspapers in a hotel shop and café so that he could cut out and keep all the pictures of himself.

Clay was also developing his own inimitable style. Instead of holding his hands up high to guard his head like most boxers, he held his gloves down low, and while most boxers stepped or ducked aside to avoid being hit, Clay leaned away from blows, risking throwing himself off balance. This unorthodox style worked for him because he had very fast reflexes and could throw a quick punch and dodge out of the way before other fighters could react. Soon, reporters, referees, and judges were talking about his presence and prodigious talent.

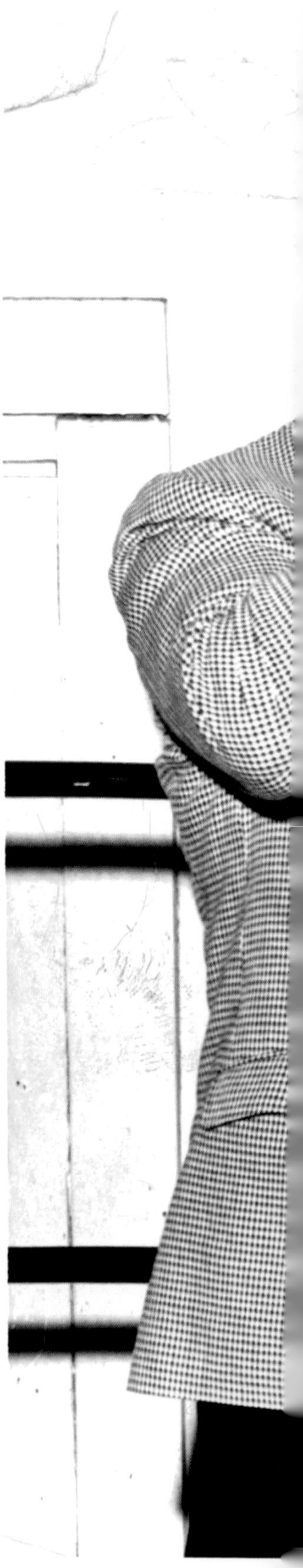

This is Clay in 1960 posing with Maxie Rosenbloom (left), Light Heavyweight Champion in 1932, and Solly Krieger (right), World Middleweight Champion in 1938.

Cassius Clay fighting against Gary Jawish during a Golden Gloves bout.

ON THE WAY TO THE OLYMPICS

Clay continued to train with Joe Martin and a more experienced coach named Fred Stoner. By the time he was 18 years old, he had fought a total of 105 amateur bouts, with 100 wins and just five losses. He won six Kentucky Golden Gloves Championships and two national Golden Gloves tournaments, in 1959 and 1960. He also won two national AAU titles.

This run of exciting wins had made Clay a local celebrity but he was yet to become really famous. This all changed when he was selected to represent the United States at the 1960 Olympic Games in Rome. Clay did well in the Olympic trials, but the trip to California for the trials was his first time on an aeroplane. It was such a rough flight that he declared he wouldn't fly again and that if he couldn't travel to Rome by train or boat, he wouldn't go at all. In the end he knew that if he wanted to be Heavyweight Champion of the world one day, he had to face his fears, so agreed to go but he bought a parachute from an army surplus store to wear on the flight!

Eighteen-year-old Cassius Clay raises his arm in victory after knocking out Gary Jawish in the 1960 Inter-city championships at Madison Square Garden.

When the Olympic team gathered in New York before the flight to Italy, Clay took the chance to try to meet one of his heroes, Sugar Ray Robinson. He waited all day outside Robinson's club but when the boxer finally appeared at ten o'clock and Clay stepped forward to talk to him, he remembers Robinson just patted him on the shoulder and said, "Later boy, I'm busy right now." Crushed, Clay vowed there and then that he would be different when he was a famous champion and that he would speak to, shake hands with or sign autographs for every fan he met.

At the Olympic Village, Clay stayed true to his vow and devoted attention not only to his training but also to meeting and greeting as many people as possible. He did as many interviews as he could and was often photographed. An unnamed team-mate said, "You would have thought he was running for mayor. He went around introducing himself and learning other people's names and swapping team lapel pins. If they'd had an election, he would have won in a walk." In fact, Clay even earned the nickname "the mayor of the Olympic Village".

Clay stands tall and proud wearing his gold medal for light heavyweight boxing in the centre of the winners' podium at the 1960 Olympic Games in Rome. On the right is Zbigniew Pietrzykowski of Poland who took silver. On the left are Giulio Saraudi of Italy and Anthony Madigan of Australia who took joint bronze.

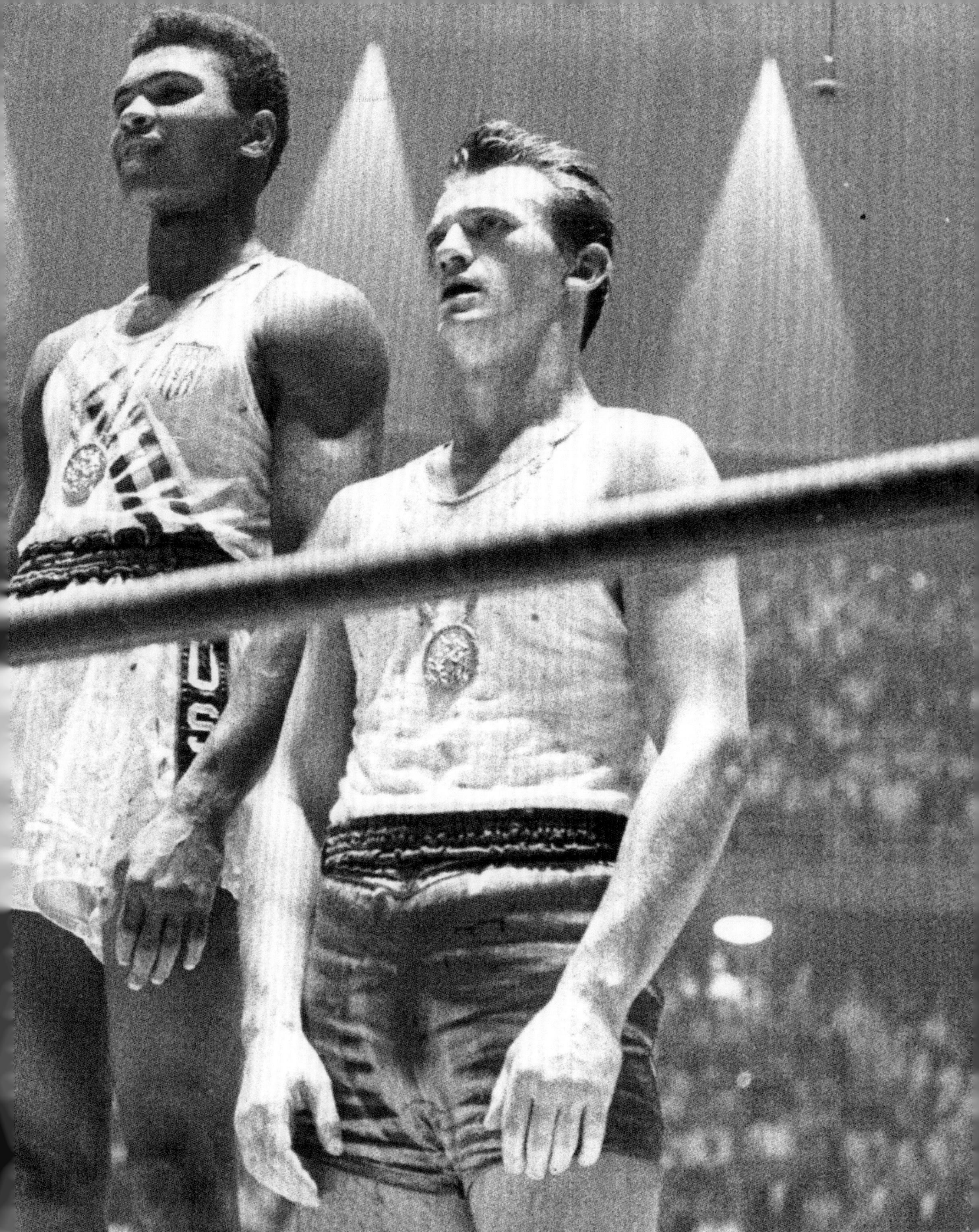

TAKING GOLD

Clay's opening fight was against the Belgian Yvon Becot. It was stopped by the referee in the second round. He then beat the Russian Gennadiy Shatkov, who had won the middleweight gold medal at the 1956 Games in Melbourne in a unanimous points decision. In the semi-final Clay won again in a unanimous decision against Australian opponent Tony Madigan. In the final battle for the light-heavyweight gold medal, Clay fought Zbigniew "Ziggy" Pietrzykowski, an older, stronger and more experienced opponent. The first round didn't go well, with Clay taking some serious punches. The second went a little better, as he managed to throw four hard rights to Pietrzykowski's head, but he was still behind on points. Clay came alive in the third and final round. He was quick, coordinated and displayed perfect timing, with a flurry of both left and right punches, almost winning by a knockout blow, but in the end taking the match on points.

A spokesperson for the US Olympic Committee told The Associated Press that Clay "is putting on an amazing performance. In the ring he murders 'em with his fists. Outside the ring he kills them with kindness and his solid Americanism."

When Clay returned to Louisville after a three-week absence he received a hero's welcome. Crowds cheered as he passed through the streets in a 30-car motorcade escorted by the police. At a celebration at his school, he was met by Mayor Bruce Hoblitzell, cheerleaders and about 200 friends and fans. The mayor, on behalf of the Louisville Chamber of Commerce, told him that his gold medal was the key to the city. Clay read aloud what would be his first published poem: 'How Cassius Took Rome'.

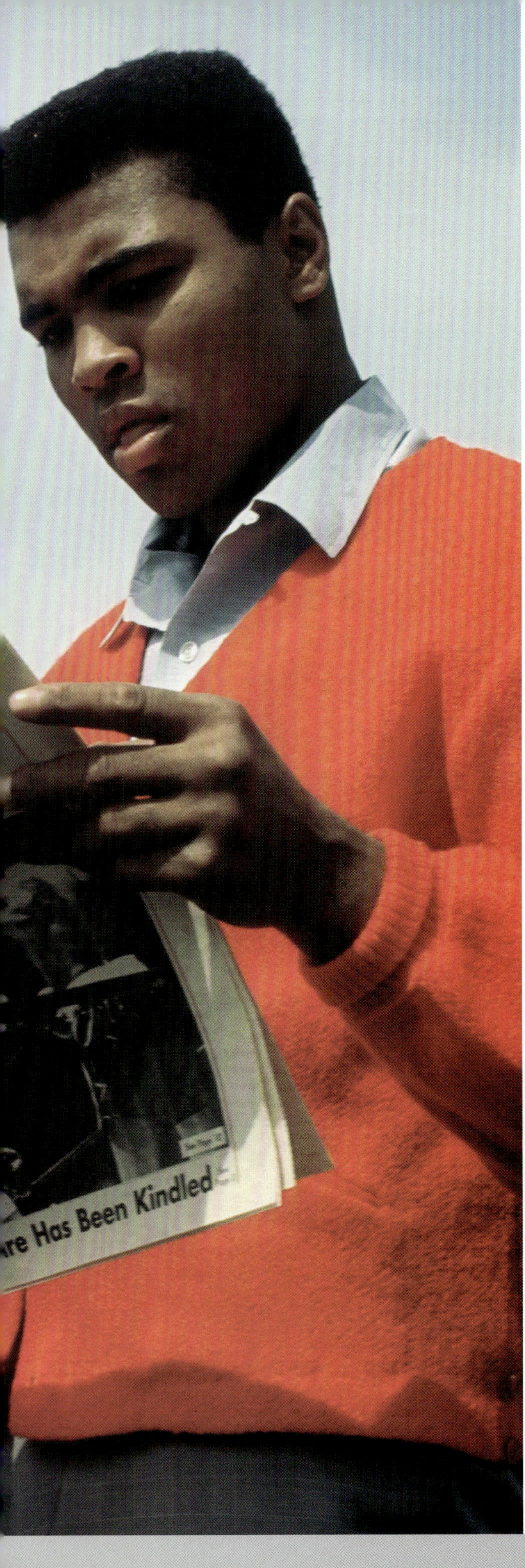

HOW CASSIUS TOOK ROME

To make America the greatest is my goal,
So I beat the Russians, and I beat the Pole,
and for the USA won the Medal of Gold.
Italians said, "You're Greater than the
Cassius of Old."
We like your name, we like your game.
So make Rome your home if you will.
I said I appreciate your kind hospitality,
But the USA is my county still,
'Cause they're waiting to welcome me
in Louisville.

Clay was so proud of his medal that he even wore it to bed. He believed that the medal could change more than his career prospects. Sadly, it didn't. Before he had left the Olympic Village, a Russian reporter had asked him how it felt to win the gold medal for his country when there were still restaurants in the United States that wouldn't serve him. He replied that there were qualified people working on that problem and to him, the United States was the best country in the world. However, when Clay returned and he and a friend were refused service at a local whites-only restaurant while he was wearing the Olympic medal round his neck, he was furious. Legend has it that his response was to angrily toss the gold medal straight into the Ohio River.

When he was young, Clay loved to read about his victories in the newspapers.

AMPRO

ALI'S PROFESSIONAL CAREER

THE CONTRACT

After the Olympics, Cassius Clay was possibly the hottest property in boxing. His earning potential was huge. This attracted the attention of investors in Louisville who were prepared to pay big bucks to get a piece of the action.

The first interested party was Billy Reynolds, a Louisville metals millionaire. Clay never signed the contract Reynolds offered owing to his father. Reynolds stipulated that Joe Martin should play a role in Clay's professional career but Clay Sr. disliked cops in general, and Martin in particular.

A consortium of white businessmen turned boxing enthusiasts quickly came up with a better deal. The prime mover in the Louisville Sponsoring Group (LSG) was Colonel Bill Faversham, who was Vice President, sales, of the Kentucky distillers responsible for Jack Daniels and other popular drinks. Faversham and his friends, horse breeder Pat Calhoun and tobacco magnate Bill Cutchins, reckoned on $25,000 to launch Clay professionally so they contacted some investor friends, asking, "How would you like to buy a piece of a prizefighter?" Pretty soon there were ten in the consortium, each putting in $2800.

On 26 October 1960, Clay signed the contract and became a professional boxer. His deal included a $10,000 bonus, a minimum annual salary of $4,000 for two years and $6,000 for four years. Everything Clay earned, in the ring or otherwise, was to be split 50–50 with the syndicate, who paid all expenses, from his trainer's salary to housing rent.

US boxing promoter and prime mover in the Louisville Sponsoring Group (LSG) Bill Faversham is shown here speaking with Clay in 1963.

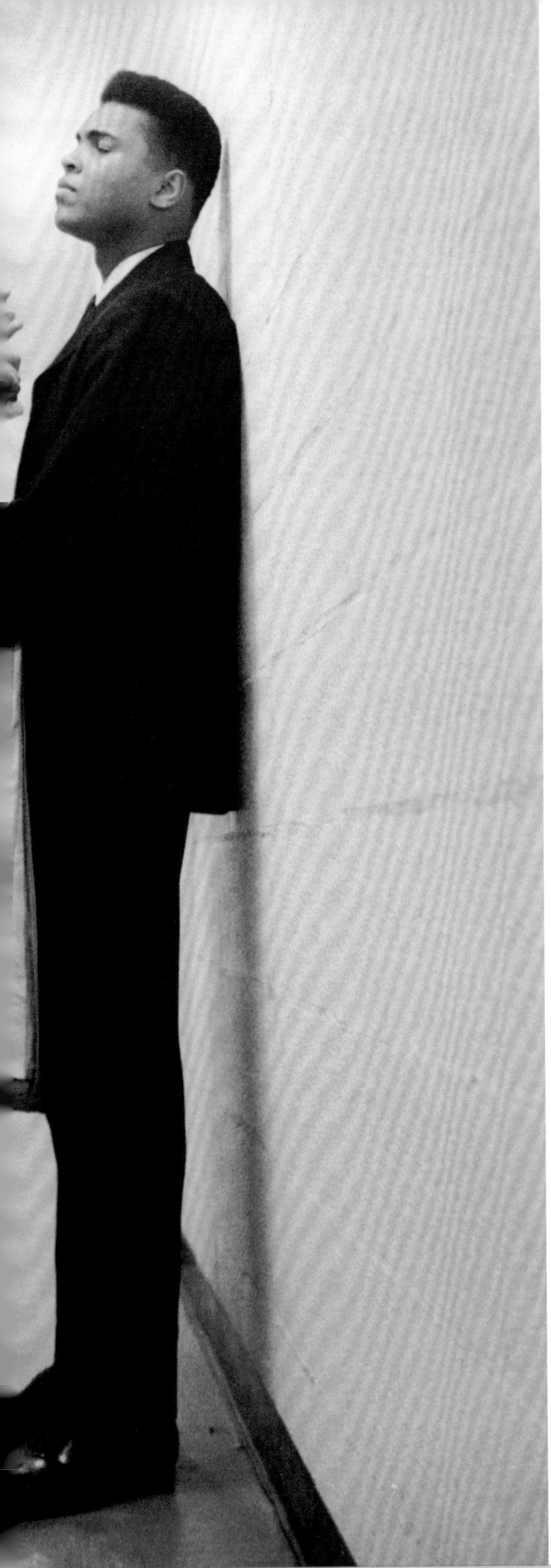

Clay celebrated the contract with a splurge: a pink Cadillac. He was soon cruising the streets of Louisville showing it off. In the following years the LSG became very rich from Clay's fighting, but also had to pay out a lot on anything from first class flights to the legal fees that kept Clay out of jail after speeding in the Cadillac.

Clay celebrated signing his first professional contract by buying a new Cadillac.

THE FIRST PRO BOUT

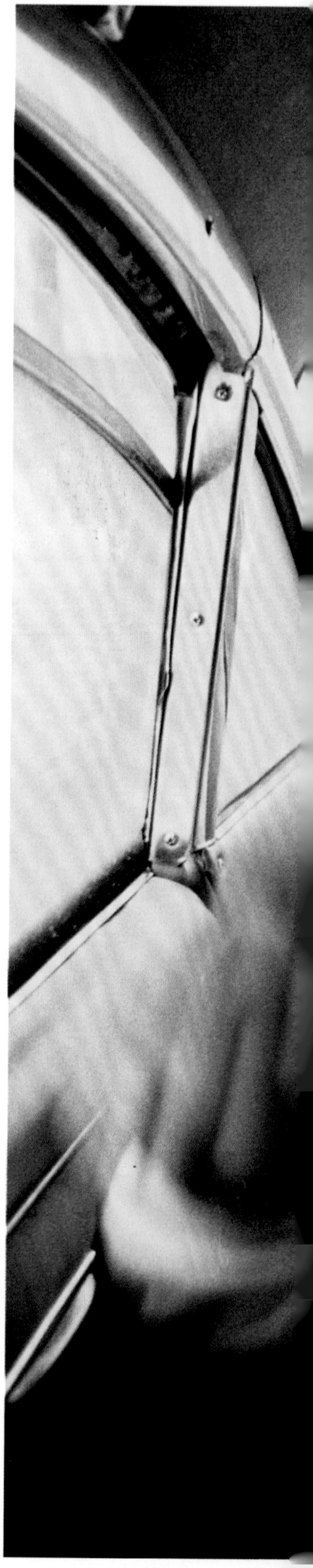

The LSG's official line was, "We are behind Cassius Clay to improve the breed of boxing, to do something nice for a deserving, well-behaved Louisville boy". They said they stepped in to make sure Clay was not prey to contracts with underworld mobsters. This was the case with the Heavyweight World Champion of the day: Sonny Liston. But the truth was that they knew Clay could make them richer. This was not just through their cut of his winnings in the ring, but also from sales amongst black boxing enthusiasts of the whisky and cigarettes they made and could advertise at Clay's fights.

Just three days after signing his contract, Clay fought his first professional bout. It had been organised over the preceding weeks by the LSG. Clay was to go up against one Tunney Hunsacker. Hunsacker was the 30-year-old chief of police of the little town of Fayetteville in West Virginia. Clay arrived at the Freedom Hall fight venue at the Louisville fairgrounds in his Cadillac. Hunsacker later recalled being 'pretty impressed' by the 'brassy young boy' and his entourage of supporters.

The police chief was a seasoned fighter who had fought more than 30 bouts. He soon realised that he was, "too old to be fighting an 18-year-old fella", once he got in the ring, even though he gave Clay, "some good chops to the stomach in the second and third rounds", that allegedly almost made the youngster bring up his hamburger dinner. However, Clay was too big and fast for Hunsacker, and had a trickily varied repertoire of punches. The six-round fight ended with a unanimous points decision for Clay and Hunsacker's eyes swollen shut. Clay was far from the finished article, but still gave the LSG cause for celebration that their investment was already paying dividends.

Clay's first professional bout against Hunsacker's was just the first on his road to success. At this point Cassius Clay knew he was going places.

Trainer Angelo Dundee was Clay's (Ali's) trainer from 1960 until the boxer retired.

A NEW TRAINER

In December 1960, the LSG syndicate made a move to back up their investment in Cassius Clay. They hired him a new trainer: Angelo Dundee. Dundee, based in Miami, had a great pedigree. He had trained 1955 World Welterweight Champion Carmen Basilio, and worked with title hopeful Willie Pastrano. Clay knew of Dundee because three years earlier, the 15-year-old boxer had stalked Dundee to a Louisville hotel, blagged a brief meet, and then quizzed Dundee for hours about all aspects of the boxing art.

Dundee quickly appreciated Clay's raw talents. The boxer was unusual in combining heavyweight power with the speed typical of the lighter divisions. Clay produced stinging jabs, usually to the head, that his friend and doctor Ferdie Pacheco called 'snake-licking'. But Dundee saw the faults, too. Clay often held his guard low and back-pedalled to evade punches. This could leave him off-balance or out of range for punching back, even with his long reach.

Dundee got to work. He further developed Clay's movement and balance. This was aided by sparring with Pastrano who was widely admired for his fleeting footwork. Dundee did not try to get rid of all the rough corners on his protégé. He once said, "Training fighters is like trying to catch fish," meaning that you have to go with what is already there.

The pair formed a close bond. Dundee was to remain as Clay's trainer through the coming years. His extraordinary abilities at training champions were sought by many other fighters, too. These included George Foreman, who in 1994, became the oldest Heavyweight Champion in history at the age of 45, and Sugar Ray Leonard who became World Champion in five different weight divisions.

Angelo Dundee was a brilliant motivator and was with Clay for virtually his entire career.

BOXER FOCUS: WILLIE PASTRANO

Wilfred Raleigh Pastrano was a pudgy child known as 'fatmeat' from the French Quarter in New Orleans. He took on a bully who was smacking him after his father, Frank, gave him the ultimatum: fight back or get a licking from me. Willie decided to take up boxing to lose weight at the suggestion of his friend Ralph Dupas. He went to the gym at night when there were fewer people around.

Pastrano lied about his age to fight his first professional bout when he was 15 years old and still at school. He was fined and had to remain amateur until he was 18. He started to spend summers in Miami at the training gym of Angelo Dundee, along with Dupas, who was a junior boxing champion. After high school, Pastrano moved to Miami where he further developed his fast hands and feet, and technical skills. In the early 1960s, Pastrano started to work with Dundee's new recruit, Cassius Clay.

Pastrano fought at heavyweight in the early professional years but with Sonny Liston rising to prominence, dropped down a division. In 1963, Pastrano's career had its high point. He won the Light Heavyweight World Championship, on a narrow points decision, against the overwhelming favourite Harold Johnson in Las Vegas. He only got the fight because other boxers had backed out. Pastrano defended the title twice, with unexpectedly hard hitting, before losing to José Torres in New York in 1965. This was when he retired. Pastrano by then was using drugs and had little money left. After working as nightclub bouncer and casino greeter, he eventually escaped the mean streets of Miami. He ran a municipal gym back in New Orleans where he trained many young fighters.

US heavyweight boxer Willie Pastrano training in 1958.

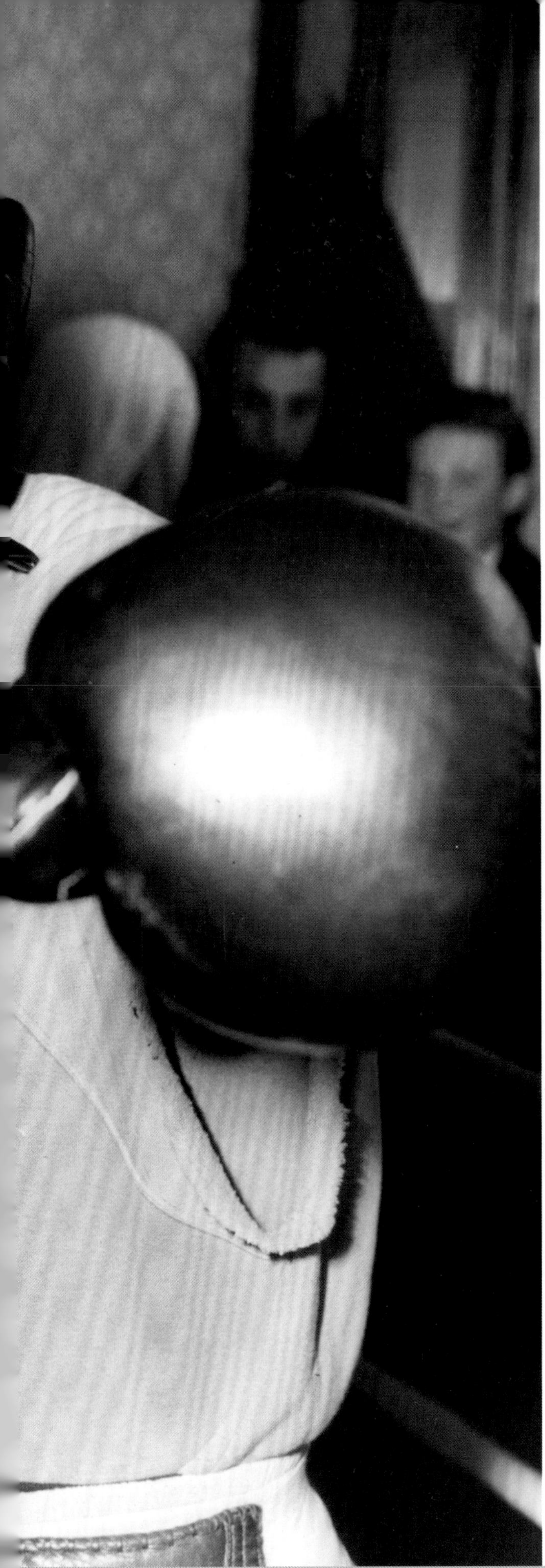

Pastrano held the World Light Heavyweight crown from 1963 until 1965.

STATISTICS

BORN	New Orleans (LA), November 1935
DIED	New Orleans (LA), December 1997
TURNED PROFESSIONAL	1950
NUMBER OF PRO BOUTS	84
WINS-LOSSES-DRAWS	63-13-8
NUMBER OF KNOCKOUTS	14
RETIRED	1965

Clay showing why he earned the nickname 'The Louisville Lip' at a press conference after he signed to fight Sonny Liston in 1963.

THE LOUISVILLE LIP

In the early 1960s, Cassius Clay was morphing into the boxing personality that the world came to know. At this time across the United States, the Civil Rights Movement was hitting its stride. There was pressure from black people to remain quiet and modest, aware that the opposite traits might offend some whites and derail the movement for race equality. Clay was a proud, loud, arrogant black man, happy to tell anyone who was listening about his boxing gifts. He also knew what he said – the boasts and the taunts – could impact his opponents, which is why Angelo Dundee called him 'The Louisville Lip'. The next step was to hone his public persona.

A seminal figure in this was the professional wrestler, George Wagner, who in his late 20s was transformed from a jobbing wrestler into the personality Gorgeous George. He became one of the first wrestling stars of the early days of colour television. Gorgeous George looked dramatic with long, curled blonde hair and sparkly robes. He entered the ring with special entrance music and valets threw roses and sprayed perfume into the crowd. He bad-mouthed his opponents and boasted at his triumphs. Crowds cheered or booed him.

Clay went to see Gorgeous George in Las Vegas in 1961 and was star-struck with his persona. And so he mimicked the wrestler's swagger, without the costumes and perfume. He proclaimed phrases such as, "To beat me, you have to be greater than great," and, "I will be the youngest champion in history". Some older boxers, such as Joe Louis, cautioned Clay; some people hated his self-praise, but as his fights and victories notched up, it was becoming clear that Clay did have something to shout about.

Henry Cooper jokingly looks at Clay's scales during the weigh-in before their fight at the Arsenal Stadium, London, in 1966.

SPREADING REPUTATION

Between his professional debut in 1960 until early 1963, Cassius Clay fought 18 different opponents and he won each fight: 14 by knock-out or technical knock-out. He fought across the United States, from Miami and New York to Las Vegas and Los Angeles. His reputation was growing fast and boxing was more popular than ever before, buoyed by increasing television audiences and the clamour for tickets to live boxing bouts.

Clay occasionally faced adversity in the boxing ring. In February 1962, he faced Sonny Banks in his 11th professional bout. This was the first time that Clay was ever knocked over. Near the start of the bout, Banks threw a left hook to the jaw that sent Clay flying but he got straight up. Angelo Dundee saw then that Clay could not only take punches, but also come back stronger. "That's when I knew I had a guy with greatness. It was remarkable how he survived that one punch. God he was exciting." Clay went on to win inside four rounds.

Clay devised a game with Dundee around this time. He started to predict the outcome of fights – how many rounds it would last. A good example of this is his fight against Archie Moore later in 1962. Moore was an old professional champion who had briefly trained Clay after the Olympics, but Clay did not like his authoritarian style. He correctly predicted a fourth-round knock-out, chanting, '"Archie Moore... Must fall in four."

Cassius Clay reached an even wider audience by travelling to London in 1963 for his 19th fight and first overseas professional bout. He took on British Heavyweight Champion Henry Cooper in front of 55,000 people and, again, correctly predicted a win in five. But Clay was lucky – he was floored by a phenomenal left from Cooper. Clay struggled to get up, but was saved by the bell marking the end of the round.

Henry Cooper and Clay in action in 1966.

BOXER FOCUS: SIR HENRY COOPER

Henry Cooper and his twin George were born in London and grew up during the Blitz years of the Second World War when the city was under attack. The boys came from a boxing lineage. Their father was a good amateur boxer in the Royal Artillery, and their horse trader grandfather was a bare-knuckle fighter who could fight 20 rounds. Henry and George joined Eltham Boxing Club and moved through the amateur ranks in England. Cooper won 73 of 84 contests, including the Amateur Light Heavyweight Championship in 1952.

Cooper became a dominant force in British professional boxing. In 1959, he won both the British and Commonwealth heavyweight titles. Back then he was still living at home, sharing a bedroom with George. He moved out only in 1960 when he got married. In the mid-60s Cooper was becoming internationally known for his crushing left hook – his left fist was popularly known as 'enery's hammer'. Buoyed by his close loss to Clay in 1963, Cooper challenged for the world title in a rematch against Muhammad Ali in 1966. History repeated itself as Cooper lost again after swelling and persistent bleeding above the left eye where the skin was thin – his jagged brow did him no boxing favours.

Cooper remained British champion until his narrow defeat to Joe Bugner in 1971. He became a national celebrity following release of a popular autobiography, appearances on BBC's *A Question of Sport*, television advertising for Brut aftershave and flu jabs, and his dedication to charitable work. His fundraising bought 100 coaches enabling sick or disabled children to go on holiday. Henry Cooper was knighted in 2000.

British boxer Henry Cooper at a function with his old rival Muhammad Ali in 1984.

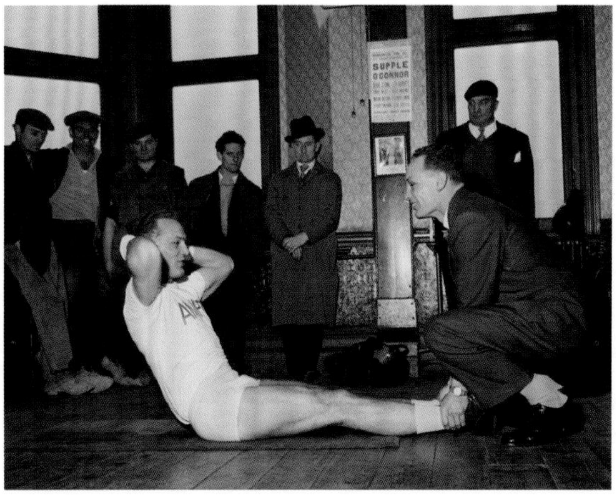

Henry Cooper and his brother George during a training session in 1958. Henry was preparing for a Commonwealth heavyweight title fight against Brian London.

STATISTICS

BORN	London, May 1934
DIED	London, May 2011
TURNED PROFESSIONAL	1954
NUMBER OF PRO BOUTS	55
WINS-LOSSES-DRAWS	40-14-1
NUMBER OF KNOCKOUTS	27
RETIRED	1971

WORLD CHAMPION

Joe

Cassius Clay talks up his chances of beating Sonny Liston at a press call before the fight in 1964.

GETTING A SHOT

In early 1964, boxing in the United States was massive. It had far more press coverage than basketball, tennis and athletics were still amateur-only sports and it was the quiet season for baseball and American football. Heavyweight was the most talked about boxing division. The two biggest stars in this division were the champion, Sonny Liston, and the young pretender, Cassius Clay.

The contrast between the two men fascinated the nation and the boxing world. Clay was handsome, eloquent and brilliant but his near defeat to Henry Cooper suggested he was an unfinished article. Liston, however, was a sullen and quiet, unstoppable force of nature.

Clay had had Liston in his sights for years and in 1964, thought he was ready. The boxers' handlers fixed a match for 25 February at Miami Convention Hall. In the run-up to the match, Clay trained hard in Miami, with the occasional break for press events including meeting the phenomenally popular Beatles, who were on tour. He also took time to plague Liston with taunts and boasts. At 3 a.m. outside Liston's rented Miami house, Clay parked a vehicle sign-written with 'Cassius Clay Enterprises' and shouted out that he was 'bear hunting' until the furious Liston ran out with a poker in his hand. At a press conference Clay read out a poem in which he imagined he'd punch Liston out of the ring:

"Who would have thought when they came to
the fight,
That they'd witness a launching of a human satellite.
Yes the crowd did not dream when they put down
their money
That they would see a total eclipse of the Sonny."

Clay noisily predicted he would knock out Liston in eight rounds. When reporters asked Liston how long Clay would last, he simply raised two fingers. The public antipathy between the men only pumped up expectations for the fight.

BOXER FOCUS: SONNY LISTON

Charles 'Sonny' Liston was the youngest of 25 children. His abusive and alcoholic father, Tobe, worked in cotton fields near Little Rock, Arkansas, and forced Sonny and his other children into hard labour, too. Sonny and his mother Helen escaped Tobe's domination when she started a new life working in St. Louis.

Sonny was 6 feet (1.82 m), 200 pounds (90 kg), incredibly strong and illiterate. Out of place amongst city kids, he fell into gang fighting and armed robbery. In 1950, he was jailed for five years at Missouri State Penitentiary Life. In jail a priest encouraged him to take up boxing and Liston soon rose to jail heavyweight champion.

Liston was paroled in 1952 by boxing handlers with alleged links to organised crime. He shot through the amateur ranks and turned professional in 1953. He became known as 'The Bear' owing to his frightening power, 15-inch (38-cm) circumference fists, and record of short bouts with knockouts. After a stretch in the St. Louis Workhouse for assault in 1956, Liston relocated to Philadelphia, where his professional contract was bought out by Mafia bosses. Liston defeated the popular fighter Floyd Patterson to take the World Heavyweight Championship in 1962. After two defeats to Clay in 1964/5, he carried on boxing for a further five years.

Sonny Liston was found dead at his Las Vegas home on 5 January 1971. Many suspected a mob execution, probably by enforced overdose, as there were traces of heroine in Liston's blood and needle marks on his arm and Liston had always been afraid of needles. It is alleged that he signed his own death warrant by refusing to throw a fight.

Sonny Liston in 1958.

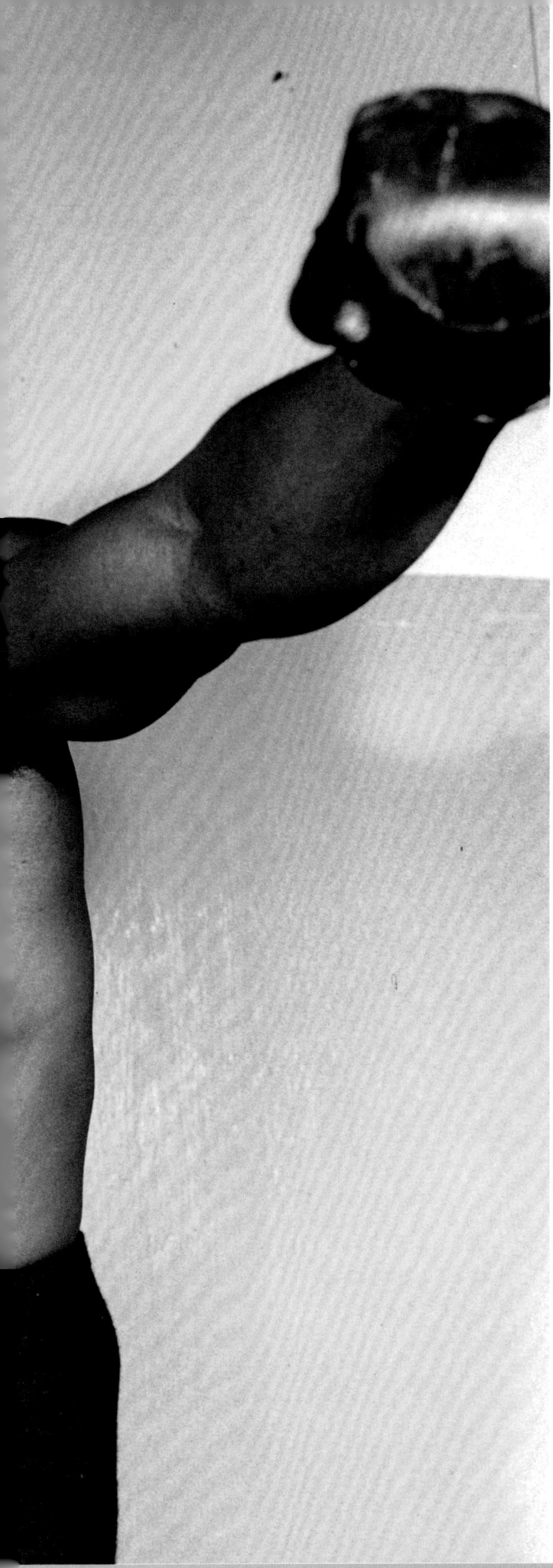

Sonny Liston and Floyd Patterson (left), during a championship fight won by Liston in just one and a half minutes.

STATISTICS

BORN	St. Francis County, May 1932 (uncertain)
DIED	Las Vegas (NV), December 1970
TURNED PROFESSIONAL	1953
NUMBER OF PRO BOUTS	54
WINS-LOSSES-DRAWS	50-4-0
NUMBER OF KNOCKOUTS	39
RETIRED	1970

8-1 CHANCE

It was not looking good for Cassius Clay. The bookmakers were giving odds of 8-1 for a Liston whitewash. In the days before the fight just 3 out of 46 boxing writers predicted a Clay victory. At the weigh-in on fight day Clay was pumped up more than anyone could remember. He screamed at Liston, "Someone's going to die at ringside tonight!"

The Convention Hall was only half full owing to limited hopes for a long fight, but many ex-world champions, including Sugar Ray Robinson, Willie Pastrano, Rocky Marciano and Joe Louis, were there to see how Clay would fare, and maybe even witness an upset.

Onlookers saw how Clay was taller than Liston and refused to be stared down by 'The Bear'. The fighters started warily with Cassius evading jabs and wild punches from Liston, but then Clay threw a rapid combination of punches. Liston staggered, outboxed. The champion fought back in the second round, but in the third he was hurting as Clay ramped up the head blows. Liston was cut on the cheekbone and reeling.

In the fourth round, Liston landed his best punch and Clay started blinking, rubbing his face, ducking and backpedalling. At the bell, he told Angelo Dundee he couldn't see properly, and Dundee demanded he continue but stay out of the way of Liston. Later it was alleged that Liston had put stinging liniment on his gloves to slow his opponent. Clay's eyes were wide open by the start round six and he laid into Liston's face, punch after punch. Liston appeared dazed as he slumped in his chair at the bell. He didn't come out for round seven.

There was pandemonium in the ring. Clay bounded around, arms raised, shouting, "eat your words" at the assembled press. Cassius Clay was the new Heavyweight World Champion.

Cassius Clay's expression says it all in the moments after he beat Sonny Liston and became Heavyweight Champion of the World.

Cassius Clay shows off his World Champion belt.

THE GREATEST

"I don't have a mark on my face. I upset Sonny Liston. I just turned 22. I must be the greatest. I shook up the world! I shook up the world! I shook up the world! I shook up the world!" Cassius Clay

Cassius Clay's victory was one of the biggest upsets in boxing history. He had talked the talk and walked the walk. But he had had severe doubts he could win. Clay's doctor, Ferdie Pacheco, later said, "This was the only time I saw him nervous... he had no idea if he could do what he had been saying he could do."

Clay put his victory down to being too fast for Liston. But there were other factors. One was complacency on Liston's part. In the three-and-a-half years preceding their bout, Liston had been in the ring for just more than 13 minutes! That was because he kept beating opponents quickly. Another was an alleged injury. Straight after he quit on the night, he told a reporter that his left shoulder "feels like it's broke". He later claimed he could not punch properly after the flurry in the initial round owing to a strained muscle, possibly resulting from extravagant punching in round one, or a training injury. Many thought the claims were just sour grapes. After all, Liston could fight through pain – his only defeat as a professional before the Cassius Clay fight had been against Marty Marshall, when he had suffered a broken jaw and carried on fighting until the end.

Suddenly Clay's claims in interviews, at the ringside or even on later records and in books, to being 'The Greatest', were no longer sounding like hollow boasts. Everyone witnessing his performance now knew that he was the real deal. His boasts still irritated many, but their substance was undeniable.

Cassius Clay ponders his stratospheric rise in US and world sport, and boxing opportunities to come. What would happen to top his achievements in the early 1960s?

Smok
Joe
MUHAMMAD
ALI

BECOMING MUHAMMAD ALI

I'M FREE TO BE ME

Two days after his victory in the Liston fight, which had made Cassius Clay the youngest Heavyweight Champion in history, he made an important announcement. He told a press conference that he was a follower of the religion of Islam, and that among the reasons for his conversion from Christianity was the discrimination against black people in the United States and his refusal to support integration. By making this stand, Clay was telling the United States, "I don't have to be what you want me to be. I'm free to be me."

Clay had first stepped into a mosque in 1961 and later said it was the first time he felt truly spiritual. He liked what he heard and started to read the Islamic newspaper *Muhammad Speaks* and attend regular meetings. He was soon seriously considering becoming a Muslim. He was linked to an organisation known as the Nation of Islam and the teachings of one of their leaders called Elijah Muhammad, a man who preached powerful messages of emancipation and believed Islam was the only religion for black people and that Christianity was the religion of white people. This argument proved a powerful one to Clay, who had seen injustices all his life and faced discrimination every day.

Clay attended meetings in the temple and read and learned from the Quran – the only difference between him and other Muslims was that he didn't have the same duties to carry out because of his profession. Clay also introduced his brother Rudy to his mosque and to Islam, and although he had discovered Islam later than Clay, it was Rudy who converted first, changing his name to Rahaman Ali. Clay waited to make a public declaration of his faith because he feared he would not have been allowed to fight in the championship if people knew that he had converted to Islam.

Clay's victory against Liston gave him the confidence to pursue his beliefs.

Cassius Clay with Malcolm X (left).

FROM CLAY TO ALI

Residents of Ghana cheer for Muhammad Ali during his visit there in 1964.

Clay was also influenced by his friendship with Malcolm X, who he met in 1961 at a Nation of Islam meeting. Malcolm X supported Clay and stayed at the Miami training camp before the Liston fight. In March 1964, Malcolm X met Clay in New York and took him on a tour of the United Nations where they were photographed with African delegates. While at the UN, Clay signed his name Cassius X Clay and later that day, he rejected what he'd come to see as his slave name and accepted a new name, as given to him by Elijah Muhammad, Muhammad Ali. Muhammad meaning 'worthy of praise' and Ali the name of a great general and cousin of the Prophet Muhammad.

Many in the boxing establishment and the press did not respond well to Ali's change of religion and name. Some treated it as a fad he'd soon get over; many believed he was being used as an instrument of hate and refused to call him anything other than Cassius Clay. When Ali went to watch a fight at Madison Square Garden in March, the President refused to use the name Muhammad Ali when introducing well-known boxers in the audience. When Ali walked out by way of protest, the audience booed.

In May 1964, to get some respite from these tensions and the glare of the press, Ali began a month-long tour of Africa, visiting Ghana, Nigeria and Egypt. He met Egyptian President Gamal Abdel Nasser and Ghanaian President Kwame Nkrumah and was greeted by cheering crowds wherever he went, repeatedly calling out, "Who's the Greatest?" for the response, "You are!" In a speech during his trip, he announced, "In America everything is white. I am glad to be here among my own people."

Muhammad Ali sits attentively listening to Elijah Muhammad giving a speech at a Nation of Islam meeting in 1964.

TIME OF TENSIONS

Muhammad Ali returned from Africa to rising tensions in the Nation of Islam. A rift between Elijah Muhammad and Malcolm X had become publicly apparent when Malcolm X said President Kennedy's assassination in 1963 had been, "chickens coming home to roost", which went against the Nation's stance of no comment on the popular leader's death.

In early 1964, Malcolm X had made a pilgrimage to Mecca where he witnessed people of different colours worshipping together, making him question the Nation's core belief of Islam being a black religion. In spite of Malcolm's attempts to persuade him otherwise, Ali chose to side with Elijah.

In Africa, Ali snubbed Malcolm, and after Malcolm X was assassinated in early 1965, Ali was not there at the funeral. In later life Ali expressed his regret at his treatment of his former close friend.

Ali also faced tension from his parents. His mother was convinced her son would not have converted if the LSG had not sent him far from home to Miami. His father was concerned that the Nation was just after Ali's money. Elijah had asked his son, Herbert, to help with Ali's business dealings with LSG and other white sponsors. Herbert became Ali's personal manager and also spiritual advisor, and was a constant presence in the Ali entourage. Ali's parents were concerned that Herbert would ruin Ali's professional life. They were also aware of their diminishing influence over Ali. A prime motive in Ali's life was now that of pleasing Elijah and, in many ways, the Nation had become his close family.

Ali also faced the threat of physical danger in the world outside the ring as a result of being in the Nation of Islam. In the days following Malcolm X's funeral, there was a mysterious fire in Ali's apartment, which was unoccupied at the time, and the Nation's headquarters were firebombed.

People queued to pay their respects at the funeral of Malcolm X. Malcolm X was a divisive figure in the United States and in the Nation of Islam. Although he had uncompromising beliefs, his powerful speeches attracted large crowds of people. He played an important role in Ali's life by introducing him to Islam.

Ali, wearing a white towelling robe, wades through members of the press to reach the ring for his rematch with Sonny Liston in St. Dominic's Arena, Lewiston, Maine, on 25 May 1965.

LISTON REMATCH

In early 1965, Ali was focussing all his energy on his rematch with Sonny Liston. The fight had been postponed from November 1964 in Boston when, three days before the fight, Ali was rushed to hospital for surgery on a swelling hernia. Liston, who after training was in better condition than the first match, had little sympathy for Ali, saying the hernia had been caused by, "all that hollering".

The fight was rescheduled for 25 May 1965, this time in Lewiston, Maine, rather than Boston, owing to concern about attacks by anti-Nation of Islam factions. The crowd in Lewiston was just a few thousand strong, but the fight was shown in movie theatres and on television nationwide. Liston was 9-5 favourite and people expected a closer, longer encounter. Ali predicted victory in the ninth.

Ali won in round one with his third punch, which became known as 'the phantom punch'. Ali had set his feet before throwing a fast, powerful right into Liston's jaw. Liston was up-ended onto the canvas. Ali stood over Liston shouting: "Get up and fight, sucker!" He was livid to be denied the chance to demonstrate he was champion by rights – Ali felt that Liston's claims of a bad shoulder had devalued his earlier victory. Liston did get up before the count had finished, but the referee called the fight a few seconds later.

There were allegations that the fight was fixed and that Liston took a fall so his mafia connections could make good betting money. It was rumoured that Liston was in poor shape having been taking heroin in the run-up to the rescheduled bout. Liston said that Ali standing over him at the count prevented him getting up. Just after the fight, Liston said of the phantom punch that he, 'saw it too late'.

Ali reacted angrily to Liston's first round defeat in 1965. He had won again but had also been denied the chance to prove his mastery in the ring.

A relaxed Floyd Patterson (left) sniggers at one of Ali's jibes at a press conference announcing their title bout in 1965.

BATTLE OF IDEALS

On 22 November 1965, Floyd Patterson challenged Ali for a championship fight. Patterson and Ali were old friends. Patterson as a past (1952) Olympic champion had mentored Ali at the 1960 Olympics. The pair had been in contact ever since. Patterson had been World Champion in 1956 and again in 1960, before losing badly to Liston in 1962, and was now aiming to regain the crown for the third time.

Ali typically decided that adding an edge of jibing before the bout would generate interest. Although friends, there was a fundamental difference in ideals of how to empower African Americans. Patterson was vocal in the Civil Rights Movement and wanted to end all segregation. The Nation of Islam supported segregation. For some, the bout pitted the two sides against each other. Frank Sinatra implored Patterson, his friend via civil rights rallies, to, "win the title back for America".

So, at press conferences, Ali called Patterson 'Uncle Tom' meaning he was subordinate to white people and 'rabbit' suggesting he was running scared of standing up for himself in society. He even showed up with a bag of carrots at Patterson's training camp. Patterson called Ali 'Cassius' to taunt him, although later he said he did it because a speech difficulty made it hard for him to say Muhammad.

The fight itself was a mockery. It was clear from the start to all, including Ali, that Patterson had an injured back – a slipped disc during training – and could not defend himself properly. Both fighters thought the bout would be stopped but the referee kept it going. The press viewed the match as an attempt by Ali to humiliate Patterson by keeping on punching and not delivering a knockout until round 12. But Ali did not want to hurt his friend unnecessarily. Patterson later said he had never felt such soft blows.

BOXER FOCUS: FLOYD PATTERSON

Floyd Patterson was the third of his parents' 11 children. He grew up in poor tenements in Brooklyn, New York. Floyd was a regular truant from school, stealing to try to help the family make ends meet. After several court appearances at age 11, he was sent to live in an upstate New York school for emotionally disturbed boys, for 18 months, where he learnt to read and write, and also took up boxing. Floyd turned amateur in 1951, and professional after winning Olympic heavyweight gold in 1952. For his first professional match, Floyd earned just $300.

Floyd was a leading professional when Rocky Marciano retired in 1956. He fought Archie Moore for the title in Chicago, in November that year. Floyd was sufficiently relaxed that he had a nap before the match, which he won on a technical knockout in the fifth, becoming the youngest heavyweight champion in history at that time. He defended his title twice before being beaten by the right hand – called the Hammer of Thor – of Swedish fighter Ingemar Johansson in 1959. Floyd regained his belt the next year but in 1962, was knocked out in round one by Sonny Liston. Floyd was so embarrassed that he left the venue afterwards wearing a false beard, moustache and dark glasses.

He failed to beat Liston again and Ali twice before retiring in 1972, after 20 years professional fighting. Patterson was a quiet, thoughtful man who became chairman of the New York State Athletic Commission and promoted boxing as a way out for children living in inner city ghettos. He suffered from Alzheimer's in later life to the point that he could not remember who he had fought for the title in 1956.

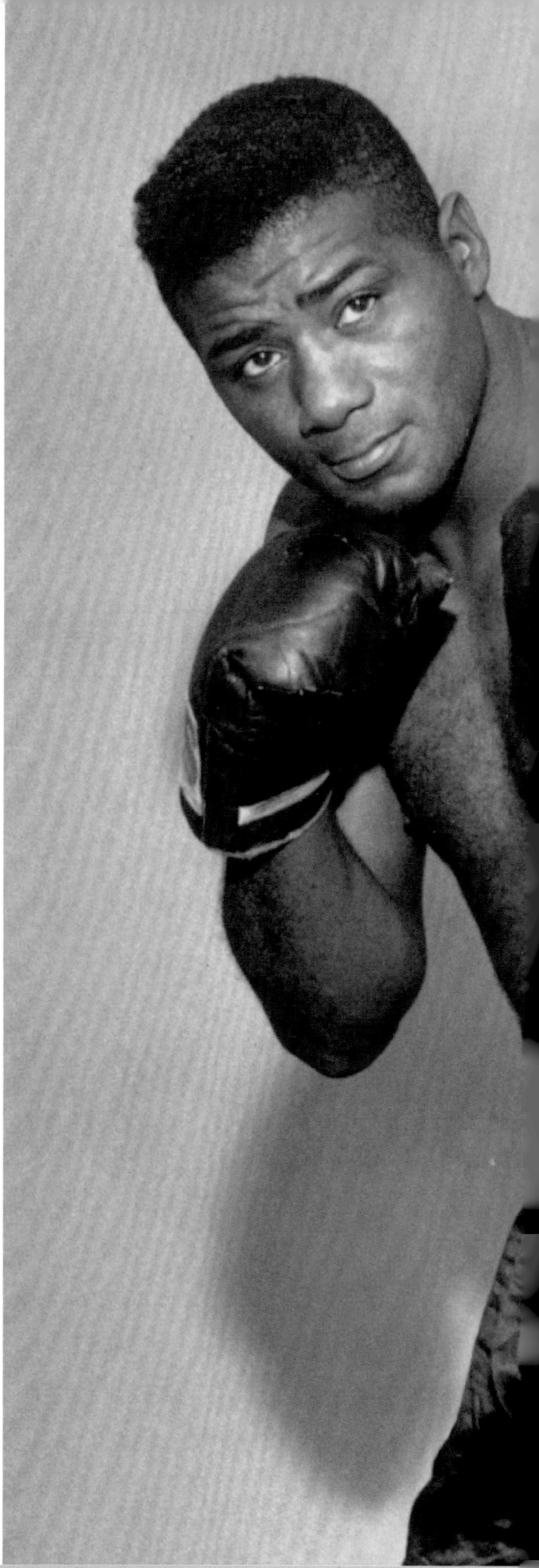

Boxer Floyd Patterson strikes a pose.

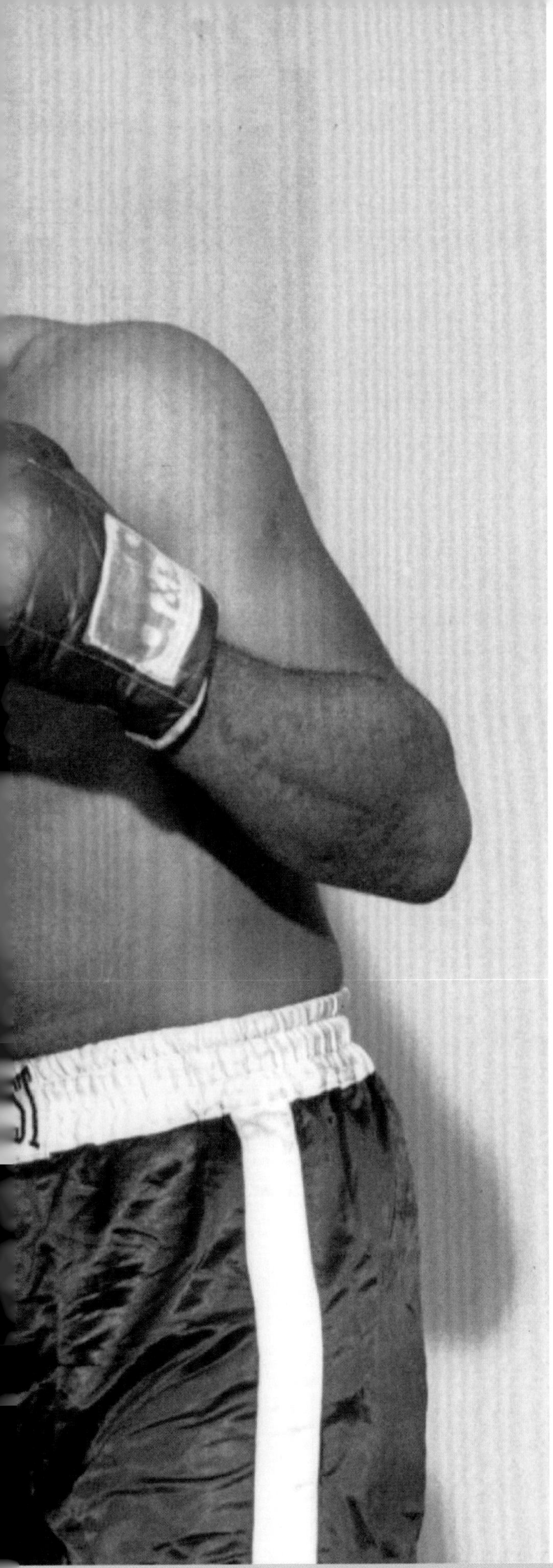

Patterson is declared victor. He retained his World Heavyweight title after a technical knockout in round 12 against Tommy Jackson in New York on 30 July 1957.

STATISTICS

BORN	Waco (TX), January 1935
DIED	New Paltz (NY), May 2006
TURNED PROFESSIONAL	1952
NUMBER OF PRO BOUTS	64
WINS-LOSSES-DRAWS	55-8-1
NUMBER OF KNOCKOUTS	40
RETIRED	1972

CALLED TO SERVE

In 1964, Ali had failed a mental aptitude test that would have qualified him to fight in the Vietnam War, a fact that caused him some embarrassment, especially when his less-than-impressive school records were publicised, too. By 1966, the Vietnam War was escalating and Ali was declared eligible and received his draft notice to join the US Army. He objected on the grounds of his religious beliefs and his response to the press: "Man, I ain't got no quarrel with them Vietcong," soon made front-page news. Many in the media and many ordinary US citizens, who at this time still supported the war, were vitriolic in their condemnation of his stand.

In Chicago, feelings ran so high that Ali's much-publicised fight with Ernie Terrell, scheduled for March, was cancelled and although promoters tried for venues in other cities, soon Terrell himself wanted no part in it either. An alternative opponent was found, Canadian heavyweight champion George Chuvalo, for a fight in Toronto, but there were calls for people to boycott this bout, too. The fight went ahead, and although Chuvalo was a tough nut to crack, Ali had more talent, and won 14 out of the 15 rounds.

After Chuvalo, Ali's promoters decided the best way to make money was to have him fight abroad. Three European bouts were scheduled. In May 1966, Ali fought and won a rematch against Henry Cooper. In August Ali was in England again and knocked out Brian London in three rounds. Then as undefeated Heavyweight Champion, he fought Karl Mildenberger in Frankfurt, Germany. Mildenberger put up a good fight, but Ali ended it in round 12 with a right hand that sent his already-bloodied opponent staggering against the ropes, prompting the referee to stop the fight.

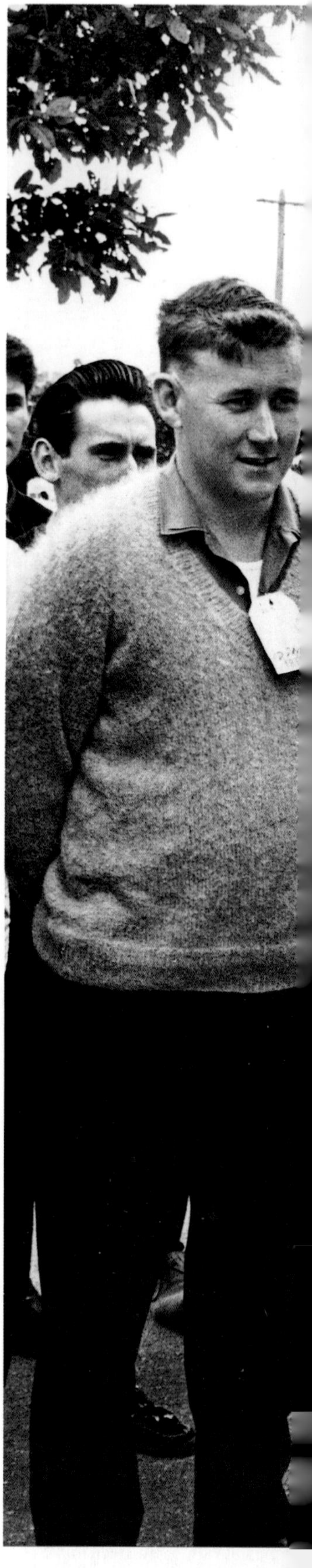

New conscripts group after being conscripted to fight in the Vietnam War. By the mid-1960s there was a major drive to draft men over the age of 18 in the United States and other countries, including Australia, to bolster ground troop numbers in the escalating conflict. Part of this was making changes to eligibility so fewer fit people were exempt from the draft.

Ali eyeballs his challenger Ernie Terrell at the weigh-in before their championship bout in Houston, Texas, in 1967.

GRUDGE MATCH

There was no love lost between Ernie Terrell and Ali in the run-up to their bout in the Houston Astrodome on 6 February 1967. In a television interview the previous December, Ali read a poem, probably written by his friend and cornerman, Drew 'Bundini' Brown, about how Terrell, "will catch hell at the sound of the bell".

Terrell responded, repeatedly calling Ali 'Cassius' to which Ali angrily asked why he could not call him by his chosen name. The two scuffled on camera. Two days before the fight, Ali announced that he wanted to 'torture' Terrell. Terrell later claimed: "I had no animosity. I understood it's a fight. What he say, all that don't count."

The fight was brutal. Terrell's defence of holding his hands high with his elbows together worked in the opening round. Ali could not hit Terrell's head and had to keep his distance from Terrell's arms. In round two, Terrell was cut under his eye. He later said it was the result of Ali intentionally poking his thumb in his eye. Round four was Terrell's best, with a right that sent Ali staggering against the ropes.

Round five, Ali had gauged Terrell's hitting radius and had started to move closer, close enough to make his rapid, hard punches count. Terrell grew gradually groggier with multiple head shots. In round seven Ali almost knocked him out with a violent right-left combination. In round eight Ali started to repeatedly taunt Terrell saying: "What's my name? What's my name," before hitting his head. By the 12th round, Dundee was telling Ali to "finish him" as his fighter was tiring, but the bout did not finish until the end of round 15.

Terrell's defence proved increasingly inadequate against Ali's speed and power as their fight progressed.

ARREST AND TRIAL

By March 1967, the issue of Ali's stand against the Vietnam War was coming to a head. He received an order to report for induction into the army on 11 April, which his lawyers had changed to 28 April so that he could fight Zora Folley on 22 March at Madison Square Garden. Ali knocked out Folley in the seventh round.

As 28 March approached, Ali became more vocal about his protest, saying: "Why should they ask me to put on a uniform and go 10,000 miles from home and drop bombs and bullets on brown people in Vietnam while so-called Negro people in Louisville are treated like dogs?" His stand made him a figure of hate for many people and even his supporters received death threats and had their car windows smashed. When the day finally came, Ali went through the morning's formalities and health checks, but when the time came for him to step forward, he refused. He was taken back into the room and given a second chance to take the oath, but he again refused. He then signed a statement to that effect.

Within an hour of Ali refusing the induction, the New York State Athletic Commission suspended his boxing licence. The rest of the boxing world soon followed suit, and Ali was stripped of his heavyweight title. His trial began on 19 June 1967. Ali argued he was entitled to exemption as an appointed minister of the Nation of Islam. However, exemptions from military service on religious grounds were allowed only for conscientious objectors who opposed war in any form, whereas when questioned, Ali acknowledged that he would take part in an Islamic holy war. He was convicted of refusing induction into the US Army and given the maximum sentence allowable – five years in jail and a fine of $10,000.

Ali holds up the cover of Nation of Islam newspaper. Muhammad Speaks referring to his trial to the watching media in 1967.

Ali appealed against his conviction and he was allowed to remain free, out on bail, while the appeal was processed. As he was banned from fighting in the United States and his passport was confiscated, he could not travel abroad to fight so he could not box to earn a living. It seemed that Ali was going to take his hardest hits outside, not inside, the ring. "He did not believe he would ever fight again," Ali's wife at the time, Belinda Ali, whom he married on 17 August 1967, said: "He wanted to, but he truly believed that he would never fight again."

Ali spent much of the next three-and-a-half years, while the courtroom fight ensued, going to Nation of Islam meetings and travelling the country giving talks at university campuses. He talked about the war in Vietnam, about integration and segregation, black pride, his views on being stripped of his title and denied the right to fight, and even on the financial hardships that brought him to make those lecture tours! He often got a mixed reception. In some places he was heckled and abused but even many of those who supported his anti-war and civil rights views, were shocked by some of his anti-gay, sexist and conservative statements.

These were tough times. Earnings from the lecture circuit didn't cover attorney fees for the ongoing appeal and Ali was still under constant government surveillance. In December 1968, he served ten days in jail for driving without a valid licence. Another blow came in April 1969. Elijah Muhammad had never agreed with boxing and after a statement Ali made to the press about wanting to go back into boxing if the money were right, Elijah suspended Ali from the Nation of Islam for a year.

Ali greets students while visiting St. John's University, New York, in May 1968. Ali's presence and messages of racial equality – by separation – transfixed student audiences across the United States during the years when he was banned from boxing.

Clay and Marciano battle it out in the ring.

FANTASY FIGHTING

Ali was running out of money and was desperate to find ways to earn outside the ring. In early 1969, he took a part in a documentary called *a.k.a. Cassius Clay* for $1000 a day to shoot interviews and recollections of his fights, which would be interspersed with archive footage.

Ali's next payday was more bizarre – a fantasy fight. A Miami advertising man named Murry Woroner had created a fantasy boxing tournament between the best heavyweights of all time in 1967. He input data about each fighter into a computer – such as speed, killer instinct, how prone to cuts – and then pitted each set of data against another in a "bout". Woroner presented this information as a blow-by-blow tournament radio show, which he successfully sold to many stations and gathered millions of listeners by 1968. Ali was outraged to hear that he had lost in the tournament to Jim Jeffries who he considered 'history's clumsiest' heavyweight, and sued Woroner for $1 million.

Woroner cleverly turned the situation around, offering to pay Ali $10,000 to film a fantasy fight supposedly controlled by computers against Rocky Marciano. The two champions met in a blacked-out gym in Miami and got on famously. Both were overweight and in poor fighting shape. Their job was to film 70 one-minute rounds of fake but realistic fighting, avoiding any hard or head punches – although Ali did accidentally knock off Rocky's toupee! They simulated cuts using ketchup as blood and filmed different knockout endings. No one knew who won until the film was presented in 1,000 movie theatres across the United States in 1970 – Rocky beat Ali. People in the audience booed, cried and yelled, not believing their eyes. Ali's supporters said he had humiliated himself: "They want your ass whipped in public... and not just by anybody, but by a real Great White Hope."

BOXER FOCUS: ROCKY MARCIANO

Rocco Francis Marchegiano's parents left Italy, during the depression era, for the United States in the hope of starting a new life. They settled in Brockton, MA, an area favoured by other Italian immigrants. Although his father found work in the city's shoe industry, the Marchegiano family lived in poverty. Rocco, who came to be known as Rocky Marciano, was one of six children and between casual jobs, was a keen amateur baseball player.

He was drafted to the US Army in 1943 and took up boxing to avoid duties such as washing dishes and cleaning latrines. He turned professional after leaving the military in 1947. Within two years he had knocked out 16 opponents and established his nickname: the Brockton Blockbuster. He was considered tough and rough but too short at under 6 foot (1.82 cm), too light at just 13 stone (82.5 kg), old (at 25) and lacking great technique. But he continued to improve and by 1951, faced up to his boxing hero, Joe Louis. Rocky knocked him out in round eight and then cried in Louis's dressing room afterwards in guilt.

In 1952, he took the World Heavyweight Championship in style by knocking Jersey Joe Walcott unconscious in round 13. Days afterwards, a triumphant Rocky rode in a convertible amongst crowds 10,000 strong – one of their own had become a sporting hero. Rocky defended his belt six times, coming close to defeat after a nose cut against Ezzard Charles. He retired in 1956, having never been beaten as a professional. For the following decade or so, Rocky made many personal appearances capitalising on his fame. He died in a private plane crash aged 46.

Rocky Marciano holds a victory pose after knocking out Jersey Joe Walcott to take the World Heavyweight Championship on 23 September 1952. Until that punch, Rocky had been trailing badly on points and an upset looked highly unlikely.

Rocky lands the right-hand piledriver that took out his childhood idol, Joe Louis, in their 1951 bout.

STATISTICS

BORN	Brockton (MA), September 1923
DIED	Des Moines (IA), August 1969
TURNED PROFESSIONAL	1947
NUMBER OF PRO BOUTS	49
WINS-LOSSES-DRAWS	49-0-0
NUMBER OF KNOCKOUTS	43
RETIRED	1956

Track and field athletes Tommie Smith (centre) and John Carlos (right), first and third place winners for the United States in the 200 metres, protest with the Black Power salute at Mexico City Olympics in 1968.

BLACK POWER

In 1969, Black Power was a mainstream issue in the United States. In in the previous year, millions of television spectators had witnessed two US athletes giving the Black Power salute from the Olympic medal podium in Mexico City. It symbolised that many African Americans believed white politicians were failing them and that they needed Black Power to help themselves.

The Black Panther Party was an extreme faction of the Black Power Movement. In this political party the members carried guns and believed that violence was justified in bringing about black justice. Many in the movement disagreed with their aggressive tactics and rhetoric, while endorsing their work in helping poor black communities.

In 1969, the musician, social activist and playwright Oscar Brown Jr opened and starred in his musical comedy about Black Power, *Buck White*. It was about the confusion and conflict in a black social organisation when a militant black leader, Buck White, addresses its members. The play did so well in California that producers decided to run it at the George Abbott Theatre on Broadway. The producers surprisingly cast Ali as Buck White in hope of drawing in crowds. Ali was 'dignified and impressive', singing songs such as 'We Came in Chains' with 'pleasant' voice. Unfortunately New York audiences were not taken and the musical ran for just seven performances. Theatre critic Kushauri Kupa said Ali had made a mockery of genuine protests by presenting a militant leader as a buffoon.

While on Broadway, Ali made a point of seeing the play *Great White Hope* about brilliant black heavyweight champion of the early 20th century, Jack Johnson. Johnson was a rebel in the Jim Crow era, dating white women, racing cars, openly displaying his wealth and bragging about his abilities. Ali said: "That's Me. You take out the white women, and that play is about me."

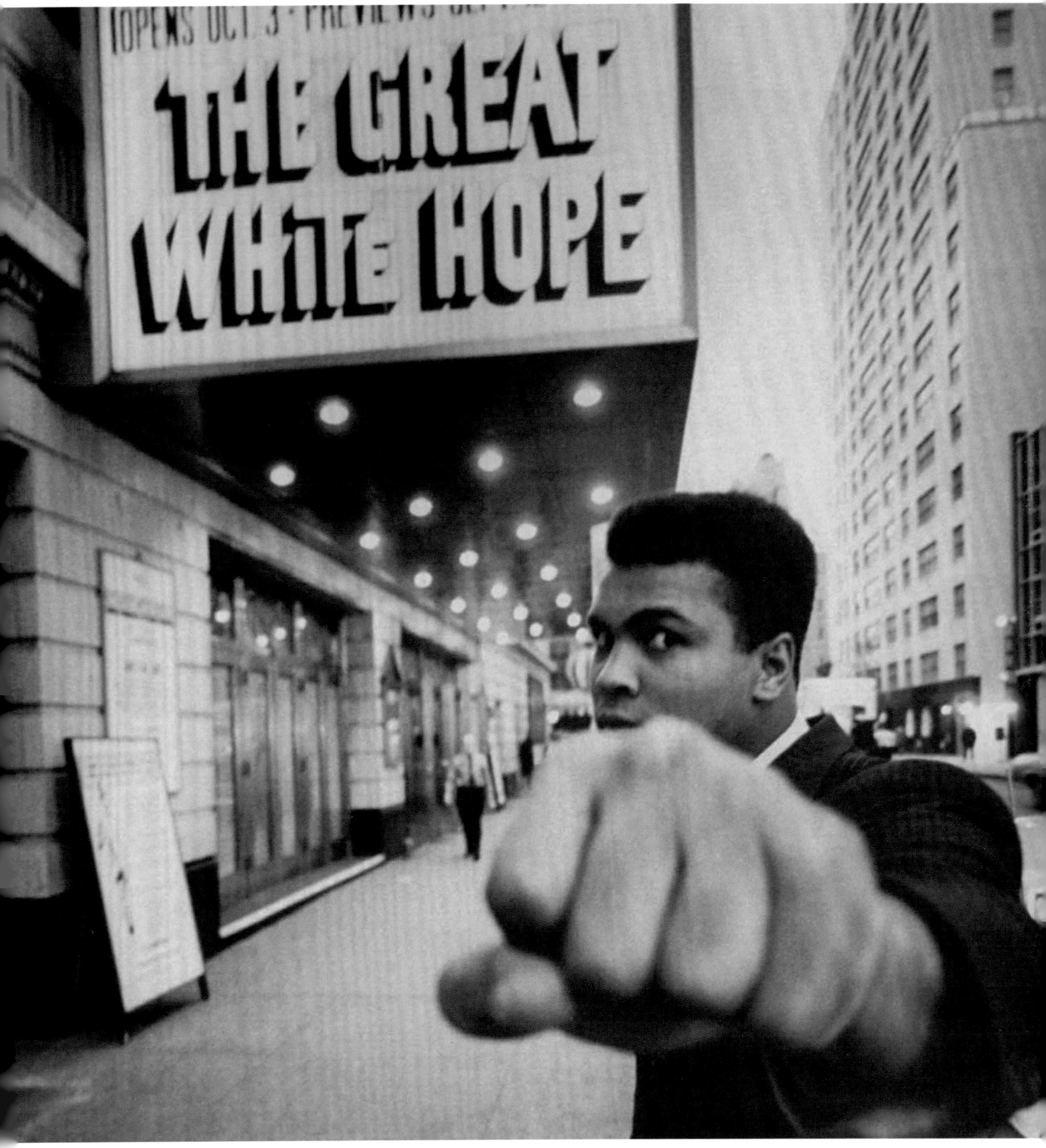

Ali poses outside the Broadway theatre showing a play about Jack Johnson, the revolutionary black boxer of the early 20th century. Ali saw deep parallels between his own outspoken stance and Johnson's views.

RETURN TO THE RING

abc
abc

Ali had to put in hard hours in the gym to get himself mentally and physically ready to fight at an elite level once more after his ban.

THE COMEBACK

In 1970, Ali's struggle to get back in the ring and win back the title of Heavyweight Champion of the World, now in the hands of the talented fighter Joe Frazier, heated up. Ali's lawyers and promoters worked hard to get permission for him to fight in different states but were denied time and again. Finally, a mayor in Atlanta, Georgia, was persuaded to allow Ali to fight against Jerry Quarry there, in spite of attempts by several members of Congress to stop it.

And so it was that on 26 October 1970, Ali fought again. It was a big moment for Ali and a stressful one: Quarry was strong and younger, a world-class opponent. The arena was filled with the rich and famous from the black community including Sidney Poitier, Bill Cosby and Jesse Jackson, and the crowd roared a delighted welcome to Ali as he entered the ring. Although Ali started well, he was slowing noticeably in rounds two and three, when he suddenly dealt Quarry a right punch that opened a huge, deep cut over the boxer's eye. This injury ended the fight and Ali was declared the winner but unsurprisingly, after three and a half years out of the ring, Ali's fitness was clearly not what it had once been.

While Ali's absence from the ring might not have been good for his training, the publicity that came from it certainly increased his fame and earning power. Ali was paid more for the Quarry fight than he had ever been paid before. While Ali's refusal to go to war and his exile had made him unpopular to begin with, by 1970, protests against the Vietnam War were growing and more people were thinking that perhaps Ali should not have been punished for his beliefs.

A deflated Jerry Quarry (left) looks past a triumphant Ali at the referee Tony Perez as he signals the end of Ali's comeback fight on 26 October 1970. Ali had won but he was not yet convincing championship material.

BOXER FOCUS: JOE FRAZIER

Joe Frazier was the seventh of 13 children of a sharecropper in South Carolina. He was a hard worker and strong – at age 12 Joe was making money filling sandbags – but to become fitter, he joined a gym. At the gym he discovered boxing and sailed through the amateur divisions until he faced Buster Mathis in the 1964 Olympic trials. Mathis beat him on points but then had to pull out of the event with a hand injury. Joe took his place, and the opportunity, winning heavyweight gold.

Joe turned professional in 1965 and sealed his reputation as a scrapper who could take heavy punches and still come through, with the help of a fearsome left hook, earning him the nickname 'Smokin' Joe'. In 1968, after Ali was banned, Joe fought Mathis again, this time for one of the several world championship titles being contested at that time. He took the New York State title on a technical knockout in round 11. He defended this title several times before beating Ali, who had returned after his ban and held one of the other heavyweight titles. With a famous left hook and unanimous points decision, Smokin' Joe became the undisputed Heavyweight Champion in 1970.

Smokin' Joe defended his title over the next two years but was then beaten by George Foreman – Olympic champion from 1968 – in Jamaica in 1973, Ali (twice) in 1974, and Foreman again in 1976. He then announced his retirement but five years later, returned to fight and draw a professional bout just once more. Joe went on to train fighters in his gym, but died after a long battle against cancer.

Joe Frazier in his mid-20s poses in a fighting stance in the ring with his trainer, Eddie Futch, looking on.

Frazier stands jubilant on 16 February 1970 after taking the World Heavyweight title against Jimmy Ellis on a technical knockout in New York.

STATISTICS

BORN	Beaufort (SC), January 1944
DIED	Philadelphia (PA), November 2011
TURNED PROFESSIONAL	1965
NUMBER OF PRO BOUTS	37
WINS-LOSSES-DRAWS	32-4-1
NUMBER OF KNOCKOUTS	27
RETIRED	1981

THE FIGHT OF THE CENTURY

After the Quarry fight, Ali won permission to fight in New York and on 7 December 1970, he took on Oscar Bonavena, winning in round 15 with a crowd-pleasing left hook. Now it was Ali's chance to win back his title by fighting Joe Frazier, who knew that he needed to defeat Ali before he would truly be accepted as the best in the world. Their meeting on 8 March 1971 at Madison Square Garden was billed as 'The Fight of the Century'. It was watched by 300 million people in 35 countries around the world. It made $1.3 million on the gate and guaranteed each fighter a fee of $2.5 million.

The promotional build-up was as tense as the fight itself. Ali infuriated Frazier by calling him 'Uncle Tom' and saying that anyone black who supported Frazier was an Uncle Tom, too. He even called Frazier ugly and dumb. Ali was clear afterwards that this was all pre-match hype, but Frazier never forgave him and this dislike formed a backdrop to this and their subsequent fights.

Ali was famous for nifty footwork and fast hands. Frazier's style was to stand firm and keep delivering hits. The two fought with skill and style and traded punches for an electrifying 15 rounds. In round six, Frazier pinned Ali to the ropes and battered him relentlessly, while in round nine it was Ali who dominated, hammering Frazier with right-left combinations. In round 11, Ali was nearly knocked to the floor by a Frazier hook but in rounds 12 and 13, Ali took the fight to Frazier. In round 15, Frazier knocked Ali to the floor and although Ali got up again, the fight was awarded to Frazier. Ali had lost his first professional fight since returning to the ring and he had officially lost the heavyweight title.

The moment when Ali's dream of becoming Heavyweight Champion once more was dashed by the power of Smokin' Joe Frazier at the end of the Fight of the Century.

Ali shows off the spangled robe given to him by Elvis Presley, before his fight against the Briton Joe Bugner in February 1973.

FREE TO FIGHT AGAIN

The loss in March 1971 was a huge blow to Ali and his supporters but after a rest, he resumed training. On 28 June, he received good news when the Supreme Court reversed his conviction. At last, Ali was free to fight anywhere again and his conscientious objection had been accepted.

While Ali waited for his next meeting with Frazier, he toured the world defeating opponents in Switzerland, Japan and Ireland as well as in the United States. In February 1973, he beat Joe Bugner in Las Vegas in an uninspiring bout that is mainly remembered for his jewel studded robe emblazoned with the words 'People's Choice' – a gift from Elvis Presley. Then in March 1973, a little known opponent, Ken Norton, surprised everybody by breaking Ali's jaw in the second round of a fight. Ali continued to fight on but finally lost in round 12. It took six months for Ali's jaw to heal. When the two fought again, it took 12 rounds for Ali to get even, winning a close but unanimous victory.

At last, Frazier agreed to a rematch with Ali and the date was set for 28 January 1974. By this time Frazier had lost the title to George Foreman, but Ali had a point to prove and Frazier hated Ali. In the build-up to the bout, the two traded bitter insults and were even involved in a brawl in a television studio. The event was another sell-out. On the night, the boxers kept up the brutal pace that had characterised their first meeting but this time, after 12 rounds, Ali was awarded a unanimous decision over Frazier. The two rivals had taunted each other throughout the bout and although Frazier had made Ali wait almost three years for a rematch, he was demanding another as soon as this one was over.

Ali was the People's Choice because he was a magnetic performer but many boxing experts were concerned that his best fighting days were over.

PROMOTING A LEGEND

Don King was a new boxing promoter on the block in 1972. King wanted to use Ali's legendary status to help him find fortune. After organising a hospital fundraiser featuring Ali in 1972, his ambitions stretched to putting on a heavyweight title bout between Ali and the incumbent champion, George Foreman. He promised the two fighters $5 million each but hit a brick wall in finding funding. Magically, a funder emerged: President Mobutu Sese Seko of recently independent Zaire would pay but only if the fight happened in his capital, Kinshasa. King met with Mobuto's advisers in Paris to forge a deal.

Don King and his friend Lloyd Price came up with King's up-combed hairstyle to give the promoter a distinctive look to accompany his distinctively flamboyant approach to boxing promotion.

Mobuto wanted to bring a major sporting event to Africa for the first time and thus demonstrate that he was a major player on the continent. African Americans including Ali and Foreman liked the symbolism of returning to their ancestral 'home' – Africa – for such a big fight.

Mobuto also had strong links with the United States. He had seized power in a military coup after killing the previous democratically elected leader, Patrice Lumumba, who Ali had met on his earlier African trip, with the clandestine aid of the CIA. The US government was concerned that Lumumba was giving too much power to 'communist' influences. Mobuto stabilised the country after years of turmoil, which earned him the friendship of several US presidents, but at a high cost. He amassed a massive personal fortune based on Zaire's mineral wealth while the vast majority of the population was living in poverty and brutally repressed by his state police and army. Tales abounded of Mobuto feeding opponents to crocodiles, and executing known criminals to maintain law and order in the months before the fight.

Ali poses for the press with fight posters advertising his Zaire Foreman fight in 1974.

In late September 1974, Ali was in intense training so he remained fighting fit while Foreman's eye injury healed.

ALI BOMAYE

When fight organisers arrived in Kinshasa in March 1974, they were shocked by what they found. The tiny runways at Kinshasa's airport were unsuitable for jumbo jets, there was a dirt track rather than road to the fight stadium and there was a lack of satellite technology so the fight could not be broadcast worldwide. However, when Ali and Foreman arrived in September, Mobuto had transformed the capital's infrastructure. Billboards along the airport road pronounced, "Black power is sought everywhere in the world. But it is realised in Zaire".

From meeting the locals to audiences with Mobuto, Ali felt at home in Zaire. Foreman was a more closed-off figure at this time, who stuck mostly with his entourage. Ali was 32 years old to Foreman's 25 years and the 3-1 underdog following Foreman's defeat of Frazier. Yet he talked up his chances of regaining his crown using speed and skill, repeating a famous phrase first coined by Bundini Brown:

'Float like a butterfly, sting like a bee
His hands can't hit what his eyes can't see'

Ali learnt a phrase, "Ako bomaye," meaning, "I will kill him", in Lingalla dialect. From that point on the crowds that came to see him chanted, "Ali bomaye", meaning, "Ali, kill him".

Eight days before the fight, Foreman's eye was badly cut by an accidental elbowing from a sparring partner. The fight was delayed for five weeks so it could heal, which was worrying for organisers as the impending rainy season risked making the open stadium event a washout. In the wait for the fight, Ali enjoyed spending time with musicians such as James Brown and Hugh Masakela at the Zaire '74 music festival, organised by Lloyd Price, a friend of King's, to take advantage of the fight's media attention.

Ali enjoys the noise from the adoring crowd lining his route, held in check by Mobuto's army, as he travelled around Kinshasa in late summer 1974.

Foreman tries in vain to scramble to his feet in round eight, still reeling from Ali's championship-winning punch combination. For all his power, Foreman had been outsmarted by Ali's tactics.

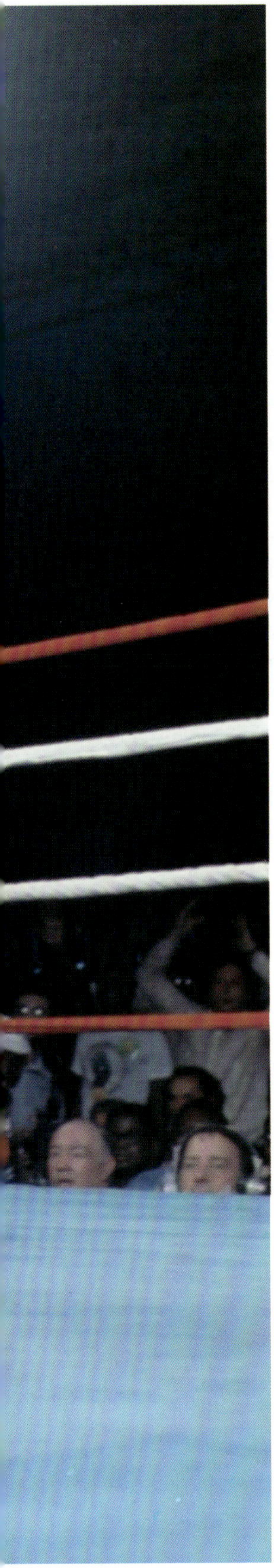

RUMBLE IN THE JUNGLE

In the early hours of 30 October, Ali and Foreman arrived at the Zaire national football stadium, the Stade du 20 Mai, in darkness. Ali, wearing a white satin robe trimmed with an African blanket, and his vast entourage arrived to the sounds of, "Ali bomaye" from the 60,000-strong crowd. In contrast, Foreman arrived in a simple red velvet robe. Mobuto was not even there. He watched the fight on television as he feared being assassinated in the open stadium.

Two national anthems, the Star Spangled Banner and Le Zarois, were played while the United States' and Zaire's flags were shown off in the ring. Ali said to Foreman: "You have heard of me since you were young... Now you must meet me, your Master." And then the fight began.

Ali landed two powerful head shots to signal his intent and then started to defend. He took whatever Foreman could throw at him. By the middle of round eight, Foreman started to tire after all that punching. Ali taunted him: "George, is that all you got?" then leapt at the opportunity when Foreman's guard was down. He summoned a fast, sledgehammer left-right combination that floored Foreman. Ali had predicted that Foreman would fall on his face from exhaustion in the tenth round, but his punches proved to be knockout blows. Foreman was counted out before he could stand up.

After a seven year gap, Ali was World Champion once more, only the second heavyweight after Floyd Patterson to regain a title. It was Foreman's first defeat in 41 bouts. Ali crowed: "I did it. I told you he was nothing but did you listen? ... I told you I was going to take all his shots. I told you he had no skill. I told you he didn't like to be punched."

Ali started fast against Foreman to remind his imposing opponent of his speed and power. But much of the bout was about a war of attrition.

ROPE-A-DOPE

The Rumble in the Jungle was a stark demonstration of Ali's changed tactics following his return to the ring. Ali remained confident of his phenomenal speed of hand. A 1969 photographic analysis in *Sports Illustrated* magazine showed he could deliver a six-punch combination of jabs, hooks, body and head shots in just more than 2 seconds. Ali knew, though, he was slower on his feet and could no longer dance around younger opponents.

He and Angelo Dundee devised a risky tactic for the Foreman fight. Instead of trading blows toe-to-toe, Ali stayed on the ropes and let Foreman hit him! This was astounding to onlookers because Foreman was known as the all-time hardest-hitting heavyweight. Ali would then lean forward inviting a knockout head punch and rapidly lean back out of the way. Ali was well prepared to take rib and belly shots because he had spent months before leaving for Zaire in the gym practising being beaten up by sparring partners such as Larry Holmes, a future Heavyweight Champion. Also he relied on give in the ropes to limit the damage. Dundee later confessed his part in the tactic: adjusting the rope tension to help Ali use the ring edge to his advantage.

Ali called the technique rope-a-dope, but it was not new. Ironically, Archie Moore, who was in Foreman's training camp, had called the tactic of absorbing heavy punches until the time was right to counter-attack, 'the turtle'. Rope-a dope almost failed for Ali in round two when he was pinned to the ropes and appeared to wobble and grabbed Foreman's shoulder. Before round six, a Zairean official accidentally loosened the ropes – if Dundee had not noticed and told Ali, he may have leant back and fallen from the ring!

Ali is shown here on the ropes using his rope-a-dope tactic while defending against Foreman's onslaught.

BOXER FOCUS: GEORGE FOREMAN

George Foreman grew up in Texas in a poor family, and as a teenager was a mugger and brawler on the streets of Houston. He fell into boxing by chance when he was put on a job corps programme to teach vocational skills to the disadvantaged. One of the corps counsellor's was also a boxing coach and saw the punching potential in George's 6 foot 3 inch (1. 9 m), muscular frame.

George proved to be so good that he became 1968 Olympic Heavyweight Champion in his 25th amateur fight. Within three years of turning professional, he had knocked out opponents 35 times in 37 matches. By 1973, he was crowned World Champion when he floored the mighty Joe Frazier. A year later, he was defeated by Ali in Zaire, and in 1977, announced his retirement after a claimed religious experience in the dressing room following his last fight. George was ordained a minister the next year.

By the early 1980s, he was a boxing commentator for the HBO network and had set up a youth centre. However, he was short on funds so returned to professional boxing ten years after retiring.

George resumed where he left off, knocking out opponents. However, there were allegations that his promoter bribed officials to up his ranking to get a title shot, first against Evander Holyfield, which he lost on points, and then Michael Moorer in 1994. At age 45 Foreman became the oldest ever World Heavyweight Champion when he knocked out Moorer. When Foreman retired for good in 1997 he had already started promoting a range of electric cookers branded Lean Mean Grilling Machines. By 2014, an estimated 100 million Grilling Machines had been sold. Foreman continues to juggle evangelism, developing and marketing products, and running a ranch in Texas.

George Foreman at ease out of the ring.

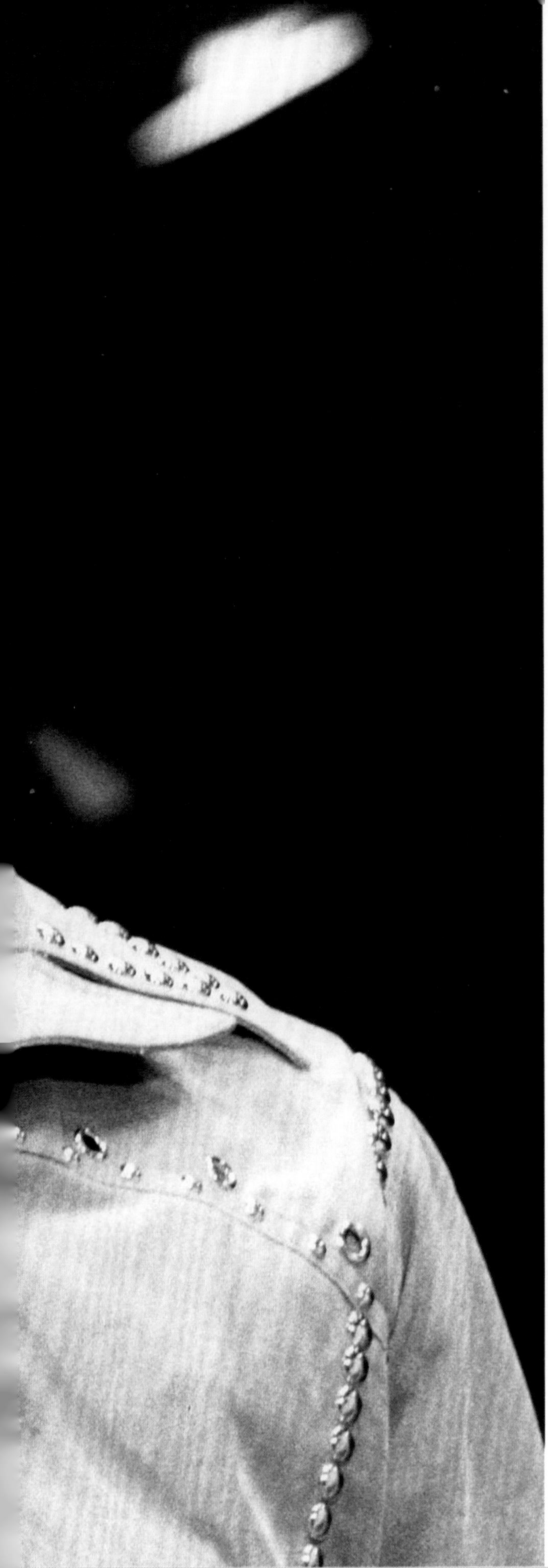

Foreman poses as he trains in 1972 in New York.

STATISTICS

BORN	Marshall (TX), January 1949
TURNED PROFESSIONAL	1969
NUMBER OF PRO BOUTS	81
WINS-LOSSES-DRAWS	76-5-0
NUMBER OF KNOCKOUTS	68
RETIRED	1997

Ali in his pomp, mocking Joe Frazier's predictions of a victory, in a press conference in 1975.

RESURRECTION

Ali was now king of the boxing world and suddenly a national treasure on his return to the United States. In December 1974, he was invited to visit President Gerald Ford in the White House. Ford wanted to meet Ali as a boxing enthusiast but also out of national reconciliation now that the US troops were out of Vietnam and racial divisions were declining. He said prophetically: "Because of his principles... Muhammad Ali will be remembered for more than just excellence in athletics."

Ali became a darling of the media, featuring in many photoshoots and pictured attending numerous events. Of course, Ali fed the hero worship, reading from epic poems about his achievements such as:

"This is the legend of Muhammad Ali, the greatest fighter that ever will be."

In 1975, Elijah Muhammad died and the Nation of Islam changed course. Led by Wallace Muhammad, it stated that the Quran taught that colour does not matter and that Muslims hate any injustice and evil. Ali said: "We're in a new phase, a resurrection." This change in tack created deep divisions in the Nation and was the beginning of its end.

By now Don King was looking for the next payday after Zaire for himself and for Ali. Allegedly using mob money, King matched Ali against Chuck Wepner, 'the Bayonne Bleeder' as he often got cut. It wasn't much of a contest, but King negotiated a $1.5 million payout for Ali. Soon King had made Ali's wish come true: a return bout with Joe Frazier. Again the big match was to be held overseas, this time in Manila, Philippines, on 1 October. The country was under martial law and its autocratic leader President Ferdinand Marcos thought a sporting event would take attention away from his mistreatment of his own people.

Ali wearing a Manila Gorilla T-shirt mock punches Frazier at a press conference in Quezon City, Philippines, in front of invited television crews, reporters and boxing enthusiasts.

THRILLA IN MANILA

**'It will be a killer
And a chiller
And a thrilla
When I get the gorilla
In Manila'**

Ali was ruthless in his pre-match taunting of Joe Frazier. At a press conference with Frazier he mocked Frazier for saying, "gonna" not "going to" and "inta" not "into". He christened Frazier "the gorilla" and repeatedly thumped a black rubber gorilla, saying: "All night long, this is what you'll see."

Before the fight, Frazier's trainer, Eddie Futch, made plans for victory. He negotiated replacing the planned US referee with a Filipino, as the former had officiated Ali versus Frazier II and he felt had insufficiently penalised neck holding by Ali. Futch also trained his man to avoid rope-a-dope by hitting Ali's arms to weaken him. It later emerged that Frazier had a cataract in his left eye, and an arthritic left shoulder. Ali was 2-1 favourite for this battle.

The fight was an intense war of attrition in sapping tropical humidity. Ali outboxed Frazier in the first third of the bout, delivering many big punches that made Frazier wobble. In the middle third, Frazier took the upper hand. In round six he whacked Ali so hard that Ali's head turned away. In the final third, Ali took control and doled out the punishment. Frazier's left eye was closed and his right closing. In the heat, there was insufficient ice to reduce the swelling. In the 14th Frazier was a sitting duck for Ali's punches but the round finished with both men slumped in their corners.

Before the bell for the 15th, Futch threw in the towel, and Ali begged Dundee to cut his gloves off as he was done. Ali had won again – netting in the region of $6 million – but this victory had taken its toll.

In the sapping heat of the Philippines the bout ebbed and flowed between both fighters, Frazier taking the upper hand mid-fight, but Ali finishing stronger.

In this classic duel, Ali only won because he was not first to quit. Both men were completely spent at the end of the fight.

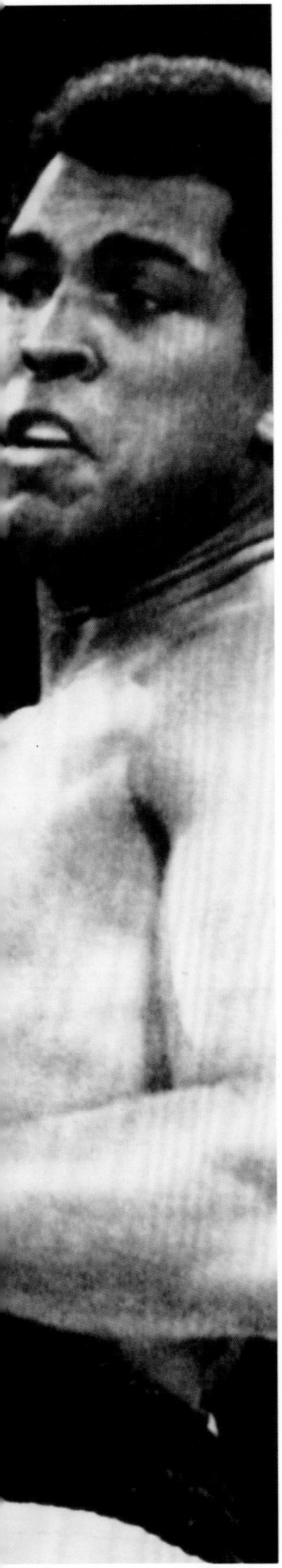

THE CLASSIC DUEL

For many people Ali v Frazier III was one of the best boxing matches in history. It was between two boxing legends who threw everything they had at each other. Ali said it was the closest to dying he had ever been. The fight had the ebb and flow of many classic fights and a gladiatorial fight-to-the-death spirit. In 1997, *The Ring* magazine awarded it, 'Fight of the Century' and in 1999, ESPN's Sports Century Series pronounced it the fifth greatest sporting event ever.

Some boxing aficionados believe the match has been overhyped, partly because Ali finally convincingly beat his nemesis, whereas in reality it was rather uninteresting. In 2012, boxing historian Mike Silvers described his sadness at seeing, "two former giants of the ring struggle and suffer."

Many people thought that Ali crossed a line in his verbal attacks on Joe Frazier out of the ring. They said that he had called Frazier ignorant, slow in speech and ugly for the sole purpose of entertaining a predominantly white audience and thus reinforced some unfortunate and persistent stereotypes about black people.

Frazier said of Ali the fighter: "In Manila, ... those punches, they'd have knocked a building down. And he took 'em... and he came back, and I got to respect that part of the man." He could never forgive how Ali tainted his image. In 1991, when Ali was first having difficulty speaking, Frazier said: "He can't talk no more because he was saying the wrong things. ... Tell me now. Him or me; which one talks worse now?" Ali himself saw the taunts as merely part of the game and retained immense respect for Frazier the warrior: "If God ever calls me to a holy war, I want Joe Frazier fighting beside me."

EVERLAST

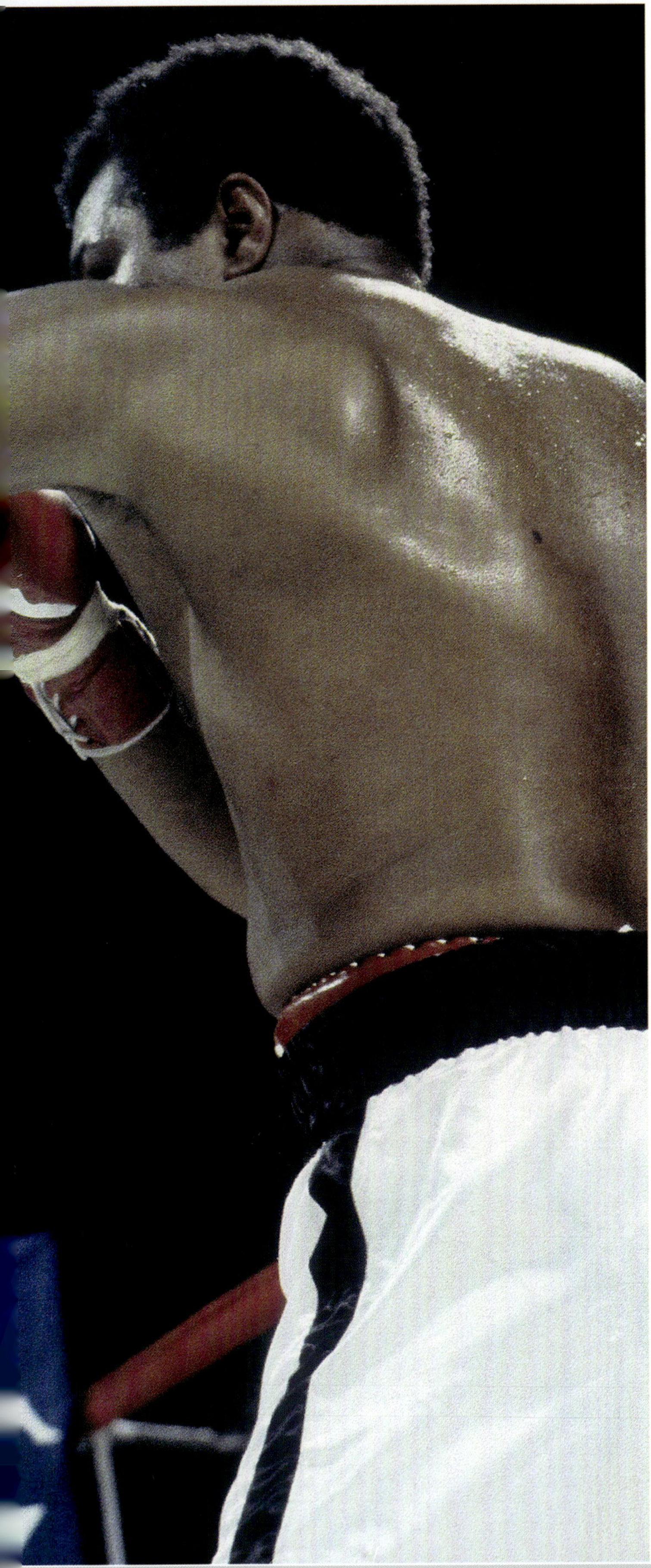

THE LAST FIGHTS

THE ALI ROAD SHOW

After beating Frazier in Manila, Muhammad Ali was probably the best-known and one of the most popular celebrities in the world. Those around him say this was not just because of his fame, but also because of his personality.

He was warm and friendly to those he met and generous to those in real need, for example handing over $100,000 dollars to save a Jewish community centre for old people, after he saw a feature about it closing due to lack of funds on the news.

Ali skipping before his World Championship bout with Jimmy Young. At this point, Ali was his heaviest weight ever and taking a lot of less-than-taxing fights against also-rans.

People loved to watch Ali fight, but they loved to watch him win more. In the years after Manila, Ali fought several opponents that did not stand a chance of beating him but were happy to fight the champion and, like him, entertain audiences while reaping great financial rewards.

On 20 February 1976, Ali fought Jean-Pierre Coopman, the heavyweight champion of Belgium. Ali justified the fight against this lesser opponent saying he needed a rest after the major workout in Manila. Coopman was so delighted to meet Ali that he kept trying to kiss him at press conferences, making it hard to build up too much drama or excitement about the event, which Ali won all too easily.

Two months later, Ali fought Jimmy Young in Maryland. Ali was slow and at 230 pounds (104 kg), he was the heaviest he had ever been. He took 15 rounds to win a fight that was universally panned as boring. Less than a month after that, Ali was on primetime television fighting England's Richard Dunn in Munich, Germany. Tickets sold badly and Ali was open to the press about his regret at having let the public down so he put on a better performance in the fight, knocking Dunn down four times before knocking him out in round five. The Ali Road Show seemed to be back in town but in reality, this was to be the champ's last ever knockout win.

The Coopman fight in Puerto Rico in 1976 was a simple workout for a boxer of Ali's skill.

POWER STRUGGLE

In the background at this time, there was a power struggle going on for the control of Ali's career. Herbert Muhammad, who was Ali's manager, was pulling away from Don King, because he believed King wanted to take over. King's efforts were to no avail however, because Herbert's friendship with Ali was so strong and long-standing, and because he distanced Ali from King, choosing promoters like Bob Arum to promote Ali's future bouts, such as his next, a controversial fight against pro-wrestler Antonio Inoki in Tokyo on 25 May 1976.

The fight was billed as a battle between the two toughest men on the planet but many viewed it as a staged circus show. When asked his reasons for taking part in a fight that many felt demeaned the boxing title, Ali was honest: "$6 million, that's why,' he replied. Nevertheless, the fighters tried to build-up some tension at press events, with Ali calling Inoki 'The Pelican' because of his big chin and Inoki presenting Ali with a crutch for after the match.

There are still disputes about whether the fight was genuine but it is known that Ali's camp renegotiated the rules of the meeting just before it took place, stating that Inoki was not allowed to do things like leg-dive or tackle. Whatever the truth, the result was 15 rounds of dull, almost farcical fighting, with Inoki bending the rules by spending much of the bout lying on the floor kicking at Ali's legs. At one point Ali tried to grab Inoki's ankle but got flipped on to the canvas with Inoki sitting on his chest and squatting over his head. The fight was scored as a draw but no one really saved face: it had been a humiliating spectacle for everyone involved. There was a cost to Ali, too: blood clots and muscle damage in his legs from all those kicks.

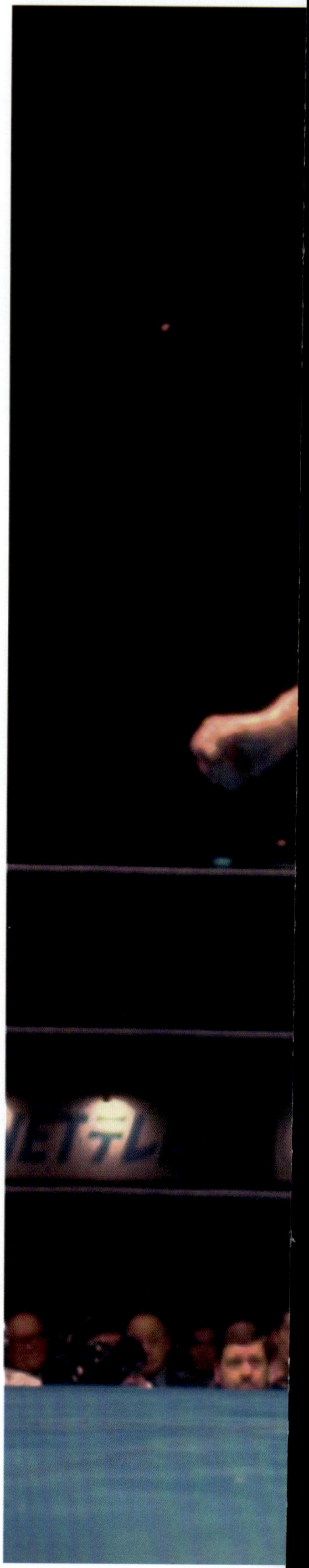

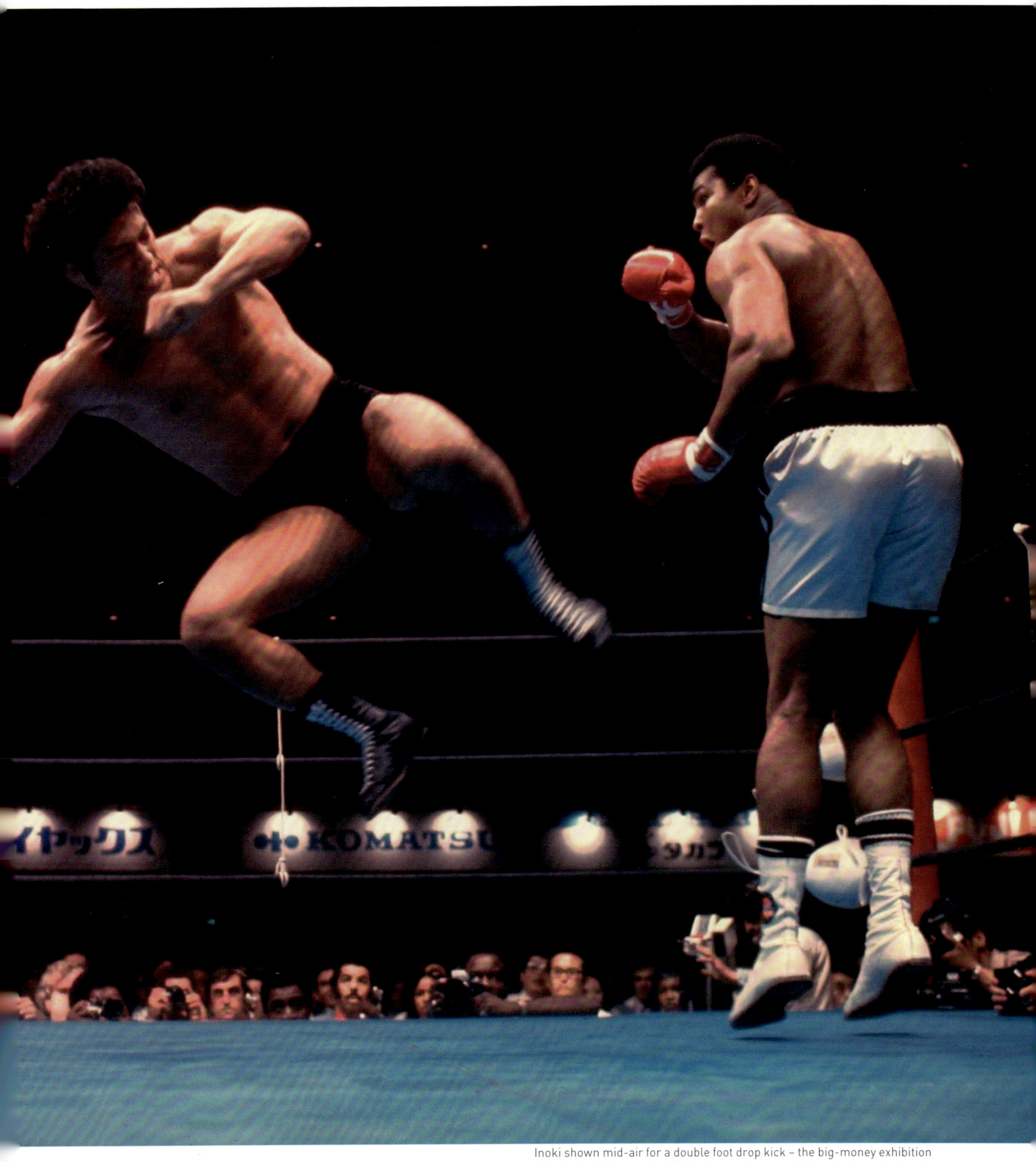

Inoki shown mid-air for a double foot drop kick – the big-money exhibition fight had a high cost for Ali: his famously powerful legs took such a beating, that Ali's movement was probably permanently slowed.

The powerhouse Ken Norton defends himself against an Ali blow during their 1976 encounter. Ali took revenge for the jaw-busting points defeat of 1973 but was a less-than-convincing victor.

ALI V NORTON

Bob Arum and Ferdie Pacheco were worried by infections to Ali's leg injuries, yet Ali spent a minimal period in hospital before starting to train for a bout against Ken Norton at Yankee Stadium, on 28 September 1976. Norton dominated the early rounds, but after round eight the tables turned as Ali, with superhuman effort, started to claw his way back. Ali, spurred on by Dundee, won the next three rounds, lost round 12, and won the next two, making the fight even by round 15. He won on a close and disputed points decision. It was clear to all that the leg problems had taken their toll on Ali's mobility.

Ali did not step into the ring again until spring 1977, for what proved to be a tedious win against Spanish newcomer Alfredo Evangelista. Even Ali was more interested in what was going on outside the ring, where his marriage to Belinda was breaking up, he had a nine-month-old child with his soon-to-be new wife Veronica, and an autobiography and a movie of his life, *The Greatest,* about to be released. It seemed that Ali's focus was on his personal ventures, not his boxing.

Just as people were speculating that Ali might retire, he booked a fight against Earnie Shavers on 29 September 1977, at Madison Square Garden. Shavers was tough and Ali was out of shape, but Ali fought 15 hard rounds to scrape another win. However, he had been hammered in the head by Shaver's brain-jarring punches so many times he suffered severe head trauma and other injuries. Several prominent people called for Ali to retire before permanent damage was done, including Pacheco, for whom the Shavers fight was the final straw. When Ali refused to stop fighting after this, his doctor of 15 years quit.

Ali makes a breakthrough against Norton.

BOXER FOCUS: KEN NORTON

Ken Norton was born and brought up in Jacksonville, Illinois, the son of a fire service engineer and a hospital therapist. After school, Norton won a football scholarship to Northeast Missouri State College. He didn't start boxing until after he joined the Marine Corps in 1963. He was a formidable athlete who took to the sport quickly.

Norton turned professional after taking the All-Marine Heavyweight Champion title three times during his four-year stint in the forces. He fought many great fighters in his time, including George Foreman, for the title in 1974. He also put his 6 foot 3 inch (1.92 m), 220 pound (99.7 kg) physique to good financial use by starring in Hollywood films such as *Mandingo* (1975), with Susan George, and *Drum* (1976), with Pam Grier, as well as television shows including *The A-Team* and *Knight Rider*.

Norton was bitterly disappointed when he lost to Ali in 1976, but he went on to take three wins in 1977 against the likes of Duane Bobick and Jimmy Young, and became the mandatory challenger for WBC Heavyweight Champion Leon Spinks, who claimed the title in 1978. The World Boxing Council stripped Spinks of the title and awarded it to Norton instead after the former agreed to a rematch with the ageing Ali instead of Norton. Norton lost the title to Larry Holmes in June the same year, after an intense 15-round fight ending in a split decision. Norton was never the same fighter again.

In 1986, Norton almost died in a car accident in which he suffered multiple injuries, including a fractured skull and a brain injury that left his speech slurred. He died after a long period of declining health, after a succession of strokes and a heart attack, since which he'd lived in a care home.

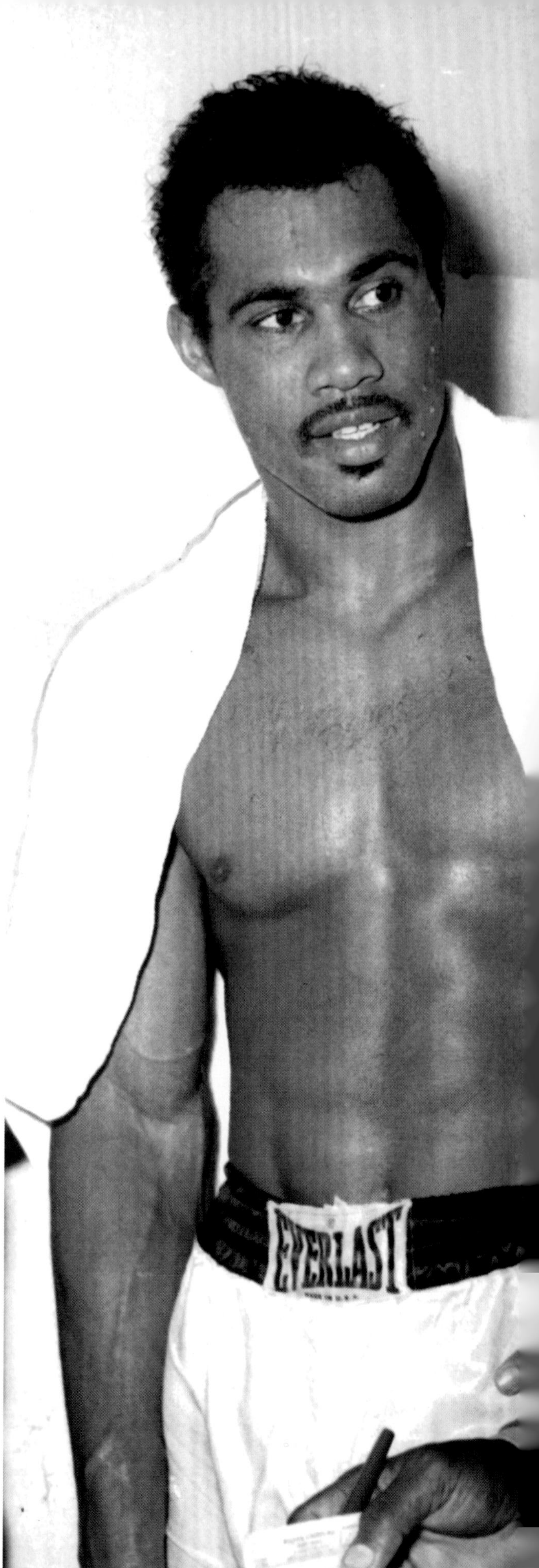

A young Ken Norton (centre) with Joe Frazier (right) in 1950.

Norton chalks up a win against Ron Stander in early 1976, before his Ali rematch.

STATISTICS

BORN	Jacksonville (IL), 9 August 1943
DIED	18 September 2013
TURNED PROFESSIONAL	1967
NUMBER OF PRO BOUTS	50
WINS-LOSSES-DRAWS	42-7-1
NUMBER OF KNOCKOUTS	33
RETIRED	1981

ALI V SPINKS

Ali's next match was in February 1978 in Las Vegas against Leon Spinks, an Olympic gold medal winner who only had seven professional bouts to his name. Ali seized the chance to take down another gold medal winner and declare himself the greatest again, but he did not bother training much, assuming it would be an easy win. It wasn't. Spinks was young and strong and went on punching Ali for the entire 15 rounds, never tiring as Ali expected. Ali tried to make a comeback in the final round but it was too late. The judges awarded the win and Ali's World Heavyweight title to Spinks. The loss hurt Ali badly and as soon as the fight was over, Ali was calling for another, to win back his title.

The rematch was arranged for 15 September that year in New Orleans. Ali began training harder than he had ever trained in his life, including sparring more than 200 rounds in the ring. On the day, Ali soon settled into his rhythm, moving and punching solidly and using improvised moves that could only come from a fighter of his experience. Over the course of the match, he jabbed and hooked with ever increasing confidence and accuracy. He even displayed the odd speedy and devastating mix of hooks and uppercuts, and landed overhand rights, which left his opponent frustrated and helpless. Ali won by unanimous decision and at 36 years old, became the first three-time Heavyweight Champion in history.

After the match, Ali said: "I've always planned to be the first black man to retire undefeated, and to do it now after being champion three times would be something no one could ever equal. I have made suckers out of all of you." He announced his retirement the following June.

Ali backs away from a punch thrown by Leon Spinks during their 15 September 1978 bout in the Superdome, New Orleans. Ali trained incredibly hard to make sure he did not make the same mistakes as before against Spinks.

BOXER FOCUS: LEON SPINKS

Leon Spinks was born in a rough area of St. Louis, Missouri, and brought up by his mother on welfare assistance. He left school after the tenth grade and went into the US Marine Corps where he joined the All-Marine boxing team. He won light heavyweight bronze at the World Games in Cuba in 1974, silver at the Pan-American Games in 1975, and gold at the 1976 Summer Olympics in Montreal. His brother Michael won gold in the middleweight, making them the first brothers in history to be champions in the same sport at the same Olympics.

In 1977, Spinks turned professional and moved up to the heavyweight division. He took the World Heavyweight title from Muhammad Ali in 1978, in one of the greatest upsets in boxing history, but was stripped of the title after agreeing to fight Ali rather than the number-one contender: Norton. In 1981, Spinks challenged Larry Holmes for the title but lost in three rounds. His last championship chance was in 1986 when he fought Dwight Qawi at cruiserweight level but he lost in six rounds. Financial problems forced Spinks to continue fighting autograph shows and boxer-versus-wrestler matches long past his prime until he retired in 1995.

Although he and Michael were the first brothers in boxing history to win World Heavyweight titles (Michael defeated Larry Holmes in the IBF Heavyweight Championship in 1985), their later lives took divergent paths. Michael Spinks left boxing with his health and his money. Leon Spinks allegedly squandered his winnings on alcohol and gambling, and for a while was homeless and living in a shelter. Since then he has worked in restaurants, at a YMCA and has done other odd jobs. He has also helped to start a gym in Detroit, and in Nebraska, he volunteers at an after-school programme for youth.

Spinks in training before his first Ali fight, which catapulted him to boxing stardom.

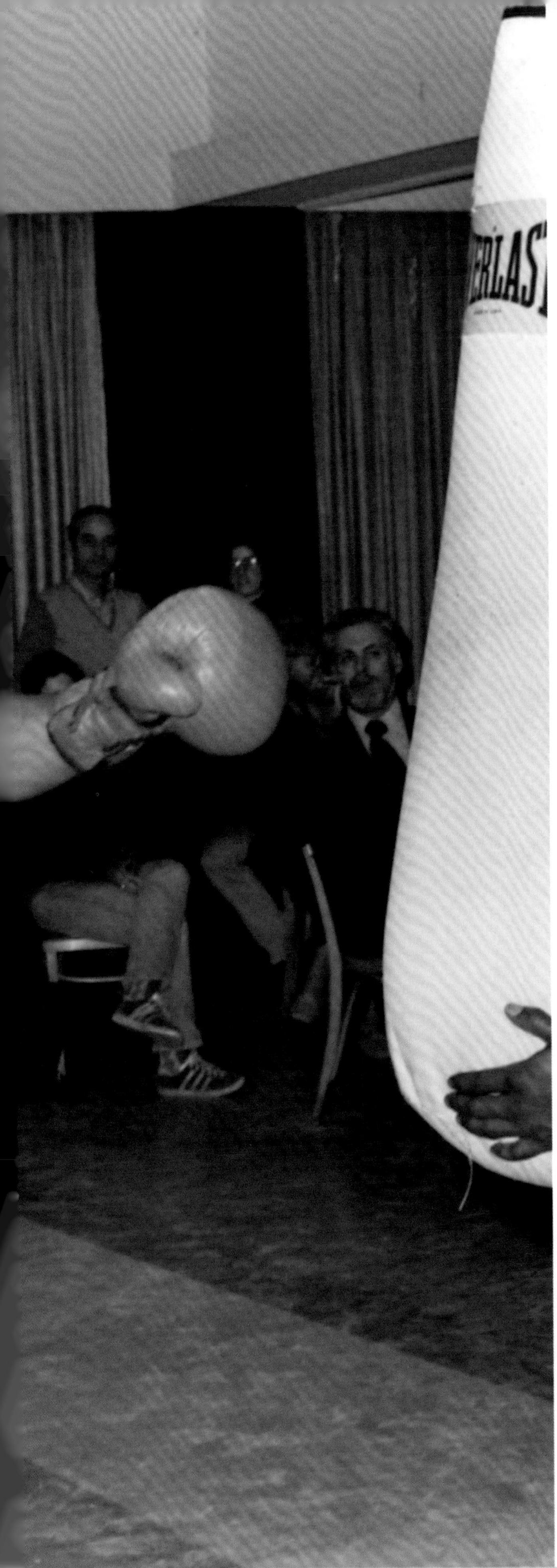

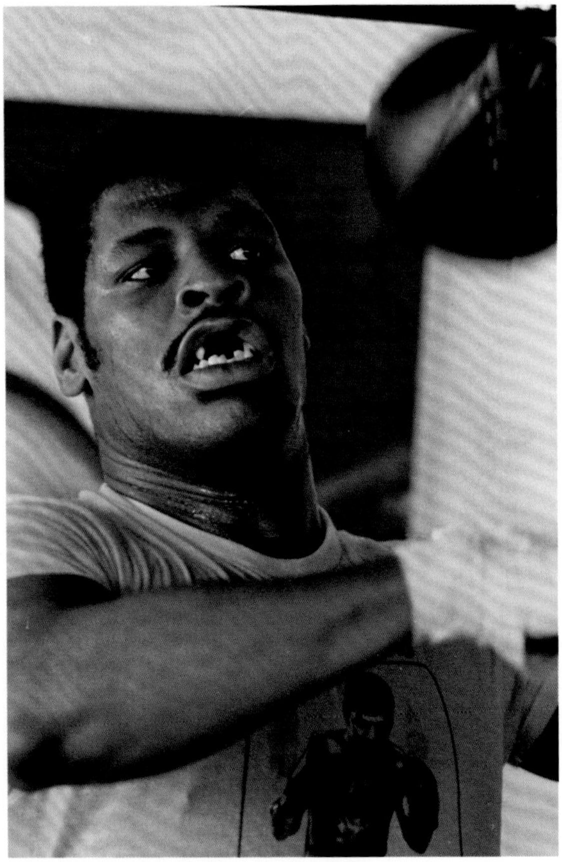

Spinks had his front teeth loosened by boxing and then removed in 1971 while in the marines. He often wore false front teeth, but they were sometimes stolen as trophies!

STATISTICS

BORN	St. Louis (MO), 11 July 1953
TURNED PROFESSIONAL	1977
NUMBER OF PRO BOUTS	46
WINS-LOSSES-DRAWS	26-17-3
NUMBER OF KNOCKOUTS	14
RETIRED	1995

Larry Holmes stands victorious over Ali, who sits hurt and beaten in his corner.

THE LAST FIGHT

After the Spinks victory, Ali concentrated on other projects for a while. He played an ex-slave in a four-hour television mini-series called *Freedom Road*, with Kris Kristofferson, he moved into a huge, luxurious mansion in Las Vegas, and he travelled the world, for example to India to raise money for Indian charities. In 1979, after Russia invaded Afghanistan, President Carter asked him to visit countries in Africa to represent the United States' reasons for boycotting the Moscow Olympics.

Ali was soon planning to get back in the ring. He did it partly for the money, because although he'd earned millions over his career, he had spent a lot, given away a lot of it, and had been conned out of some, but also because he loved the roar of the crowd, loved to fight and to show people he could still win.

On 2 October 1980, and in spite of public statements issued by his mother and former doctor, Pacheco, saying he should not return to boxing, Ali stepped out of retirement and into the ring at Caesars Palace, Las Vegas, to face Larry Holmes, a former sparring partner and current heavyweight champion.

It was a disaster. Ali never had a dominant moment in the fight, but he would not stop or drop. He just absorbed the severe beatings that Holmes dished out. In round nine, an uppercut from Holmes threw Ali against the ropes and as Ali turned away and covered his face with his gloves, Holmes delivered a right hand to his kidney that made Ali scream with pain. After round ten, Ali's trainer, Angelo Dundee, finally stopped the sad spectacle. This time there was no denying that Ali was in terminal decline.

Ali eyeballed Trevor Berbick in vain at the weigh-in in Nassau, the Bahamas, but many knew his boxing days were near the end and he did not have the moves to back up his pre-match talk. Berbick would prove to be his last ever boxing opponent.

Ali was hurt in more ways than one after the Holmes disaster. He refused to accept the decision and wanted to prove his worth in the ring. At the age of 39 he was fixated with the idea of becoming champ for a fourth time: "Why do people go to the moon? Why did Martin Luther King say he had a dream? People need challenges."

In September 1981, a ten-round fight against the Jamaican-Canadian, Trevor Berbick, was announced. Berbick had recently lost closely to Holmes, too. But US boxing commissions were officially concerned about the state of Ali's health and would not sanction the fight on US soil. US networks were not interested in televising the bout, planned for Nassau, the Bahamas, and promoted by a Bahamian company, Sports Internationale. They tagged it 'The Drama in Bahama'. Pre-fight things were shoddy – ringside tickets were on sale in a supermarket and there were concerns Sports Internationale would go bust. In early December, to soothe anxieties about the fight, Ali publicly released a medical report from UCLA Medical Center stating: "There is no evidence from a health standpoint that he should be limited whatsoever in his activities."

On the evening of 11 December Ali and Berbick stepped into the ring. Shambolic organisation meant the referees had to ask around for a stopwatch and bell. Ali looked fresh at the start, dancing round and flicking jabs, but it was immediately apparent that he could not move out of the way of Berbick's solid head shots. By round three he was tiring. Ali traded blows but they had little effect on the 27-year-old. Ali's reactions and speed had gone and he could not dodge Berbick's blows. He put off the inevitable until the final bell: a Berbick victory. This sad fight was the last in Ali's auspicious career in the ring.

A SECOND LIFE

RETIREMENT

"Father Time caught up with me. I'm finished. I've got to face the facts. For the first time I could feel that I'm 40 years old."

In the press conference in Nassau the morning after Berbick fight, Berbick described beating Ali as his, "great honour and also a sad one". However, journalists were far more interested in the main story: the end of Ali's boxing career. At the conference Ali teased Berbick for beating up an old man and proclaimed Berbick, "as good as any man I ever fought". But out of Berbick's earshot he said: "If I was 27, Trevor would have been my sparring partner."

Ali said he would have retired even if he had won because he felt conclusively that during the rounds he could not, "make certain attacks". At the end of the conference, to everyone's surprise, he suddenly pronounced: "I shall return!" But then added: "To Los Angeles", where he lived.

For Ali the early 1980s were difficult times. He had the trappings of success such as an enormous mansion, he had a glorious boxing record, international renown, and had met a pantheon of famous people. But he was bereft to be out of the boxing cycle of talking up his chances against opponents, training, competing and so on. Angelo Dundee said: "He met every big name in the world but what really energised him was being around fight guys." He knew he had left the ring with a whimper rather than a roar and that the boxing world believed he had brought the sport into some disrepute by fighting on when he was not really able. Ali retained close advisors who organised public appearances, but he was no longer surrounded by a large entourage. For the first time in years, Ali felt all alone.

Muhammad Ali with actor Tony Curtis in 1982.

When Ali visited China in 1985, he was already suffering from the effects of Parkinson's disease.

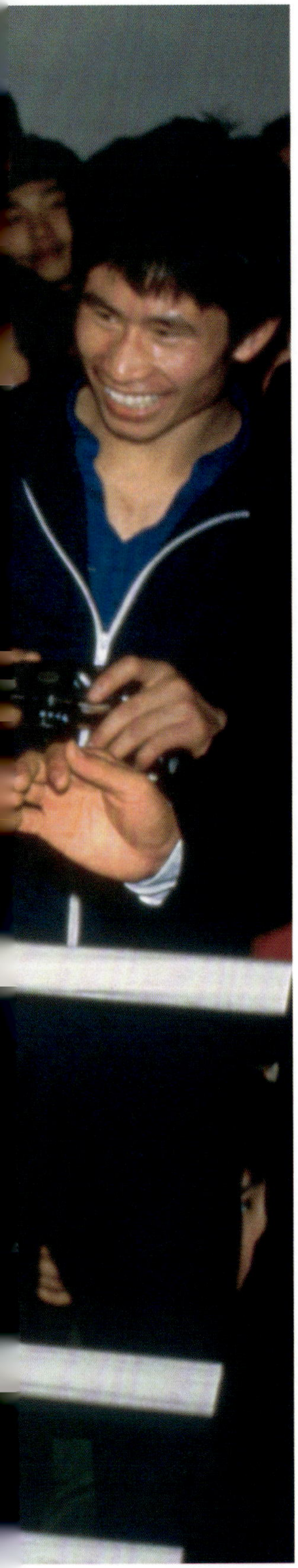

ILLNESS

Ali knew he was struggling with neurological symptoms before his last fights. At the time of the 1980 UCLA report, he blamed the symptoms on the thyroid pills that he took to help lose weight before the Holmes fight. He kept quiet the findings of a report from the Denver Mayo Clinic, which found he could not accurately touch his finger to his nose tip, he had trouble coordinating speech and could not hop well on one foot. Publicly he kept up pretences that all was OK: "You listen to me talk. Do I sound like I've got brain damage to you?"

After retirement Ali's health was under great scrutiny. It was apparent that his speech was more slurred than in the past, he moved more slowly and had tremors. He had many more tests at leading neurological institutions in the United States over the following years, and finally a PET scan in 1984 revealed that Ali had damage to his brain stem. This, along with response to medication and other tests, confirmed that he had Parkinson's Disease. Parkinson's symptoms, from tremor, slowness and rigidity to fatigue, pain and sleeplessness, result from the brain not producing a neurotransmitter called dopamine.

Parkinson's resulting from head trauma has been the prevailing theory since Ali's diagnosis, especially given that other boxers, including Sugar Ray Leonard, have also suffered neurological damage post-career. Many people blame the punishing later fights including those with Frazier and Holmes. Henry Cooper blamed it on Ali's fighting style: "We were always taught as kids that you never turned your head on a punch... But [Ali] used to turn, and he took [too] many punches to the back of the head." However, Parkinson's has many causes, from family history to viruses and exposure to toxins. Some doctors think Ali may have got the disease even without stepping into the ring.

PUBLIC APPEARANCES

After the world finally knew for sure that Ali was suffering from Parkinson's, the ex-champion reassured people that he was far from finished and that he would get on with life. He said that on Parkinson's medication to lessen the symptoms, he felt fine and that he was in no pain, even though he admitted that he was, "older and fatter, but we all change." Ali remained firmly in the public eye.

In 1985, Ali got back in the ring but this time, a wrestling ring. The event was called WrestleMania, which was held at Madison Square Garden – the scene of some of Ali's most famous fights. The main event in this pay-per-view match was a tag-team bout between the professional wrestler Hulk Hogan and the television actor Mr T against 'Rowdy' Roddy Piper and 'Mr. Wonderful' Paul Orndorff. The 19,000 crowd saw Ali dressed as referee, along with Liberace as timekeeper, introduce the wrestlers. Ali did not actually stay in the ring to referee, fearful of being bowled over by the wrestlers but he remained ringside to mock-punch people thrown from the ring. He held Hogan's hand aloft in victory at the end.

Ali retained a strong interest in heavyweight boxing and in particular, the emergence of Mike Tyson. In 1985, Mike Tyson had just turned professional at age 18 and was setting the heavyweight world on fire. In about 1977, Ali had inspired Tyson to focus on boxing when he visited the detention centre in the Bronx where Tyson was staying. Tyson was also promoted by Don King. In 1986, he became the youngest world champion in history when he knocked out Trevor Berbick, who was by then trained by Ali's close friend Dundee.

Ali is shown getting ready to participate as a guest referee in the inaugural Wrestlemania at Madison Square Garden, New York, in 1985.

Ali poses with released hostage Royce Smart, on 4 December 1990 after the latter's arrival at Kennedy International Airport.

MEETING SADDAM

In August 1990, Iraqi military forces invaded Kuwait and annexed it as part of Iraq. Saddam Hussein, the Iraqi leader, said it was retaliation against Kuwait drilling into their oil reserves. NATO condemned the invasion and the United States threatened Saddam with war if he did not withdraw Iraqi forces. Saddam took Western hostages to act as a 'human shield' to prevent military strikes on Iraq. The United States used sanctions and also took part in diplomatic moves to try to release US hostages. One venture, organised by a former US Attorney General, was sending 'celebrity diplomats' to Baghdad to meet with Saddam to try to make him release captives. Ali was asked to be one of those diplomats.

Ali arrived in Baghdad in November 1990. He was well-known in the Middle East owing to his very public Muslim faith and his past history of standing up to his own government. He was considered a reasonable person to with whom to negotiate. Ali met people on Baghdad's streets and in schools, and visited important holy shrines. He waited a week before Saddam would meet him, in which time he ran out of his Parkinson's medication, making it difficult to talk.

Back in the United States some questioned his presence in Baghdad: was he there for self-promotion? Did he break sanctions by negotiating with Saddam? According to Ali, Saddam was a 'man of conviction' and accepted the logic that hostage release would be, "good for maintaining peace in the area". Ali managed to negotiate the release of 15 hostages, whom he accompanied back to the United States in December 1990. He said of Iraq that it was, "the Garden of Eden" and should not be bombed. He was unaware that Saddam was releasing hostages anyway because he had now built up sufficient Iraqi forces to fight a war. He was unaware, too that President George Bush was intent on fighting that war regardless of hostage release. In February 1991, US forces invaded Iraq in Operation Desert Storm.

NATION'S HONOURS

"I've always wanted to be more than just a boxer. More than just the three-time Heavyweight Champion. I wanted to use my fame, and this face that everyone knows so well, to help uplift and inspire people around the world."

In the wilderness of the late 1970s and through the later boxing years, few people in the US government or US organisations wanted to have much to do with Muhammad Ali. How things had changed then when Ali, sporting a white tracksuit, slowly jogged carrying a torch. He used it to send a flaming arrow that lit the Olympic flame in Atlanta, Georgia, in the opening ceremony of the summer games in 1996. This was symbolic of his return from the cold, especially as he was given a gold medal. This was to replace the one he supposedly threw away after his Rome victory in 1960. Ali's part in an Olympic ceremony was to be repeated in 2012 at the London Games, but this time he helped to carry the Olympic flag from a wheelchair, aided by his wife Lonnie.

Ali had been officially recognised earlier than 1996 by his nation, for non-sporting reasons. In 1987, he was selected by the California Bicentennial Foundation for the U.S. Constitution as someone who personified the vitality of the Bill of Rights in striving for the equality of each person before God, and the responsibility of government to secure the rights of all. In 2005, Ali was awarded the Presidential Medal of Freedom in 2005, which is the highest civil award in the United States, in recognition of, "his lifetime of achievement and for his principled service to mankind." In 2012, Ali won the Liberty Medal for embracing the ideals of the US constitution. President Bill Clinton said: "Ali embodies the spirit of the Liberty Medal by embracing the ideals of the Constitution – freedom, self-governance, equality and empowerment – and helping to spread them across the globe."

Ali holds the torch before lighting the Olympic flame during the Opening Ceremony of the 1996 Centennial Olympic Games in Atlanta, Georgia.

INTERNATIONAL WORK

In 1998, at a brief ceremony in New York, UN Secretary General Kofi Annan pinned a dove of peace badge to Ali's lapel and named him a Messenger of Peace. This high honour was recognition of his global pursuit of peace outside the boxing ring.

Ali had spoken against inequalities in South Africa at the UN nearly 20 years earlier at a Special Committee against apartheid. In 1993, he went to South Africa on a benevolent mission and met Nelson Mandela who had been recently released from jail. In 2013, he paid tribute to Mandela, who he said had reached for the impossible in uniting South Africa and "taught us forgiveness on a grand scale".

Ali has widely preached and acted to help those in need. As UN messenger of Peace, he took part in missions to raise awareness of the needs of people in the internationally vilified countries of Afghanistan and North Korea. In Afghanistan, Ali visited a UNICEF-backed girls' school, a rare institution as pupils and teachers were in danger from Taliban forces that banned the education of women. He also gave support to a women's bakery that employed widows of war, and a Kabul boxing club where photographs of his fighting days decorated the walls.

Ali, in his role as UN Messenger of Peace, arrives at Kabul Airport, Afghanistan, for a three-day goodwill mission in 2002.

Ali has helped to distribute food and medical supplies to Cuba during the years of US embargo, to street children in Morocco, and to a refugee orphanage in Ivory Coast. More generally he has worked with the World Food Programme and helped to facilitate more than 200 million meals for the world's hungry. In the United States he has visited and fundraised numerous ventures, from soup kitchens and hospitals to summer camps for disadvantaged children and adoption agencies. Ali may have raised more for US charities than any other single person. Little wonder that for the breadth of his humanitarian work, Ali was granted an Amnesty lifetime achievement award.

Actress Julia Roberts shares a joke with Ali at the Amnesty International Media Spotlight Awards. There, Ali received a lifetime achievement award.

Ali and fellow Parkinson's sufferer Michael J. Fox are seen here in Washington where they asked the Senate for more funds for Parkinson's research.

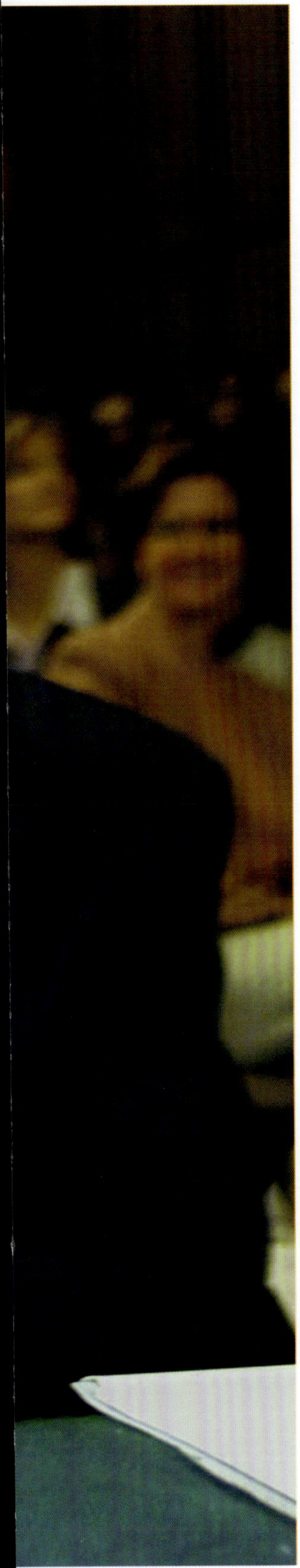

MUHAMMAD ALI PARKINSON CENTER

Jimmy Walker is a philanthropist who made his money through financial planning and investments in sports teams such as the Phoenix Giants baseball team in the 1980s. As a trustee on the Barrow Neurological Foundation, he came up with the idea of using his contacts in sports and other media to help raise funds for and awareness about a new unit specialising in treatment of Parkinson's disease. The unit was being set up by Dr. Abraham Lieberman. Lieberman has been Ali's physician since his diagnosis with Parkinson's Disease in the mid-1980s, seeing him every other week since then, and is an authority on the disease. Lieberman said: "Jimmy had the idea that if Muhammad had his name in the event, it would be a bigger deal... He's the greatest sports figure of the 20th century and I think the fact that he has Parkinson's disease makes people much more aware."

Lieberman realised that there was a pressing need for a more holistic approach to treating the disease. Rather than having patients diagnosed in one place, treated in another and having disconnected access to strategies for living with Parkinson's, the Center brought together clinical and research expertise on Parkinson's with its treatment, from using surgery such as stimulation of brain movement centres to therapies, including drugs, and teaching tactics for living with the progressive disease.

Ali was a rich man when he was diagnosed with Parkinson's and could afford to see the best medical experts, wherever they were located. He was also prey to suspicious medical advice at times, such as blood filtering to remove pesticides that some experts thought were causing his Parkinson's syndromes. So he endorsed having everything in one place, run by respected experts, and the Center's emphasis on promoting community integration and outreach, through recreational therapy programs and excellence in education about Parkinson's, for people at the thin end of the wedge – patients and caregivers.

CELEBRITY FIGHT NIGHT

In 1994, a celebrity charity fundraising event was organised in Phoenix, again by Jimmy Walker, the philanthropist. Invited wealthy guests and charity workers in tuxedoes and glamorous dresses witnessed a humorous fight in a boxing ring between two stars of local Phoenix Suns basketball team, Charles Barkley and Dan Majerle, wearing outsize boxing gloves. Auctions of objects and experiences, ticket and drinks takings raised $100,000. It was a smash hit and the next year, a long set by singer Kenny Rogers helped the event morph into an evening of entertainment. In 1996, Muhammad Ali was invited as the featured guest.

Ali's involvement upped the stakes for Celebrity Fight Night. His global name in boxing and in other fields proved a real draw for celebrities. Ali used the spotlight in 1996 to tell the world about the Muhammad Ali Parkinson Center. Since then the Center has become the focal charity for the event and has received some $45 million in donations from Celebrity Fight Night. Each year, The Muhammad Ali Celebrity Fight Night Awards, are presented to leaders in the sports, entertainment and business communities who best represent the qualities associated with Ali and his fight to find a cure for Parkinson's disease. Recipients have included Halle Berry, Arnold Schwarzenegger, fellow Parkinson's sufferer Michael J. Fox and boxer Evander Holyfield. Entertainment is kept at a high standard by multi-Grammy winner David Foster, featuring such global stars as Celine Dion, Lionel Richie, Gloria Estefan and Jennifer Lopez.

By 2013, Celebrity Fight Night had become one of the highest grossing charity events in the United States. No wonder, with tickets selling at up to $5,000 and auctions for unique experiences, such as a night with Jennifer Lopez on the red carpet in Hollywood, dinner with Billy Crystal and Robert De Niro in New York, or lunch and golf with golfer Phil Mickelson.

Ali and wife Lonnie attend Muhammad Ali's Celebrity Fight Night in Phoenix, Arizona in 2013.

THE BIOPIC

In 1994, the idea of a biopic about Ali was kicking around Hollywood. The original screenplay by Gregory Allen Howard focused on the troubled relationship between Ali and his father Cassius Sr. Directors including Oliver Stone and Steven Spielberg had contemplated making it. The charismatic young film star Will Smith was identified to play Ali but he refused as the screenplay was controversial and Ali was so universally scrutinised, saying "I didn't want to be the dude that messed up the Muhammad Ali story."

That changed in the late 1990s when a new script emerged by *Forrest Gump* screenwriter, Eric Roth, and director Michael Mann came on board. Smith confessed: "If there's a role I was born to play, this is it," and Ali said at their first meeting: "Man, you're almost pretty enough to play me." Smith immersed himself in the role by watching endless interviews with Ali to perfect the voice and getting fighting fit. He entered a professional training camp with Sugar Ray Leonard's trainer, Darrell Foster, running 3 miles (4.8 km) and boxing for 2 hours each morning, watching fight films and then lifting weights to bulk up. At the end of the camp, Foster said Smith "could fight for real. His hand speed's real good."

Mann filmed scenes as authentically as possible. For example, he recreated the Rumble in the Jungle in a football stadium in Mozambique, with a crowd of 20,000 volunteers and 2,000 paid extras plus, some cardboard cutouts! Sony Pictures was so worried about the budget that they temporarily pulled out until Mann and Smith took partial financial risk in the project. Ali opened in 2001. It had cost $100 million to make but recouped a tenth of this on opening weekend. Ali said at the Louisville premiere: "It's a great movie. Will Smith did a great job."

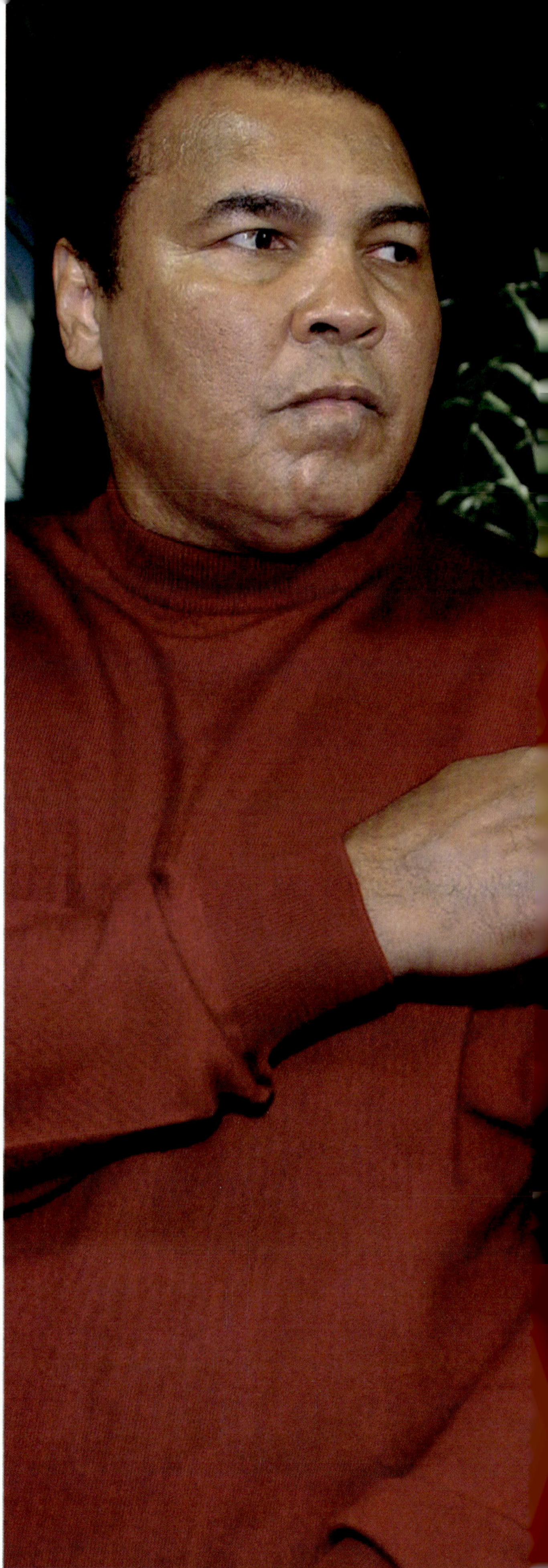

Actor Will Smith portraying Ali in a fight scene from *Ali*.

Ali jokes with US actor Will Smith, who plays him in the film *Ali* at the film's premiere in Hollywood in 2001, watched by Smith's son.

Ali holds a flame with former Heavyweight Champion Evander Holyfield during the Grand Opening Gala for the Muhammad Ali Center in Louisville in 2005.

MUHAMMAD ALI CENTER

"A visitor of the Muhammad Ali Center experiences the hows of Ali's life: how he found the courage, the dedication, and the discipline to become who he is today; how he found the conviction to stand up for what he believed; and how he turned his passion for excellence in the ring to a passion for peace on the world stage."

The other big charitable cause in Ali's life is his eponymous center in his home city of Louisville, Kentucky. Ali had always retained strong links with the place where he grew up, which had celebrated him in different ways, from naming a street after him in 1978 to naming him the greatest athlete of all time in 2000. Ali co-founded the Center in 2005 with his wife Lonnie. At its heart is an interactive museum about Ali but its mission is to promote respect, hope and understanding, and inspire greatness, in the spirit of Ali's life.

The Center is linked to the Muhammad Ali Institute for Peace and Justice at the University of Louisville. This advances the study and practice of social justice, peace building and violence prevention. It does this through initiatives such as SeeRedNow, an educational media campaign designed to encourage better understanding of root causes of violence, and The Ali Scholars Program for undergraduates to travel internationally to explore, witness and collaborate in peace and social justice work.

Funding for the Center came from the city from an anonymous donor and Ford Motor Company. City leaders invested in the project as part of urban re-development of downtown Louisville. However, the project is not without controversy. Critics have questioned the building of the Center downtown, rather than in the predominantly black, run-down West End part of the city, where Ali grew up and where re-development would have arguably had a greater impact, and the Center's goals would have had greater relevance.

The Muhammad Ali Center, in Louisville, Kentucky.

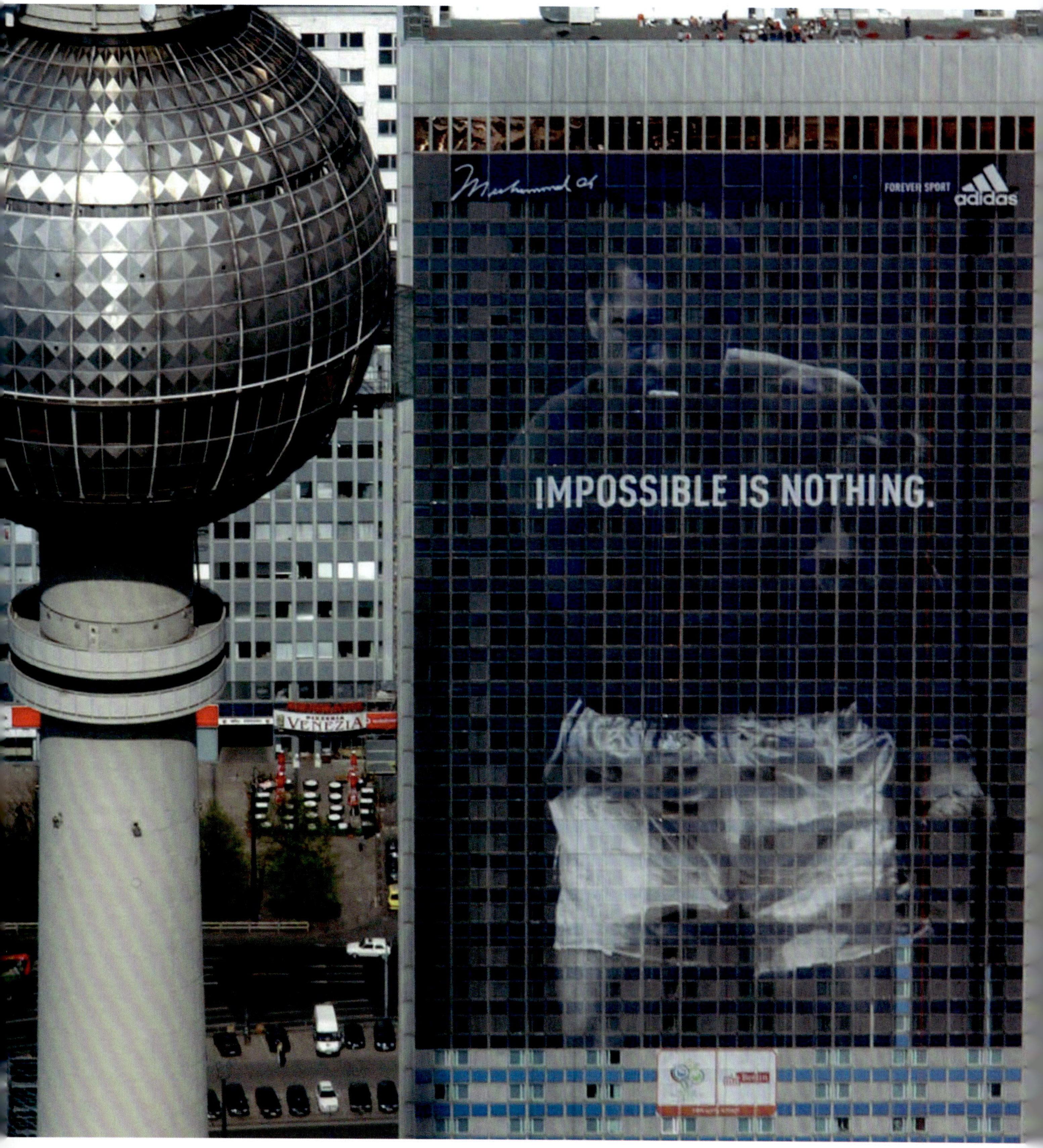

In 2004, sports company Adidas created this 1,544 square mile (4,000 m2) advert using a portrait of Ali, which covered the façade of the Berlin Park Inn.

BRAND ALI

Muhammad Ali is an icon. Ali knew his brand had a value from selling signed goods. For years the going rate was $25 and annually he might sign around 15,000 for profit, on tickets, posters, boxing gloves (that would sell for $200), statues and the like. He marketed sports collectibles through a company called Sports Placement Services, but he and his family had limited control of, and therefore limited earning power from, his wider brand, such as use of his face, of his names Cassius Clay and Muhammad Ali, and even phrases such as "Float like a butterfly, sting like a bee".

In 2006 Ali signed a $50 million deal with the Entertainment and licensing firm CKX. This was to form a new company G.O.A.T. LLC, which stands for "Greatest of All Time," in which Ali received 20 per cent and CKX 80 per cent from selling his name and likeness. CKX had many other 'partners with iconic content', including Elvis Presley's name and likeness, found on objects such as velvet paintings and commemorative shot glasses, Graceland, and the American Idol television series. Some of the first Ali-inspired goods were snack foods with names such as 'Rumble' and flavours including 'Thrill-A-Dill-A' and a limited edition luxury book. It was called *GOAT: A Tribute to Muhammad Ali*. Weighing 75 pounds (34 kg) with nearly 800 pages and more than 3,000 images of Ali and his life, it was covered in silk and Louis Vuitton leather and sold for $7,500.

In 2011, the brand giant IMG Licensing bought out G.O.A.T. and acquired the newly formed Muhammad Ali Enterprises and the Ali brand, which represents, "rebelliousness, excellence and inspiration in equal parts". Brand Ali is now in a stable that includes Ferrari, Dole bananas, World Series of Poker, and Goodyear tyres. In 2014, the first line of Adidas Muhammad Ali boxing apparel appeared in stores.

A copy of the book *Greatest Of All Time: A Tribute to Muhammad Ali* published by Taschen.

BIRTHDAY CELEBRATIONS

There were at least five parties to celebrate Muhammad Ali's 70th birthday but one of the biggest and most star-studded, was the "Power of Love Gala" on 18 February 2012, at the Grand Garden Arena, Las Vegas, the site of most of boxing's major fights in the last 20 years. Famous faces, including David Beckham, Anthony Hopkins and Samuel L Jackson, paid ticket prices starting at $1,500. The gala raised awareness about conditions such as Alzheimer's and Parkinson's Disease, and funds for the Cleveland Clinic Lou Ruvo Center for Brain Health and the Muhammad Ali Centre in Louisville. The event also raised funds through an auction, in which the pair of Ali's boxing gloves that he used to defeat Floyd Patterson in 1965, were sold for $1.1 million to Lorenzo Fertitta, a casino owner. A four-night stay at private islands in the Bahamas owned by magician David Copperfield raised $300,000.

During the 5-hour long birthday bash, the former heavyweight boxing champion was honoured by singers, athletes and actors who spoke and performed in tribute to Ali. Stevie Wonder sang Happy Birthday and there were also performances by Cee-Lo Green, Lenny Kravitz, Snoop Dogg, and LL Cool J, who rapped, "Mama Said Knock You Out". Footballer David Beckham paid tribute to Ali saying he was an inspiration and President Obama made an appearance via a heartfelt video message. The event was televised on 25 February and Samuel L Jackson told the audience: "He's done it with guts and grace, with his fists, and with his wits. He's one of the groundbreaking figures of the generation that helped make the world a more open place when it comes to who we can love, where we can go and what we can do."

Lonnie, Ali and recording artist Sean "Diddy" Combs onstage during the Keep Memory Alive foundation's Power of Love Gala celebrating Ali's 70th birthday.

ALI TODAY

By 2014, there had been numerous stories about the possible demise of Muhammad Ali. In 2011, he was taken to hospital after falling unconscious soon after attending the funeral of Joe Frazier, where although frail, Ali had stood to energetically applaud his old adversary. In 2013, there were rumours he could no longer speak and was on the verge of death, but in response, Ali's family posted a picture of him watching the Superbowl on television and striking a defiant pose with boxing fists. A year later, in April 2014, Ali was pictured with boxer Andre Berto at his home in Arizona, where Berto reported that Ali had dished out pearls of wisdom such as "Stay focused on the task" and "Don't worry about the outside noise". As at many other times in his life, the Greatest appeared to be defying expectations and fighting on when he seemed to be down and out.

Ali is rarely seen at public events and spends much of his time at home nowadays, enjoying the family times he missed out on when he was boxing. Laila Ali, his daughter, said: "...he lights up when he sees the kids, especially my son who looks exactly like him. He loves that."

One of his latest, rare public appearances was in October 2013, at the inaugural Muhammad Ali Humanitarian Awards in Louisville, proving that he may be frail but his commitment to social justice has not diminished. While Parkinson's disease has taken a severe toll on Ali, his wife Lonnie said: "Every day he gets up with a smile in his face and looks forward to whatever the day brings. He doesn't let things stop him and he does as much as he can every day and he still finds meaning in life."

Ali and his daughter, Hana Yasmeen Ali, promoting his book, *The Soul of a Butterfly* in 2004 in New York.

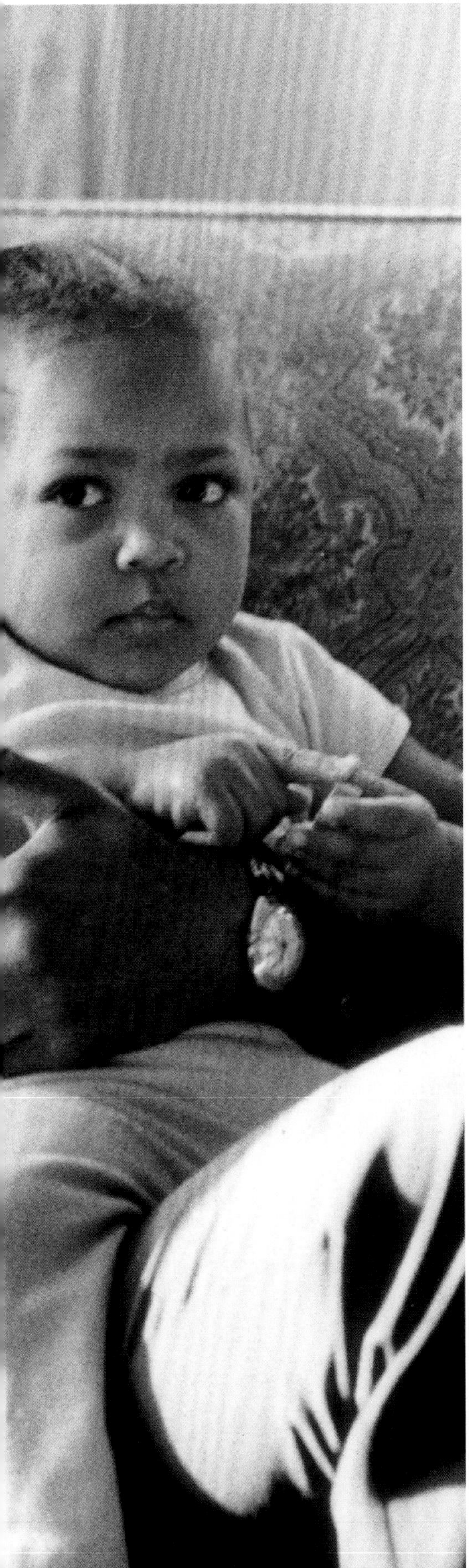

PERSONAL LIFE

Ali training for a fight in Munich while spending time with his twin daughters, Jamillah and Rasheda in 1971.

FAMILY LIFE

Being one of the most famous men on the planet and travelling as much as he did away from home must have made it difficult for Ali to maintain a home life. He has been married four times and has nine children: seven daughters and two sons. Two of his daughters, Miya (born 1971) and Khalilah (born 1974), were from affairs he had while married to his second wife, Belinda.

When Ali met 23-year-old Sonji Roi, she was working as a cocktail waitress. She was very beautiful and Ali was so taken with her that he proposed the night they met. They married in August 1964, first under Islamic law and then with a Justice of the Peace to make it legal under US law, but by June 1965 Ali filed for divorce. One reason stated was that Sonji refused to follow the religion of Islam as she had promised to, for example never wearing a headdress or veil. When the divorce was finalised on 10 January 1966, Ali sent her a note saying: "You traded Heaven for Hell, baby."

Ali met Belinda Boyd because her mother worked as a sort of companion for Elijah Muhammad's wife. They had a quiet private marriage ceremony in Chicago, after which Belinda changed her name to Khalilah Ali, although old friends and family continued to call her Belinda. She stayed in the background as she believed a Muslim wife should do and she and Ali had four children: Maryum (born 1968), twins Rasheeda and Jamillah (born 1970), and Muhammad Junior (1972). She recalled some of their happiest times were when the government stripped Ali of his title, and they travelled together to his lectures at colleges around the country and she managed their depleted finances.

Ali holds up his 4-month-old son Muhammad Ali, Jr., in 1972, outside his Deer Lake, PA, training camp.

BELINDA AND ALI BREAK UP

Ali and Belinda were married for almost ten years before their marriage broke up because of Ali's affair with Veronica Porsche. Veronica was one of four poster girls who helped to promote the 1974 Rumble in the Jungle fight. At first, Belinda turned a blind eye to the affair, believing Veronica was just, "one of the bunch", even allowing Veronica to join them on family trips, billed as the babysitter.

However, when Veronica accompanied Ali to Manila and met Ferdinand and Imelda Marcos before the big fight, she was introduced as his wife and Ali did not correct the error. Once the story broke, Ali tried to justify his need to have a girlfriend at a press conference and it became big news. Belinda flew straight to Manila and Ali's heated fight with her at his hotel became almost as big a story as the upcoming boxing match! Belinda finally admitted defeat and filed for divorce in 1976. She got a generous divorce settlement and Ali put $1 million in a trust fund for their four children.

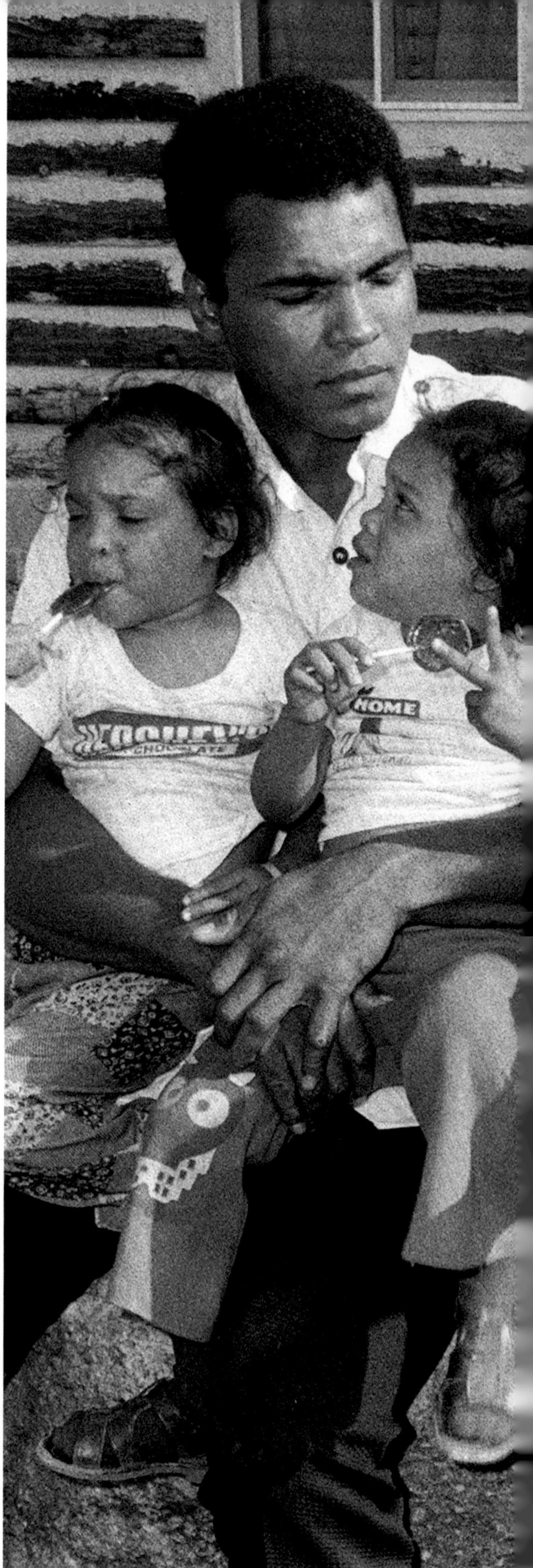

Ali with his second wife, Belinda, and three of their four children at Deer Lake, Pennsylvania, in August 1973.

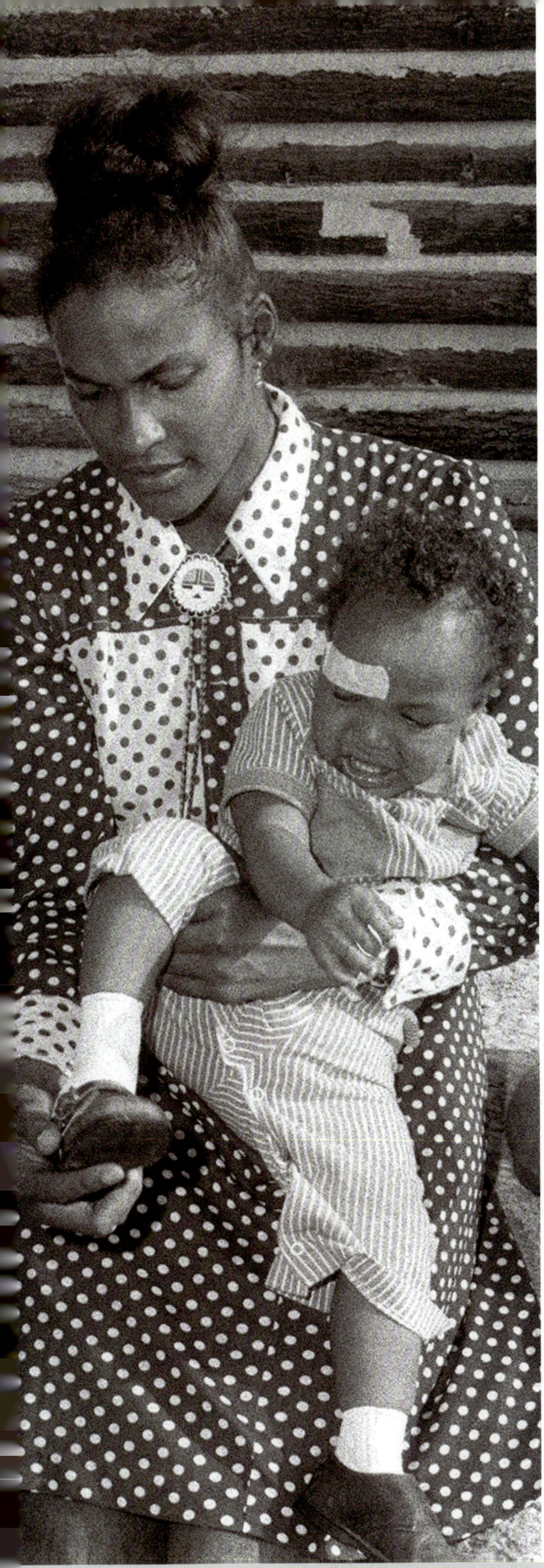

When Ali and Veronica got married on 19 June 1977 their first daughter, Hana (born 1976), was about ten months old and Veronica was pregnant with their second daughter, Laila Ali (born 1977). Veronica and Ali lived in luxury in a huge mansion in LA but the strain soon started to show on their relationship. Ali missed his busy life as a boxer and Veronica felt confined because while she wanted to continue her career, Ali wanted her to stay at home. By now Ali was also feeling tired all the time and his speech was slurred. On a visit home to Louisville in 1982 he met his fourth wife-to-be, Yolanda Williams, and by 1985, he and Veronica had filed for divorce.

Ali poses with his third wife Veronica outside his home at Freemont Place, Los Angeles in March 1982.

Ali with Lonnie Williams in Michigan, in July 1999.

YOLANDA WILLIAMS

Ali married his fourth wife, Yolanda Williams, known as Lonnie, in 1986 but they first met back in 1962, when her family moved into a house opposite his, when she was five and he was 20. Her mother recalls Yolanda, like all the local kids, being in awe of him and Ali looking after her like an older brother. She recalled Ali playing driving around town before his fight with Sonny Liston in a bus with "Cassius Clay" written on the sides, with as many kids as would fit on it, him shouting: "Who's the Greatest!" and the kids calling back: "You are!"

When Lonnie and Ali met for lunch in 1982 she was studying for an MBA at Louisville University but was upset by the noticeable decline in his health, and, with Veronica's permission, moved to a house near his in LA to help to care for him and continue her studies there. She converted to Islam and when he divorced Veronica in 1986, she and Ali were married at a quiet ceremony in Louisville. His mother-in-law said this was an example of Ali not forgetting his roots: "A lot of people, when they get famous, they forget old friends, or at least they expect you to come to them. But not Muhammad." Ali and Lonnie are still together and have one son, Asaad Amin, whom they adopted when he was five months old.

Many people who know Ali and Lonnie say she is very good for Ali and that his physical and financial state stabilised after they got married. However, there is still some controversy. In 2014, Ali's eldest son, Muhammad Jr., accused Lonnie of making it difficult for him to see his father while he and his family live on the breadline in Chicago. A similar accusation was also made by Ali's brother, Rahman.

BOXER FOCUS: LAILA ALI

Laila Amaria Ali was born on 30 December 1977 in Miami Beach, Florida. She grew up in California with her parents Muhammad Ali and Veronica Porsche-Ali, and her older sister, Hana. During troubled teenage years, she spent time in a juvenile detention centre but afterwards, earned a degree in business management and owned a nail salon. She was inspired to become a boxer after seeing a televised fight between female boxers Christy Martin and Deirdre Gogarty in 1996.

Laila had first her professional fight on 8 October 1999, knocking out opponent April Fowler 31 seconds into round one. Over her career, she fought many leading names in women's boxing, including Jacqui Frazier-Lyde, daughter of boxer Joe Frazier, who she defeated in 2001 after a fight that was widely promoted as "Ali vs. Frazier IV". In 2002, she won the IBA title with a two-round knockout of Suzette Taylor and in November the same year, she retained that title and added the WIBA and IWBF belts, after an eight-round knockout win over world champion Valerie Mahfood. Laila retired from boxing in 2007 as undefeated Super Middleweight Boxing Champion of the World. Her ring nickname was "She Bee Stingin", a nod to her father's famous phrase, "Float like a butterfly, sting like a bee."

After retiring from boxing, Laila Ali has become a television host and personality, featuring in shows such *Dancing with the Stars* (2007), *American Gladiators* (2008) and *Stars Earn Stripes* (2012), *All in with Laila Ali* (2013) as well as exercise videos. She wrote a book, *Reach!* in 2002, and launched a range of beauty products. She is married to former NFL star Curtis Conway and they have two children, son Curtis Jr and daughter Sydney.

Laila Ali poses for a portrait in August 2001 in New York.

Laila Ali with her father, Muhammad Ali, after a WBC/WIBA Super Middleweight title bout in Washington, DC.

STATISTICS

BORN	Miami (FL), 30 December 1977
TURNED PROFESSIONAL	1999
NUMBER OF PRO BOUTS	24
WINS-LOSSES-DRAWS	24-0-0
NUMBER OF KNOCKOUTS	21
RETIRED	2007

Ali prays at the Alabaster Mosque in Cairo, Egypt in October 1986.

RELIGIOUS LIFE

A belief in one God, who created everything in the universe, has been the driving force in Muhammad Ali's long life, although his religious views have developed over time. After he began to study the Quran in the mid-1970s, he converted from his mother's Baptist religion to become a follower of Islam. He joined the Nation of Islam, an organisation that combined elements of traditional Islam with black nationalist ideas, and followed the teachings of Elijah Muhammad, who proclaimed all white people were 'devils' who hated black people and that it was time for black people to unite and assert themselves. Ali was vilified by the press and the white establishment for his change of religion and the change of name that came with it.

In 1972, Ali began to turn from the Nation of Islam to a mainstream Sunni Islam faith. In this year, he also made his first hajj, or pilgrimage, to Mecca, wearing the correct orthodox ihram attire. He began to pray five times a day and to fast during Ramadan. Ali himself expressed a broader tolerance and acceptance that other religions contain truth too: "Rivers, ponds, lakes and streams – they all have different names, but they all contain water. Just as religions do – they all contain truths." He also said that no matter what religion you believe in, if you live a good life you'll receive God's blessing and go to heaven.

In 1975, Elijah Muhammad died and when his son Wallace D Mohammed became leader of the Nation of Islam, he, like Malcolm X before him, also converted to orthodox Islam and most Nation of Islam members followed him. The Nation of Islam was eventually known as the American Society of Muslims and welcomed people of all races, too.

In 2005, according to Ali's daughter, Hana, Ali embraced spiritual practices of Sufism, a mystical branch or sect of Islam, after reading Sufi teachings in a collection of books by a man named Hazrat Inayat Khan. Sufism is a belief and practice in which Muslims seek to find the truth of divine love and knowledge through direct personal experience of God.

In his later years, Ali has seen himself primarily as a holy man. He published a memoir entitled *The Soul of a Butterfly: Reflections on Life's Journey,* which he wrote over the course of two years with his daughter Hana. It is an unconventional autobiography that combines reminiscences with stories, poems, and spiritual lessons, and in which he discusses the meaning of religion. He is also the co-author of *Healing: A Journal of Tolerance and Understanding* and *The Greatest: My Own Story.*

His religious beliefs gave him the values that shaped and sustained him and continued to guide him throughout his life. In his later years, it has become much harder for Ali to follow strictly the daily pattern of the call to prayer, but he still prays or reads when he can, saying that although his physical abilities were taken from him, he was given something greater: a chance to focus completely on his journey to forgiveness and peace.

Ali sums up his belief in spirituality best in his own words: "The only true satisfaction comes from honouring and worshipping God. Being a true Muslim is the most important thing in the world to me. It means more to me than being black or being American. I can't save other people's souls: only God can do that. But I can try to save my own."

Ali watches a basketball game between the Phoenix Suns and Miami Heat at US Airways Center, Phoenix, in 2010.

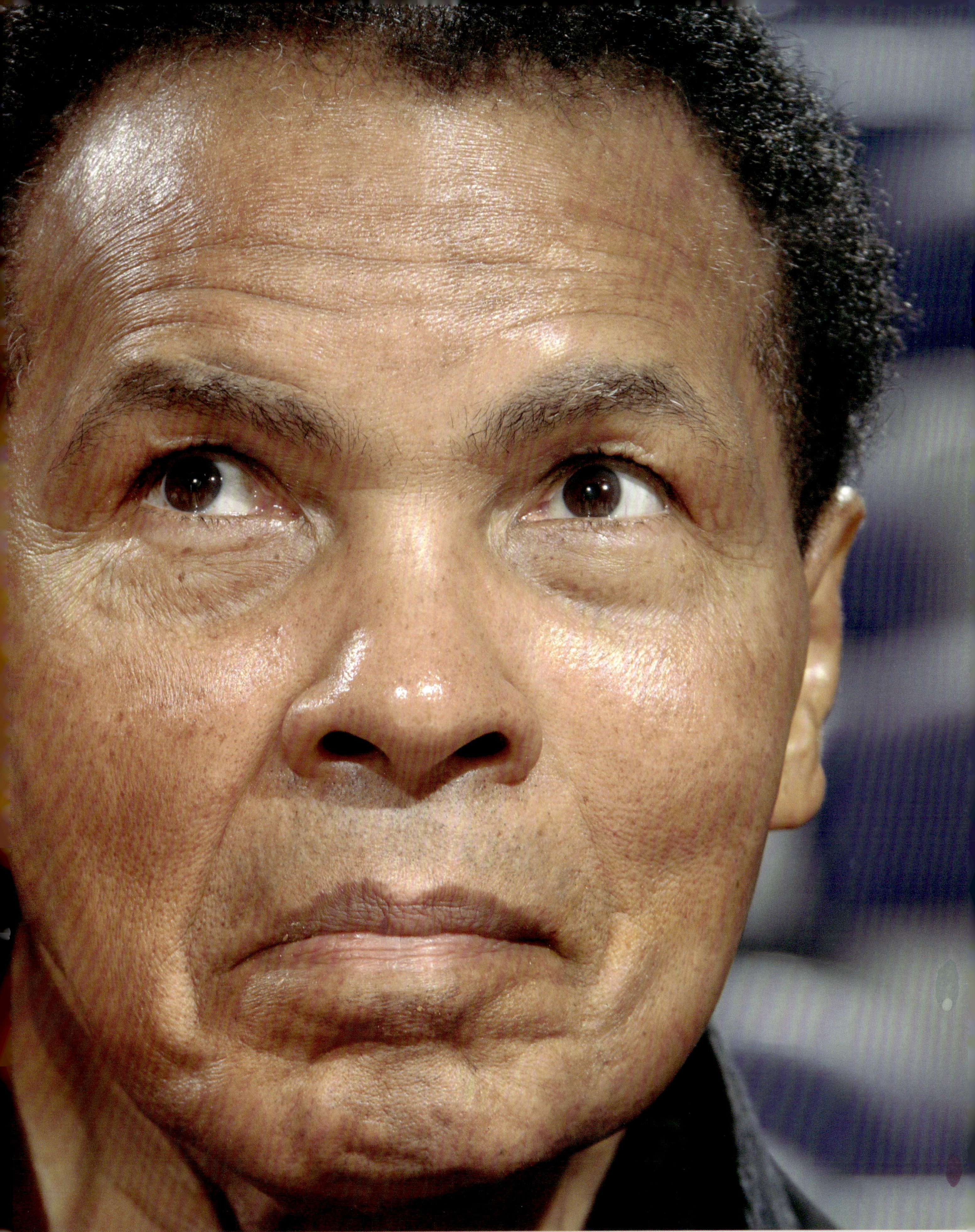

THE ALI LEGACY

Float Like
BUTTER FLY
Sting Like

Ali and fellow boxing legend Lennox Lewis pose with television presenter Harry Carpenter at the BBC Sports Personality of the Year Awards in London in 1999.

INSPIRING ATHLETES

Muhammad Ali was an outstanding athlete, who inspired generations of sportsmen and women around the world to follow their dreams. Of course, many of the athletes inspired by his determination and success, are from the world of boxing, such as Lennox Lewis, who said: "Muhammad Ali inspired me – from when I was a young boy growing up – he motivated me to chase my dreams inside and out of the ring."

Ali is also an inspiration for athletes from other sports disciplines and to both men and women. Footballer David Beckham has said of Ali: "Muhammad Ali has shown us one man can make a difference. His example of love, character, dignity, makes us want to be better." US tennis star Serena Williams said that she was inspired by Ali's fighting spirit not to give up after she struggled to get back on form after recovering from a blood clot on her lungs in 2011.

In December 1999, as the 20th century drew to a close, Ali was awarded no fewer than three Sportsman of the Century awards. He won the Sports Illustrated Athlete of the Century Award, the World Sports Award's World Sportsman of the Century and the BBC Sports personality of the century, in which he had garnered more votes than all of the other four candidates put together. Other legendary sportspeople were shortlisted for all awards, including Brazilian football star Pele and US tennis player Pete Sampras, whose sporting successes had no doubt equalled Ali's. Once again it was Ali's compelling skill, style, personality and his campaigning for causes he believed in, which made him stand out above the others. Ali collected the Sports Illustrated award at New York's Madison Square Garden, in front of many of the world's greatest athletes who gave him a standing ovation.

US tennis star Serena Williams is just one of many athletes who have been inspired by Ali's sporting skills and determination in some way.

INSPIRING ACTION

Muhammad Ali is more than an inspiring athlete. He is also a role model who encouraged people to stand up for what they believe in and to use their positions of privilege for positive action. After Australian Aboriginal sprinter Nova Peris-Kneebone presented Ali with the Olympic torch at Sydney in 2000, she explained that meeting him was important to her because, like Ali standing up for civil rights in the US, she used her celebrity to promote Aboriginal health and other issues in Australia. Standing with Ali at a press event, she said: "If you believe in something strong enough and you go out and stand for it, people start to take notice," at which point Ali said: "She's telling the truth."

Jack Newfield in *The Nation* magazine said Ali believed that if he fought he could persuade others to do so, too: "Ali believed that if he could beat Liston or Foreman or Frazier, that would inspire a junkie to get off drugs, a child to survive a terminal illness, a welfare recipient to get a job, a drunk to go to rehab. He believed his life could change other lives..."

Ali has also inspired leaders of nations. In 2005, President George Bush awarded Ali the United States' highest civilian honour, the Presidential Medal of Freedom. One year earlier and four years before being elected the first ever black US president, Barack Obama wrote about how Ali inspired him in an essay for a special edition of *USA Today:* "This is the Muhammad Ali who inspires us today – the man who believes real success comes when we rise after we fall; who has shown us that through undying faith and steadfast love, each of us can make this world a better place. He is, and always will be, the champ." Ali's picture is a reminder of this inspiration hanging in pride of place on the White House wall.

Ali never stops playing to the crowds! Here he is making a humorous gesture to George W. Bush after receiving the Presidential Medal of Freedom in 2005.

Picture Credits

4–5 Phil Greitzer/NY Daily News Archive via Getty Images; 6–7 Keystone-France/Gamma-Keystone via Getty Images; 8–9 Express/Archive Photos/Getty Images; 10 Charles 'Teenie' Harris/Carnegie Museum of Art/Getty Images; 11 AFP/Getty Images; 12–13 Jack Delano/Getty Images; 14 Buyenlarge/Getty Images; 15 New York Times Co./Getty Images; 16–17 Popperfoto/Getty Images; 18–19 FPG/Getty Images; 20 AFP/Getty Images; 20–21 Keystone-France/Gamma-Keystone via Getty Images; 22–23 The Ring Magazine/Getty Images; 24 NY Daily News Archive via Getty Images; 25 Frank Hurley/NY Daily News Archive via Getty Images; 26–27 Central Press/Getty Images; 28–29 Focus on Sport/Getty Images; 30 Tony Triolo/Sports Illustrated/Getty Images; 32–33 James Drake/Time & Life Pictures/Getty Images; 33 James Drake/Time & Life Pictures/Getty Images; 35 James Drake/Time & Life Pictures/Getty Images; 36 Ray Fisher/Time Life Pictures/Getty Images; 37 Focus on Sport/Getty Images; 38–39 Ron Case/Keystone/Getty Images; 39 Keystone/Getty Images; 40 Lee Balterman/Sports Illustrated/Getty Images; 42 Tony Triolo/Sports Illustrated/Getty Images; 43 Tony Triolo/Sports Illustrated/Getty Images; 44¬–45 Doug McKenzie/Hulton Archive/Getty Images; 45 John Pratt/Keystone Features/Hulton Archive/Getty Images; 46–47 Keystone-France/Gamma-Keystone via Getty Images; 48–49 OLDPIX/ANSA/UIG/Getty Images; 50–51 The Ring Magazine/Getty Images; 51 George Silk/Time Life Pictures/Getty Images; 52–53 Herb Scharfman/Time Life Pictures/Getty Images; 54 Popperfoto/Getty Images; 55 James Drake /Time & Life Pictures/Getty Images; 56–57 Popperfoto/Getty Images; 58–59 NY Daily News Archive via Getty Images; 60 John Peodincuk/NY Daily News Archive via Getty Images; 61 Gerry Cranham/Sports Illustrated/Getty Images; 62 Universal History Archive/UIG via Getty images; 63 Buyenlarge/Getty Images; 64 John Dominis/Time & Life Pictures/Getty Images; 65 The Ring Magazine/Getty Images; 66–67 Frank Castoral/NY Daily News Archive via Getty Images; 68–69 Central Press/Getty Images; 69 Popperfoto/Getty Images; 70–71 The Sydney Morning Herald/Fairfax Media via Getty Images; 72 Underwood Archives/Getty Images; 73 James Drake/Sports Illustrated/Getty Images; 74–75 David R. Lutman/Getty Images; 76–77 Joe Farrington/NY Daily News Archive via Getty Images; 78 The Ring Magazine/Getty Images; 80–81 Walter Kelleher/NY Daily News Archive via Getty Images; 81 Charles Hoff/NY Daily News Archive via Getty Images; 82 John Dominis/Time & Life Pictures/Getty Images; 83 Bob Gomel/Time Life Pictures/Getty Images; 84–85 Popperfoto/Getty Images; 86 Anwar Hussein/Getty Images; 87 Underwood Archives/Getty Images; 88–89 American Stock/Getty Images; 89 The Ring Magazine/Getty Images; 90–91 AFP/Getty Images; 92 Anthony Casale/NY Daily News Archive via Getty Images; 93 The Ring Magazine/Getty Images; 94 Evening Standard/Getty Images; 94–95 AFP/Getty Images; 96 AFP/Getty Images; 97 AFP/Getty Images; 98–99 Tony Triolo/Sports Illustrated/Getty Images; 100 Rolls Press/Popperfoto/Getty Images; 101 AFP/Getty Images; 102–103 Popperfoto/Getty Images; 103 The Ring Magazine/Getty Images; 104 Dieter LUDWIG/Gamma-Rapho via Getty Images; 105 Neil Leifer/Sports Illustrated/Getty Images; 106 Rolls Press/Popperfoto/Getty Images; 107 Rolls Press/Popperfoto/Getty Images; 108–109 Neil Leifer/Sports Illustrated/Getty Images; 110–111 Focus on Sport/Getty Images; 112 AFP/Getty Images; 112–113 Herb Scharfman/Sports Imagery/Getty Images; 114–115 Takeo Tanuma/Sports Illustrated/Getty Images; 116 Popperfoto/Getty Images; 117 John Iacono/Sports Illustrated/Getty Images; 118–119 The Ring Magazine/Getty Images; 119 The Ring Magazine/Getty Images; 120–121 Focus on Sport/Getty Images; 122–123 The Ring Magazine/Getty Images; 123 Tim Chapman; 124–125 Manny Millan/Sports Illustrated/Getty Images; 126–127 John Iacono/Sports Illustrated/Getty Images; 128–129 Robert Riger/Getty Images; 130–131 Time & Life Pictures/Getty Images; 132–133 Peter Charlesworth/LightRocket via Getty Images; 135 The Ring Magazine/Getty Images; 136–137 MARIA BASTONE/AFP/Getty Images; 139 Michael Cooper/Getty Images; 140–141 Paula Bronstein/UNICEF/Getty Images; 141 Richard Corkery/NY Daily News Archive via Getty Images; 142–143 STEPHEN JAFFE/AFP/Getty Images; 144–145 Mike Moore/Getty Images for Fight Night; 146–147 LUCY NICHOLSON/AFP/Getty Images; 147 Peter Brandt/Getty Images; 148 JEFF HAYNES/AFP/Getty Images; 149 Dennis Macdonald/Photolibrary/Getty Images; 150 FABIAN MATZERATH/AFP/Getty Images; 151 Michael Buckner/Getty Images for Baby2Baby; 152–153 Ethan Miller/Getty Images for Keep Memory Alive; 154–155 Kramer/Getty Images; 156–157 Frank Tewkesbury/Evening Standard/Getty Images; 158 Central Press/Getty Images; 159 Popperfoto/Getty Images; 160–161 Popperfoto/Getty Images; 161 AFP/Getty Images; 162–163 Steve Liss/Time Life Pictures/Getty Images; 164–165 The Ring Magazine/Getty Images; 165 Ed Mulholland/WireImage/Getty Images; 166 MIKE NELSON/AFP/Getty Images; 168–169 John W. McDonough/Sports Illustrated/Getty Images; 170–171 Anwar Hussein/Getty Images; 172 Craig Prentis/Allsport; 173 Mike Hewitt/Getty Images; 174–175 MANDEL NGAN/AFP/Getty Images

Endpapers: front left NY Daily News/Getty Images; front right Popperfoto/Getty Images; back left Popperfoto/Getty Images; back right NY Daily News/Getty Images
Cover: front Focus On Sport/Getty Images; back Thinkstock/Getty Images

Smok
Joe
MUHAMMAD
ALI

Successful **Glamour** Photography

REVISED EDITION

Successful **Glamour** Photography

A GUIDE TO PROFESSIONAL TECHNIQUES FOR FILM AND DIGITAL PHOTOGRAPHY

Duncan Evans • John Kelly

AMPHOTO BOOKS

AN IMPRINT OF WATSON-GUPTILL PUBLICATIONS / NEW YORK

Contents

A QUARTO BOOK

First published in US by Amphoto Books,
an imprint of Watson-Guptill Publications,
a division of Crown Publishing Group,
Random House Inc., New York
www.watsonguptill.com
www.crownpublishing.com

Original edition reprinted 1988, 1989,
1991, 1992, and 1994
Revised edition 2005, 2009

Library of Congress Control Number:
2004111882

International Standard Book Number:
0-8174-5923-5

Conceived, designed, and produced by
Quarto Publishing plc
The Old Brewery
6 Blundell Street
London N7 9BH

QUAR: SGF

Editor: Michelle Pickering
Art editor & designer: Sheila Volpe
Assistant art director: Penny Cobb
Illustrator: Kuo Kang Chen

Art director: Moira Clinch
Publisher: Piers Spence

Color separation by Provision Pte Ltd,
Singapore
Printed by SNP Leefung Printers Ltd, China

5

3

4

Introduction

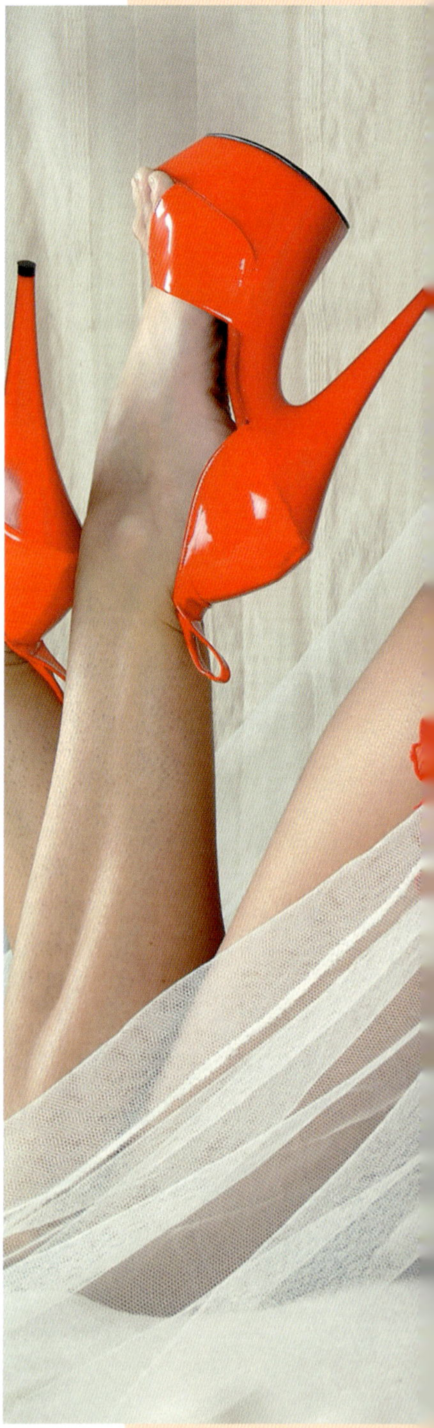

GLAMOUR PHOTOGRAPHY has changed out of all recognition in the last few years. Gone are the days of soft-focus, fluffy-haired beauties, scorch-tanned models covered in baby oil, and predictable lighting arrangements shot by photographers with a king's ransom in film camera equipment. Fashions in makeup, styling, and clothing change, of course. Even fashions in underwear are different from one decade to the next. The equipment used for glamour photography has also changed, and the photography itself is no longer the province of art-school dropouts with deep pockets.

Portable, flexible studio lighting is now affordable. Models are far more available and, with the advent of the internet, it is possible to scout, research, and find a suitable model without leaving the comfort of your computer. With the advent of digital technology, you can also easily check to see if the lighting has worked or whether the exposure needs tweaking. There is no need for expensive processing at film labs, either.

Finally, the market for glamour images has also changed, with the rise of so-called "lads mags," featuring glossy, sexy, provocative poses, but not necessarily with nudity. Here, the requirement is for clever lighting, a fresh approach, and plenty of photographic creativity. Mix in all the traditional elements of glamour photography and you possibly have the dawn of a golden age. All you need to know is how to take those photos successfully and that is where this book comes in.

Starting with photographic gear—both the film variety and what you need for a digital kit—this book provides the essential checklist for the aspiring glamour photographer. Prime lenses or zooms, camera types, lighting, reflectors, and so on are all examined. Then we move to the subject of models—how to find them, how much to pay, assessing what you need from the subject, and how to go about organizing a shoot. The art of makeup and body painting is discussed, along with props, styling, and clothes.

Once you have your model, let's head outside and scout out those ideal glamour locations, such as beaches and boats, and learn about the lighting conditions to which you need to pay careful attention. Now take the models inside and look for creative interior locations. Learn how to light them with a mixture of flash and tungsten, or even natural daylight, and how to use props, backgrounds, and accessories to make the most of the interiors where you are shooting. Plus, what about a studio of your own—how to set up a studio, the amount of space you will need, and the advantages of working in your own studio are all discussed. Finally, we turn to the professional side—how to get those jobs, sell your images, and create portfolios, presentations, websites, and promotional material.

Whatever your level of photography now, there will be something in this book to help you take better, more successful glamour photographs.

Duncan Evans

Transparent fabrics are often used to produce dreamy, romantic images but this photograph is all about seduction, created by the model's provocative pose, red lingerie and high heels, and half-hidden face as she looks up at the camera. Take care with your model's clothing because fashions change quickly. Although these shoes are highly distinctive, they have a fetish look that should stand the test of time.

90mm lens, digital ISO 100, 1/60 sec at f5.6

Camera Types

The cameras used to take the photographs in this book are indicated by the following symbols:

- Digital camera
- 35mm camera
- Medium-format camera

Cameras and accessories need to be versatile to cope with different lighting conditions. With digital cameras, you can now instantly review the result and reshoot if necessary.

Photographic Equipment

Whatever the circumstances, whether you shoot on film or digital, the advice in this chapter will help.

Types of Cameras

35mm SLR

Digital SLR

Medium format

35mm SLR Camera

The 35mm single-lens reflex (SLR) is the ideal camera for glamour work. It is light, versatile, and offers a bright, what-the-camera-sees view through the lens, delivered to the eyepiece via a pentaprism. Fixed focal-length or zoom lenses can be quickly and easily interchanged, in each case the viewfinder showing exactly the framing that will appear on film. Focusing can be automatic or carried out manually where the scene lacks contrast, by adjusting the focusing ring until the image is sharp. Modern SLRs also have through-the-lens metering, making it possible to set the aperture and shutter speed without consulting a separate light meter. Some SLRs even have automatic exposure control, although this is not necessarily an advantage in unusual lighting.

Digital Camera

Most amateur glamour photography is carried out using digital cameras, whether they are fully featured compacts with fixed zoom lenses, or digital SLRs with interchangeable lenses. If you are intending to break into the commercial field, the extra quality offered by an SLR is a must. A digital SLR has all the advantages of a film SLR in terms of shooting mechanics, but with huge bonuses on top. A digital SLR allows you to review each picture immediately to check exposure and composition, enabling

LEFT & RIGHT: These three shots are from a traditional Canon film SLR (right), an Olympus E-10 digital SLR (far right), and a scan of a medium-format slide (left). The aspect ratio of 35mm is 3:2, which is not ideally suited to reproduction in standard magazine pages. Many digital cameras use a ratio of 4:3 that is almost exactly that of a letter (A4) page. Medium-format cameras range from the 6x4.5 format, which is ideal for magazine work, to the very popular 6x7 pro format, which offers astounding detail but usually needs cropping to fill a vertical page.

Cameras, Lenses, and Accessories

In comparison to other branches of photography, the amount of equipment needed for successful glamour photography is relatively small. The basis of any kit is a 35mm or digital SLR camera, with the appropriate range of lenses. Each photographic assignment has its own individual requirements that will determine which lenses should be selected for use. In addition, there are a number of standard items that should be part of every camera kit.

Cameras

Today's camera technology is so sophisticated that there is sometimes the risk of using technique for its own sake, or buying expensive camera accessories that are little more than gimmicks. This is counterproductive as far as glamour photography is concerned; the aim is to achieve spontaneity of effect. The trick is to learn how to use your camera and then forget about it, leaving yourself free to concentrate on the image you are trying to create.

35mm SLR The single-lens reflex camera represents the pinnacle of achievement in modern camera design. Not only is the camera compact and easy to handle, but the fact that many of its functions are automatic makes its operation simple, quick, and undemanding.

Most modern 35mm SLRs, for example, have a viewing system that allows you to see precisely what the lens is imaging—not only what it is framing, but also the depth of field. Additionally, the light-sensitive cells incorporated within the camera make it possible to ensure highly accurate exposure measurements of the area to be photographed.

As far as glamour work is concerned, the SLR does have one minor disadvantage in the eyes of some photographers. The mirror arrangement of the viewing system does not allow you to see the subject at the moment the photograph is being taken. At fast speeds, this is hardly noticeable, but in long or panned exposures it can be inhibiting. Fortunately, this is not the norm in glamour. Also, under low light conditions or with lenses that do not have a very wide maximum aperture—f4 or f5.6 as opposed to a lens with f2, for example—viewing and focusing can be difficult. To overcome the problem of shooting with f16 or f22 in subdued light where you would probably see very little, most lenses have a preset diaphragm that allows normal viewing when the aperture is fully open, but stops down to the correct aperture at the moment of exposure.

Digital SLR The digital SLR also blanks out the viewfinder in exactly the same fashion as the 35mm SLR, and the compact digital camera, which uses an LCD for viewing, cuts it off at the moment of exposure. Fortunately, the viewfinders in digital SLRs tend to be very bright and offer excellent viewing, and compact digital cameras can boost the signal to the LCD so that it is always bright. Compacts have another disadvantage in that they suffer from shutter lag—the slight pause after pressing the fire button before the camera actually captures the shot.

Polaroid This is a useful additional item because it enables you to take instant reference prints as a final check before embarking on the actual shoot. Though still in use to some

an immediate reshoot to take place, or even to generate more ideas. Digital also has the advantage of being able to vary the ISO rating of every single shot, which can be very useful if moving in and out of a location like a house and garden. If shooting on location, digital can give great peace of mind when leaving the shoot that the images required are in the bag. The boon of not needing to develop film also means that it costs nothing to experiment, which can pay dividends with sophisticated lighting setups.

Medium-format Camera

When top quality and definition is an absolute must, there is nothing to beat the medium-format camera. With its large film area, it can produce far more detail than 35mm or digital cameras. The drawbacks are that medium-format cameras are large and heavy, and not suited for handheld work. You also only get 10–15 shots on a roll, making running costs higher.

degree, Polaroids have recently fallen out of favor. Some 35mm photographers use a cheap digital camera to check exposures, though most have actually switched to digital SLRs. However, the professional seeking maximum quality who uses medium-format cameras will employ a Polaroid back to generate a relatively instant shot for checking.

Lenses

Modern technology has deeply influenced lens design; the lenses of today are much more refined than their predecessors. The range of lenses available for 35mm cameras is extensive. For glamour photography, 35mm, 85mm, 135mm, and 80–200mm lenses were generally considered the most useful by professionals. If your digital SLR features a focal-length shift, then 24mm, 55mm, and 90mm are the equivalent lens sizes. However, the quality of large zooms has risen to such a degree that it is unusual to see a set of prime lenses being used on 35mm equipment now. More flexible and powerful, and far more popular, are the short telephoto zoom of 28–70mm and the big zoom of 70–300mm. The wide-angle zoom of 18–50mm is also popular.

Most SLR cameras are sold with a short telephoto lens, usually covering the 50mm mark because, of all focal lengths, this is the least obtrusive and gives a faithful, straightforward rendering of an image. However, what needs to be considered are the pros and cons of working at different focal lengths on the zoom, rather than actual lenses.

35mm Focal Length This is a moderately wide-angle view that is indispensable for indoor photography and for working in confined spaces. The perspective is much closer to that of a

Types of Lenses

There is no need to accumulate large numbers of expensive lenses—just establish the ones you like working with and stick to them. For glamour photography, the minimum requirements are likely to be: a moderate wide-angle lens for "setting" shots, and a moderate long-focus or "portrait" lens. Typically for film users, you are talking about the 28–100mm zoom and the 100–300mm telephoto zoom. Digital users will have to sacrifice either space or quality and use a wider angle lens than would otherwise be required. Just to get a standard 35mm SLR view, you need to use a 24mm lens with a digital SLR.

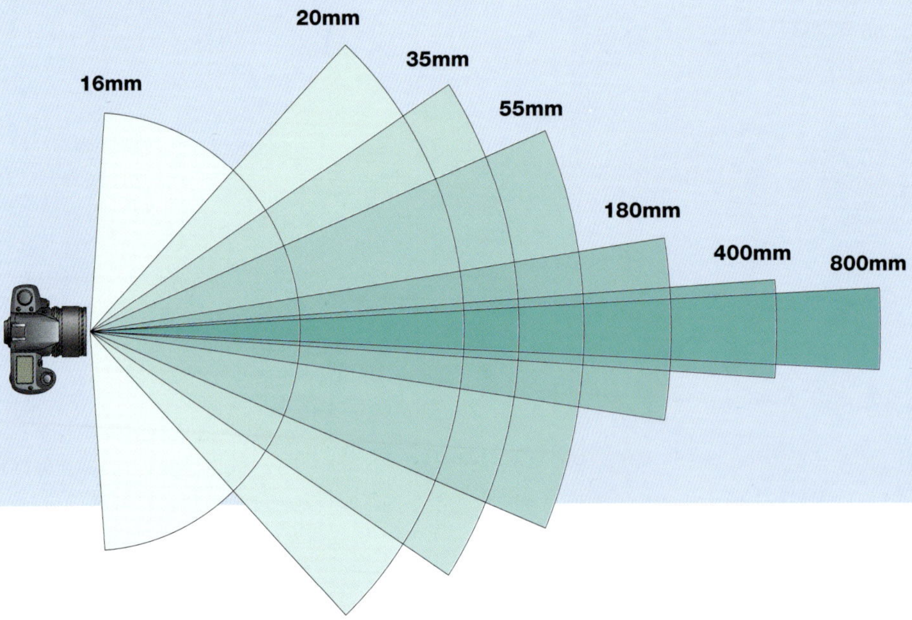

Angle of View This diagram shows the angle of view of some of the lenses that can be used by a 35mm or digital SLR camera. The longer the focal length, the smaller the angle of view seen by the lens.

LEFT: These photographs, taken in an interior location, demonstrate different angles of view produced by different lenses. The 85mm lens (far left) is ideal, closing in on the model and framing her, yet still offering reasonable depth of field. It is more flattering to the proportions of the body and face than wider angle lenses, and offers a working distance from the subject that is generally found to be convenient. The 135mm lens (near left) is similar but with reduced depth of field. It is useful when you cannot approach the model closely.

OPPOSITE PAGE: This pair of photographs, taken in an exterior location, demonstrate different angles of view produced by different focal-length lenses. The 35mm lens (top), a moderate wide-angle lens, sets the model in the environment. The 55mm lens (below) is the "standard" lens with an angle of view approximating to human vision. It is less useful for glamour photography than other focal lengths, tending to produce predictable images, neither concentrating on the model nor setting her in the location.

normal focal-length lens, but it does not possess such great depth of field as wider angle lenses at full aperture.

85mm and 135mm Focal Lengths These are long focus; the former is the most useful focal length for glamour photography, being particularly flattering for portraiture. A wide-angle lens used close up will distort features and limbs, whereas a longer lens used from farther away to give exactly the same view will not. The 135mm needs more light for its magnified image and therefore the lens has a relatively large aperture, plus a limited depth of field. This is ideal if you want to focus your subject against a blurred background. Another great advantage of a long-focus lens is that the photographer can work at a distance. This can be particularly useful for candid shots or in beach photography.

Superzoom Lenses A recent innovation is the superzoom lens, covering 28–300mm. Obviously, there is a price to pay for this kind of performance and convenience; this is usually pincushioning of the image, lack of focus at the end of the zoom, susceptibility to lens flare in bright daylight, and a lack of sharpness throughout. It generally also entails smaller apertures than less ambitious lenses, which makes it harder to use in lower light conditions.

Wide-angle and Extreme Long-focus Lenses In glamour photography, both these lenses are of limited use. As far as wide-angle lenses are concerned, their only purpose is for creating a bizarre, distorted effect. In the case of extreme long-focus lenses (300mm and over), the only useful effect they can create is a voyeuristic, "peeping Tom" image.

Choosing Lenses
Fixed focal-length lenses offer higher quality than zoom lenses but suffer from the lack of flexibility that a zoom can offer.

Camera Supports and Accessories

In glamour photography, it is common practice to use some form of camera support—usually a tripod—to avoid the risk of camera shake. This is far less acceptable than subject movement, particularly when shooting at slow speeds. At fast speeds, the camera can be handheld, but in the studio, or when precise composition is important, a support should always be used.

The ideal tripod should make it possible for you to take sharp pictures with a slow shutter speed under very windy conditions, with its legs fully extended. Points to check are the tripod's ability to hold a steady weight and its resistance to torque. Check the latter by trying to twist the head; if this moves significantly when clamped still, the design is poor. It should also be possible to spread the legs to a wider angle for a lower camera position, though an alternative is to reverse the center column so that the camera hangs from the tripod. Some center columns have a rachet and crank for raising and lowering the camera, but on cheap tripods this device can simply make them less steady.

Motor Drives, Winders, and Shutter Releases A motor drive uses a battery-powered motor to trigger the shutter and wind on the film. This is invaluable for fast action shooting, but it is also useful throughout the glamour photography field. Your aim in glamour photography is to concentrate as much of your attention as possible on the subject and anything that helps you to do this is a valuable aid. On most motor drives, the firing rate is adjustable up to 5 frames per second, though the unit can also be set to fire single frames. A cheaper alternative is an automatic winder. On digital cameras, there is no film to wind on, which is what actually takes up the time, but if shooting large size files for maximum quality, the speed of the camera will determine the frame rate. On a budget SLR you can expect 2.5 fps, 3 to 5 on a consumer model, and 8 or more on a professional model. Expect a lot less on a compact camera. The other salient point for digital is the size of the image buffer. The bigger the buffer, the more pictures you can shoot before the camera stops responding because it is too busy saving images to the memory card.

Cable releases are another way of simplifying firing when a long exposure time is required. Their use lessens the risk of camera shake, which can occur even when the camera is mounted on a tripod. The device is simply a flexible, sheathed cable that screws around or into the shutter release button. The longer and more flexible the cable, the less chance there is of vibration. An alternative is to use a timed delay.

LEFT: Many modern drives for film SLRs can be set to shoot continuously at speeds of up to 5 frames per second. Alternately, they can be used for single shots as a power winder. For sequences—in this case, the model taking off her bikini top—both modes can be very useful, allowing you to take a number of shots in a very short time without taking your eye from the viewfinder.
85–210mm zoom lens, Kodachrome 64, 1/125 sec at f5.6

BELOW RIGHT: Flare can easily ruin otherwise good pictures (far right), particularly when shooting into the sun. It may not always be obvious through the viewfinder, so be on the lookout. A lens hood will help, although it may be necessary to change the camera position (near right) as well.
35–140mm zoom lens, digital ISO 80, 1/64 sec at f8

Lens Attachments Two useful lens attachments are a lens hood and filter holders. The former is essential when working in intense sunlight or when using lamps for backlighting, because, in both cases, it is very difficult to avoid creating flare. The use of a lens hood removes this risk, since it cuts off extraneous light from outside the picture frame. Some lenses have built-in hoods that retract when not needed; most, however, take separate hoods that screw or clip onto the front of the lens.

Filter holders reduce the wear and tear on filters. This is especially the case when gelatin filters are used. These are cheaper, but more fragile, than glass filters.

Viewfinders Many SLRs have the facility for changing viewing heads and a range of these to suit particular circumstances is part and parcel of any professional's equipment. A magnifying pentaprism head, for instance, allows rapid viewing of an enlarged screen without having to press your eye close to the camera. A waist-level finder can be used for low-level viewing, while a high-magnification focusing viewer is useful for close-ups. Some digital cameras, particularly compacts, feature a flip-out LCD screen that enables low-level photography to be shot.

Accessories

An enormous variety of photographic accessories is available. Here are some of the more useful items for glamour work.

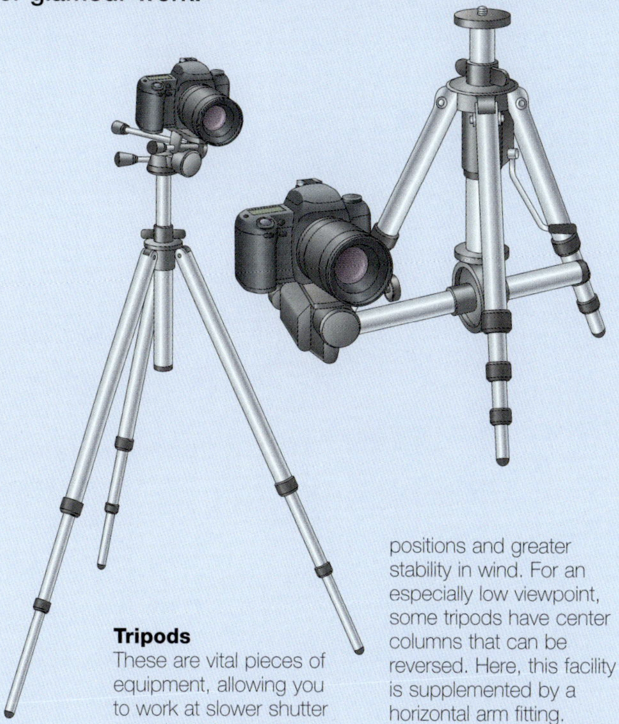

Tripods
These are vital pieces of equipment, allowing you to work at slower shutter speeds and removing the need to look through the viewfinder when the model is in position. Choose a good-quality, sturdy type. Some tripods have legs that can be spread wide for particularly low camera positions and greater stability in wind. For an especially low viewpoint, some tripods have center columns that can be reversed. Here, this facility is supplemented by a horizontal arm fitting. The tripod head is also important. Ball and socket heads allow movement in all directions, while pan and tilt heads allow you to adjust each movement—vertical, horizontal, and sidewise—independently of the others.

Motor Drives and Power Winders
These are extremely useful. Winders (left) merely advance the film automatically, while motor drives (below left) can be set to shoot sequences for as long as the shutter release is depressed. These are of no use for digital SLRs because the rate of fire is dependent upon resolution and memory buffer.

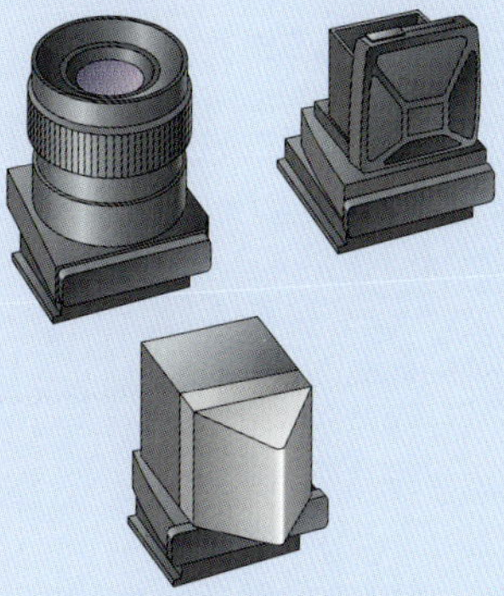

Magnifying Right-angled View and Enlarging Sports Finder
These are used for rapid action and can replace the standard prism head on some cameras. This is most commonly found in medium-format cameras.

Built-in Lens Shade
Some lenses, especially telephotos, have built-in lens shades that retract when not in use.

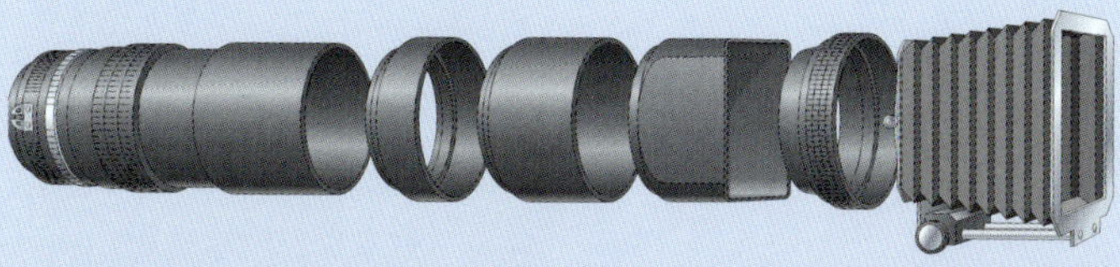

Conventional Lens Hoods
These are available in several shapes and with screw, clip, or bayonet mounts. It is important to have the right shape for the lens you are using; the wrong type may show as a dark vignette in the corners of the shot.

Gelatin Filters
These are cheap and light to carry, although they need to be mounted in special holders that fit over the lens.

Care and Maintenance

Photographic equipment is expensive and often fragile. Treat it with care and always protect it when traveling or shooting in the open.

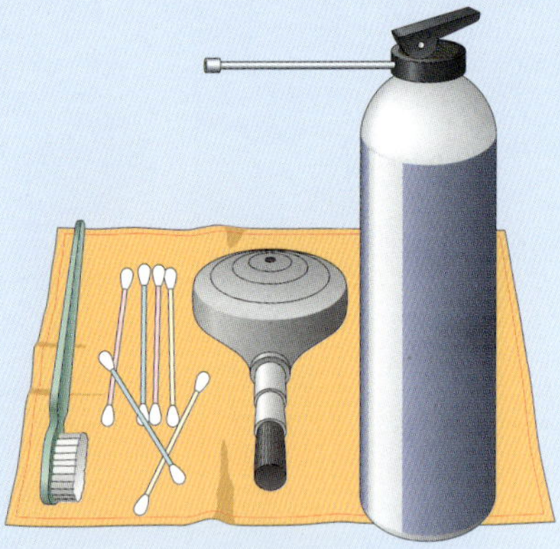

Cleaning

It is important to have the correct cleaning equipment and to use it carefully. Use denatured alcohol to clean salt spray deposits or grease off camera and lens surfaces. Remove dust from inaccessible corners with compressed air or a blower brush. Cotton swabs, a soft toothbrush, lens-cleaning tissues, and a stiff brush also have their uses for different parts of the camera, as indicated on the diagrams. Under no circumstances should you try to wipe a digital camera CCD. If it has dirt on it that cannot be blown off, have it professionally cleaned or risk fatally damaging it.

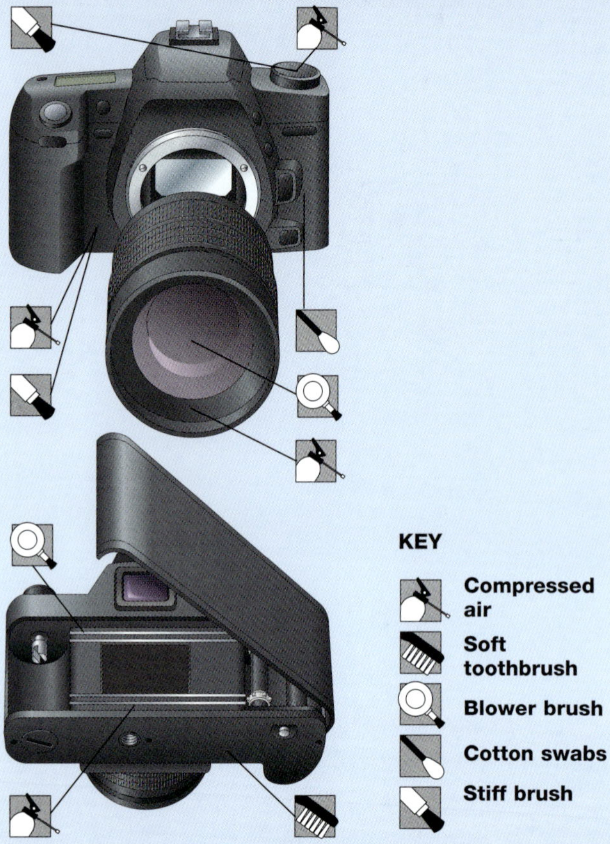

Camera Protection Proper protection and storage of delicate photographic equipment is vital. Consider the circumstances under which you will be taking photographs and act accordingly. A damp and salty atmosphere, for instance, will corrode the camera mechanism, while abrasive dust and dirt can damage lenses. Excessive heat can ruin both equipment and film. Digital SLRs are prone to dust on the CCD/CMOS chip, so try to avoid changing lenses in dusty environments. Prepare properly before the shoot by fitting the lens—a zoom would be most useful—and don't change it during the shoot. To get dust off the CCD, send the camera to be professionally cleaned by the manufacturer or use an air-blowing canister.

The chief item of protective equipment is a camera case. The best, but most expensive, are made of aluminum, gasket-lined, and water-, dust-, and grit-proof. The reflective metal finish helps keep the equipment cool, since it reflects heat. Such a case has room for other fragile items, such as lenses, as well as the camera.

Shoulder bags are acceptable alternatives. However, they will not generally offer as much protection against dust or damp as an aluminum case, so keep camera and lenses in plastic bags if you are likely to be working in such conditions. It is also

RIGHT: Tungsten lighting, from continuous photographic lights (not flash) or standard lightbulbs, gives an orange cast on daylight film. Bluish filters are needed for more accurate results. You may also get an orange cast on digital cameras, depending on how well the automatic white balance copes with the lighting.

35–140mm zoom lens, digital ISO 160, 1/15 sec at f2

advisable to protect lenses with individual lens cases if there is any risk of items of equipment scraping together. These come in hard leather, soft padded leather, or clear plastic with a screw base. Always keep a packet of silica gel in your case to absorb damp.

You will also need a changing bag and an X-ray proof bag. The former is useful if the film jams in the camera and there is no darkroom within reach. The latter is lead-lined to protect film against X-ray machines at airports. It also provides an extra measure of safety if unprocessed film has to be mailed.

Cleaning Equipment A cleaning kit for lenses and the moving parts of the camera is just as essential as an adequate form of protection. It makes no sense to buy an expensive lens and then not to look after it properly. This is especially true when photographing on location, particularly on a beach, when you should pay attention to the cleanliness of your lens.

Blow dust off with a blower brush and use a lens cloth or special cleaning tissue for surfaces. Dust and grit can be removed with denatured alcohol applied with cotton swabs.

Maintenance and Repair Equipment Complicated camera repair is a job for an expert, but there can be times when you have no option but to make temporary repairs yourself. Simple on-the-spot repairs are usually possible with the aid of a few basic tools, such as tweezers, a set of jeweler's screwdrivers, sharp-nosed pliers, and a pencil claw. Unfortunately, this really only applies to more manual cameras. Investigating the insides of a digital camera is not recommended.

Filters

Color-correction filters have their uses in glamour photography, but these are not as extensive as in other photographic fields. The quality demanded by the subject is such that it does not pay to compromise with the wrong film stock or less than perfect lighting conditions. Of course, this does not mean that filters should never be used; there may be situations—or effects may be required—that make their use desirable. For instance, the effect you want may demand the use of tungsten film in daylight. This is strictly incorrect, since the result will be dominated by a strong blue cast. However, you can eliminate this, while still preserving the other effects, by placing an orange filter over the lens. Similarly, photographing with daylight film in tungsten lighting creates an orange cast on the photograph, although the effect is more acceptable. A blue filter can be used to correct this.

Another use for filters is if you are shooting in very drab, cold conditions. Here, a pale color filter will often serve to warm up the color in the photograph. Note, however, that, if you do use a filter for this purpose, you should make sure that it will not give your model's skin an unnatural tone.

Filters can be used with digital cameras, but before use the automatic white balance feature should be manually set to match the conditions, otherwise it will interpret the filter as different weather and compensate by negating most of the effect. For most conditions the AWB can automatically compensate anyway, though this is not infallible. If shooting in low light or under artificial lighting, it is advisable to set the white balance manually to the correct color temperature.

Specialized Filters Other filters are more highly specialized. When two color-graduated filters are used together, for instance, they will produce a different hue above and below the horizon in a landscape shot. This effect is occasionally, though only rarely, used in glamour photography. Another specialized filter is the star filter. This uses cross-screens to produce a "star" effect on point sources of light. The etched pattern on the filter determines the number of points to the star. It can be used, for instance, to highlight a piece of jewelry or a sequinned dress.

LEFT: For this shot from a beach series, a graduated filter was used to darken the top half of the frame. Without it, the sky would have looked a little weak.
28mm lens, digital ISO 100, 1/500 sec at f6.7

COLOR-CORRECTION FILTERS

These require additional exposure. When using the filters recommended on page 22 to balance the color of the film to that of the light source, give extra exposure as indicated. Note that additional exposure is not needed with through-the-lens meters, which is, of course, all digital cameras and most film SLRs.

TYPE OF LIGHT	TYPE OF FILM	
	Daylight film	Tungsten-balanced film
Shade under blue sky	85C	85B
Overcast sky	81A	85B
Summer sunlight or electronic flash		85B
Photoflood lamp	80B	81A
Photographic lamp	80A	
Ordinary lightbulbs	80A	82B

A polarizing filter is similarly useful in special circumstances. When light bounces off various materials—notably glass and water—the reflected light produces intrusive clear reflections. A common example of this is the reflection of light in a store window. The filter can block this light without changing the color quality of the photograph, though it may deaden the texture slightly.

A soft-focus filter can also be used to good effect in certain types of shot. As the name implies, it is designed especially to create a soft image. It will obscure detail slightly—most lenses are intended to produce the sharpest possible detail—and cover the subject in an ethereal haze that can be very attractive for glamour shots. If you plan to produce many pictures of this kind, it could be worth investing in a soft-focus lens, but this is naturally more expensive than the filter.

LEFT: Soft focus is widely used in glamour photography, flattering the model and creating a romantic mood. Various means can achieve this effect: petroleum jelly can be smeared on the lens or a clear filter (be careful because it is almost impossible to clean off without damaging the surface); gauze can be placed in front of the camera; or special soft-focus attachments can be used to create an accurately controlled soft-focus vignette around the image. The simplest is an etched filter. The alternative for digital users is to create the effect on the computer afterward, as seen here.

35–140mm zoom lens, digital ISO 80, 1/125 sec at f5.6

LEFT: Star filters are particularly good with vehicles and other machinery. Use with caution because the images they produce can look dated. An alternative is to add effects digitally, as demonstrated here, such as motion blur.
85mm lens, Fuji Provia 100, 1/125 sec at f5.6

LEFT: Polarizing filters can block unwanted reflections. The shot on the far left, taken through the window of a boat, would have been spoilt without the filter. With it, near left, the window became almost invisible. Polarizing filters can also be used to eliminate reflections from surrounding surfaces such as water. Simply revolve the filter until the image darkens.
85mm lens, Kodachrome 64, 1/30 sec at f5.6

Portable Flash

Automatic portable flash units can be extremely versatile. They can measure the light bouncing back from the subject as the flash is fired and quench it when sufficient exposure has been given. The best types have tilting heads so that the flash can be bounced off the ceiling or a reflector for a more diffused light.

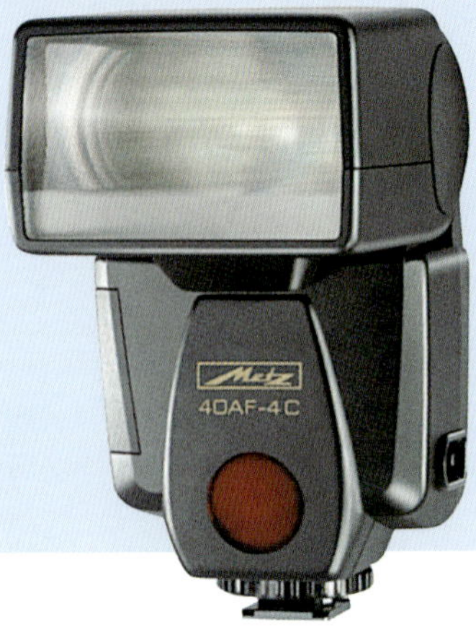

ABOVE: Portable flash units can occasionally be used for special effects in glamour photography. Their light is usually too hard to be attractive, with ugly shadows or "red eye" caused by the light reflecting back to the camera from the model's retinas. Here, however, the effect is dramatic. The fading twilight just preserves the silhouetted background, with the flash spotlighting the model in sharp relief.

35mm lens, Ektachrome 64, 1/60 sec at f8

Electronic Flash

Quite often in glamour work it is essential to provide a source of light that you can directly control. This will give you greater control over the appearance of your model. In the studio—and sometimes on location—special lights are used, but the simplest way of providing your own light source is to use an electronic flashgun.

There are two main types of electronic flash on the market. The first is battery-powered—the battery can be recharged—while the second works directly on main voltage. Battery models give up to 200 flashes per charge. After each firing, all flashguns take a few seconds to recharge; direct-powered models take twice as long to achieve this.

On most SLRs, the working of the flash is automatically synchronized with that of the camera. The flash is attached to

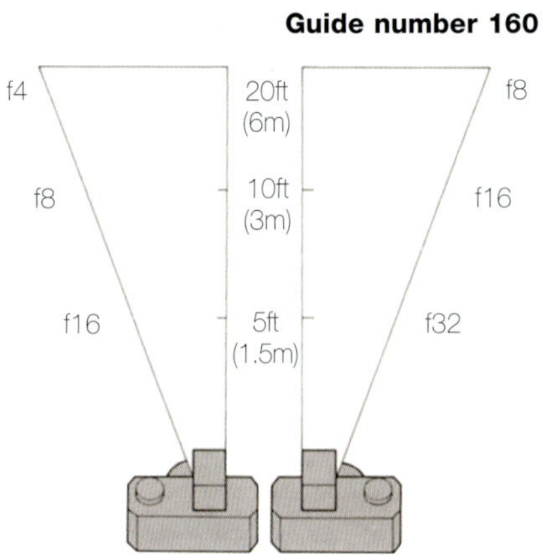

LEFT: Use the manufacturer's guide number for the speed of film you are using to calculate the aperture when using portable flash. Divide it by the distance to the subject (in feet or meters, depending on the guide number system used). For example, if the guide number with ISO 64 film is 110 and the subject is 10 feet away, stop down to f11.

the camera's hotshoe or PC sync socket. An internal circuit then triggers the flash when the shutter is fully opened. In some models, a sensor measures the amount of flash reflected from the subject and quenches the tube when the correct exposure has been achieved. It is best to avoid a built-in flash unit on a camera, except for fill-in flash, because it will create direct, ugly shadows.

Light Meters

Most SLRs incorporate their own light-metering system, but because these work on reflected light, the results are not always reliable. A reading may sometimes record too much sky or too much foreground, for example. The former, being a strong light source, tends to cause underexposure, while the latter can cause overexposure.

For this reason, professionals use handheld meters as an essential backup to the automatic system. It is always best to use them if you are photographing under difficult light conditions, or when the distribution of light and dark tones differs radically from the average. With subjects of greater than normal brightness, for instance, take two reflected light readings—one of the brightest level and one of the darkest. The compromise is the mean. However, only use these measurements as a guide to producing the image you want. There is no value, for instance, in preserving the maximum amount of detail in a backlit scene, when a silhouette would create a better and stronger photograph.

There are several types of meter on the market. Selenium cell meters generate their own energy from the light they measure; CdS (cadmium sulphide) meters, on the other hand, are battery-powered. They are far more sensitive than their selenium cell equivalents. A spot meter is a specialized, but useful, purchase. It differs from a conventional handheld meter in that it takes a pinpoint reading of whichever part of the subject you desire; the latter only produces an average reading of the entire subject. This factor makes the spot meter the most accurate.

Even with these technological aids, there may still be times when you are uncertain as to what will be the final photographic result. The trick here is to bracket your shots—that is, to make a series of exposures, varying each one by a stop or half a stop over and under the reading given by the light meter. Though this may appear wasteful of film at first sight, it is a device used by all professionals in such circumstances. You should also be prepared for any change in lighting conditions, particularly on location, by having a wide selection of film stock available. Digital users are limited only by the number of memory cards on hand and the time available to delete unwanted images.

ABOVE: In some circumstances, exposure is difficult to judge, even with a through-the-lens meter. The photo on the left shows that the metering has balanced the exposure for the darker areas, leaving the white area of the window to burn out. On the right, the model turns toward the light, giving fewer dark areas and the resulting exposure records body tone and window detail.

28–70mm zoom lens, digital ISO 160, 1/32 sec at f2.8

Handheld Light Meters

Handheld light meters can be a real boon with glamour photography. An overall reading can be influenced by a dark or light background when it is the model that should be correctly exposed. In these circumstances, use the meter to measure the light falling on the model (an incident light reading) or move closer to the model and take a reflected light reading from her skin.

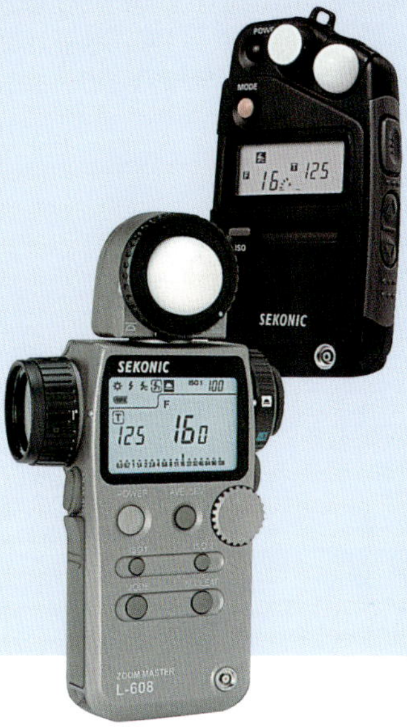

Color Film

The vast majority of glamour photographs are shot in color. Traditionally, glamour photos were shot on Kodachrome film, though these days Fujifilm has an excellent range with more modern tonality and color. Remember, however, that Kodachrome and most daylight films are not particularly suited to poor lighting conditions; they are comparatively slow films, being rated between ISO 50 and 100. In such circumstances, therefore, it may be necessary to use a faster film. There are now many stocks of ISO 200 and 400 that use fine grain and offer faster shooting speeds. It is also worth noting that film stock at ISO 200 and 400 features larger grain and therefore tends to make a model's skin look smoother. If faster film than this is used, the grain becomes so pronounced that it detracts from the image. Digital cameras use ISO ratings to depict how responsive they will be, but obviously don't use film. You may find that anything above ISO 200 creates color noise in images that is unacceptable.

Whichever brand of film you use, it is important to remember not only that no two brands are alike, but also that there can be a marked difference between the results produced by two batches of the same brand. For this reason, professionals make sure that they use films from the same batch on a shoot to ensure consistency.

Color film falls into two categories: reversal and negative (or slide and print). Professionals tend to use the former. Films are also designed to be used with different light sources and are graded accordingly. Each type of film has what is termed its color temperature, measured on the Kelvin scale. The whiter the light, the higher the color temperature.

Daylight film, for instance, is calculated to have a color temperature of 5500K. Studio lighting is now calibrated to match daylight so that standard film can be used with it.

RIGHT: Kodachrome 64 is an excellent transparency film for glamour photography, with superb color quality. It also has very small grain, making it good for enlargement.
85mm lens, Kodachrome 64, 1/30 sec at f5.6

LEFT: Ektachrome 100 gives the photographer an extra stop. It also does not have to be processed by Kodak. Professional laboratories often give a faster turnaround and are prepared to alter the film's development time if you wish. The color has excellent quality.
85mm lens, Ektachrome 100, 1/60 sec at f5.6

Color Temperature

The light from different sources has different characteristics that are not always visible to the naked eye. Color temperature, as it is called, is measured in degrees Kelvin. This table, from red (candlelight and sunset) to blue (blue sky light), gives the color temperature for some common light sources.

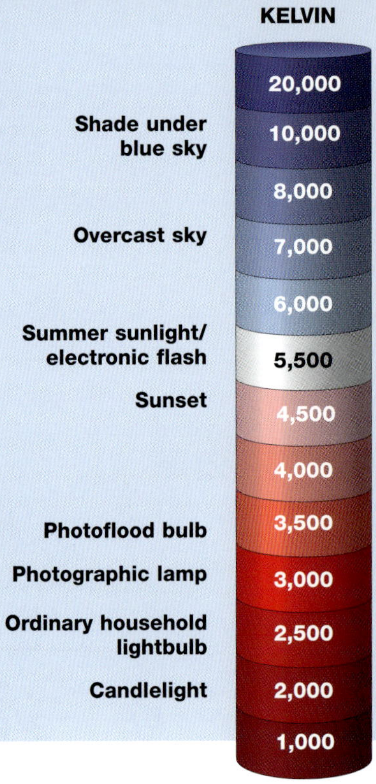

COLOR-CORRECTION FILTERS

To balance the film you are using to the light source, use this table to identify the correct filter. Read off the type of light and the type of film and use the filter designated if you want improved color balance.

Filter	Purpose	f-stop increase
YELLOWISH		
85B	Tungsten film in daylight	⅔ stop
85C	Daylight film in shade under blue sky	⅔ stop
81B 81A 81	Daylight film in overcast conditions	⅓ stop
BLUISH		
82B	Tungsten film with ordinary lightbulbs	⅓ stop
80	Daylight film with photofloods	1⅔ stop
80A	Daylight film with photographic lamps or ordinary lightbulb	2 stops

ABOVE: Fuji Provia 100 under a mix of studio flash and tungsten gives well-saturated colors and records the tungsten glow as a pleasing orange/yellow cast.
127mm lens, Fuji Provia 100, 1/30 sec at f4

ABOVE RIGHT: By comparison, this unretouched digital image taken during the same session using the same lights and exposure shows the relatively limited tonal range and weaker colors that digital offers. However, it is fairly easy to increase both to similar levels of the film shot, though without being quite as rich.
35–105mm zoom lens, digital ISO 100, 1/30 sec at f4

Tungsten-balanced film is calibrated for 3200K tungsten lighting. To put these figures in perspective, it is helpful to note that household 100–200 watt lightbulbs have a color temperature of 2900K, while 40–60 watt bulbs have a temperature of 2800K.

Correct exposure metering is vital, because reversal film has limited exposure latitude. This means that little (and sometimes no) compensation for exposure or color balance can be made in processing and that, if the metering is out by as little as one stop, the picture may be unusable. The ideal is to work with short exposures, since long exposures will lead to what is called reciprocity failure. The effect of this varies from emulsion to emulsion; you should follow carefully the manufacturer's instructions to overcome it.

ABOVE: Kodak Ektachrome 64 gives well-balanced colors with faithful skin tones under studio flash, here on medium-format 120-roll film.
127mm lens, Ektachrome 64, 1/125 sec at f8

Models need special talent. They are the most important element in glamour photography and their ability to look good in front of the camera

Models

is paramount. There are many different types of models with different strengths and weaknesses.

Choosing a Model

Without question, the model is the most important ingredient in glamour photographs. Technique, though essential, can carry you only so far because much depends on the model.

Being a first-rate glamour photographer is not simply a matter of recognizing the conventional aspects of beauty. It comes from developing an appreciation of all types of women and knowing how to assess their strong and weak points as photographic subjects. This is not easy. At the outset, any practice at all you can get in photographing women, in any situation, will be invaluable. The more you understand about yourself as a photographer and women as people, as well as models, the better chance you have of taking good photographs.

Your First Models

In the first instance, the easiest way into the glamour world is to ask girlfriends, or women you know reasonably well, to model for you. Unless you are in a position to hire professionals, it will not be easy to obtain the services of the ideal subject. However, there are many would-be models, all looking for photos for their portfolios. Check out message boards of modeling websites such as www.onemodelplace.com and www.modelheaven.com, which are worldwide sites, and place your own advert. If you can offer an imaginative approach and photographs in return for the model's time, you should be able to secure the services of a first-time model for free. This is known as TFP or Time For Prints.

Glamour modeling at its best requires flair and imagination, as well as an above average body and good looks. A professional model already knows how to pose to best advantage, understands about makeup, clothes, and accessories, and is able to take direction better than an amateur. This is not to say that an amateur cannot produce the results you want, but you will certainly have to be patient and not overpressing to secure initial agreement. When under pressure, the easiest response is a negative one. If a woman is approached tactfully, she will feel in control of the situation. If she is interested, she will contact you, once she has had the chance to think matters over in her own time.

Some women, of course, enjoy having their photographs taken and welcome the opportunity of modeling for a competent photographer. A drama or dance school, for instance, may well provide suitable candidates. Ask the principal if you can pin a card on a bulletin board, offering photographic prints in exchange for a model's services, for example. Drama and dance students are, for the most part, natural extroverts. They understand the business of projecting their personalities in front of a camera—indeed, they may well be eager to—and you will be spared the preliminary task of building up their confidence.

Test Shots

A series of test shots should eventually become an essential part of every photographic session. Their value is not simply to help you assess the model's potential; they are also a way of establishing a relaxed working relationship and of trying out photographic ideas.

Testing a Model

The purpose of test shots is to see how well you can work with a particular model, or at least discover how you can break the ice.

Test shots can produce surprisingly good results, as both model and photographer may be relaxed in knowing that the pictures are not intended for use. They can also be tense and unnatural if the model is inexperienced and nervous. Your job is to help her relax. Agencies may send models for testing, but any self-employed model will rarely agree to test shots unless they know they are getting copies for their own use. Study test shots carefully. Take note of the most successful poses and expressions and look for any visible defects. Remember the model's best and worst features and use this knowledge when subsequently working together.

BELOW & RIGHT: These test shots were taken in a studio with a white background and several large reflectors. It was the model's first session and she was good for a beginner. The two most successful shots are shown below left.

Types of Models

There are as many different types of models as there are photogenic women, so it is up to you as photographer to identify the strong features and weak points of each model and use poses, props, and settings to make the most of their individual potential. It is also important to decide the aspects of personality you want to project and organize the shots accordingly.

ABOVE LEFT: This model projects a smouldering, Latin sensuality.

ABOVE RIGHT: The "girl next door"—this model has an air of innocence. She is young, unsophisticated, and a little shy.

LEFT: Asian models tend to be harder to find than Caucasian models, but offer a different look from the more commonplace glamour shots.

FAR LEFT: With seemingly casual and untended curls, this model looks romantic, wistful, and a little vulnerable.

LEFT: Models of Afro-Caribbean origin produce striking imagery.

In any case, you should become more and more selective in your choice of models as you progress. Taking photographs can be expensive—particularly if your pastime becomes a profession—and it is therefore important that you should have as much control as possible over all the variables.

Model/photographer Relationship

Although there is no way of anticipating exactly how a model will react during a session, it is fair to assume that she is there because she wants to be there. Never press anyone who is unwilling into modeling for you; their reluctance will show on every print.

Talk to your model, establishing as many meeting points as possible, such as mutual acquaintances or similar interests. While you are talking, take discreet note of how she sits, stands, smiles, laughs, talks, and uses her hands. Learn to recognize any nervous mannerisms and use this knowledge as a cue to reassure her if any come into play during actual photography. Even the most experienced models can be nervous when working with someone for the first time and it is important that you are able to make them relax. The better photographer you are, the easier this is; if your model believes that you are going to take some great shots of her and that you will make her look glamorous, she will offer 100 percent cooperation.

A model should understand from the outset exactly what it is you want from the session. Describe what you are doing and why, and what you want her to do, but avoid baffling her with photographic jargon that she may not understand. This is especially important if your model lacks confidence in her appearance—this is a frequent occurrence when a model is asked to pose nude or semi-nude for the first time. To deal with this, make positive comments before and during the session and be sensitive about any insecurities your model may show.

Occasionally you will find that models want to be accompanied by girlfriends, boyfriends, and even their mothers. Try to discourage this, without actually refusing the request; a refusal may be misinterpreted. Inevitably, a model's tension increases if she feels she has to win additional approval. If a chaperone is necessary for any reason, make sure she or he is not within eyeshot of your model and is asked to keep quiet.

Posing

The more you understand your subject, the greater the chances of capturing the elusive moments that make a memorable photograph. To achieve this, you must do more than establish a rapport with your models; you must develop an instinct as to how you wish to portray them. This takes time, but, as you gain experience, you will learn to identify the qualities in a woman that make her particularly appealing.

If your model feels sufficiently comfortable in front of the camera to strike her own poses without direction, you have won half the battle. This does not mean, however, that all you have to do is point the camera and shoot. Your job is to create the photograph—to be constantly aware of the entire image as it appears when you press the shutter. If you are not aware of this, the results will be disappointing.

Assessing the Model

Before you begin to work, study your model and decide on the strengths and weaknesses you intend to show off or disguise. You want to portray the ideal, but you are unlikely to find a model who is perfect in every respect. Some of the features to look out for are listed below. Good skin and hair are particularly important. In general, models should be slender—the camera always exaggerates the proportions, and slim thighs and waist look best. Above all, it is the model's ability to look natural that counts.

From the Front
The overall proportions of the body are particularly evident. Short legs or a long waist, for example, will show. You can adjust the viewpoint to compensate—the legs will look longer from a low viewpoint.

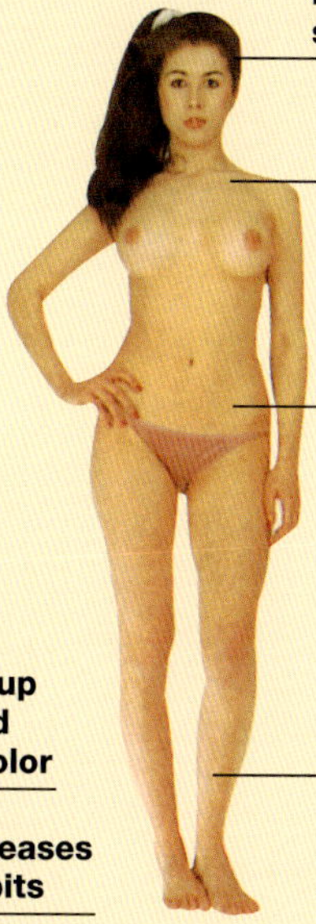

Hair should be shiny and healthy

Watch for collarbones

Wait for pressure marks from underclothes to disappear

Watch for hair on legs

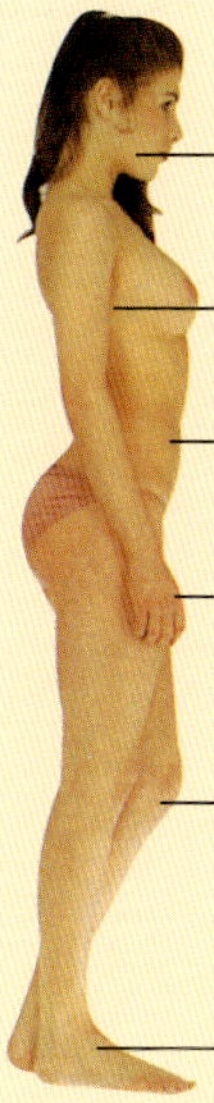

Facial makeup should blend with body color

Watch for creases around armpits

There should be no stomach bulge

Watch for veins in hands

Watch for dry skin on knees

Watch for dry skin on feet

From the Side
Posture is revealed, and also the shape of the breasts and the buttocks. Look for an upright stance and firm, high breasts.

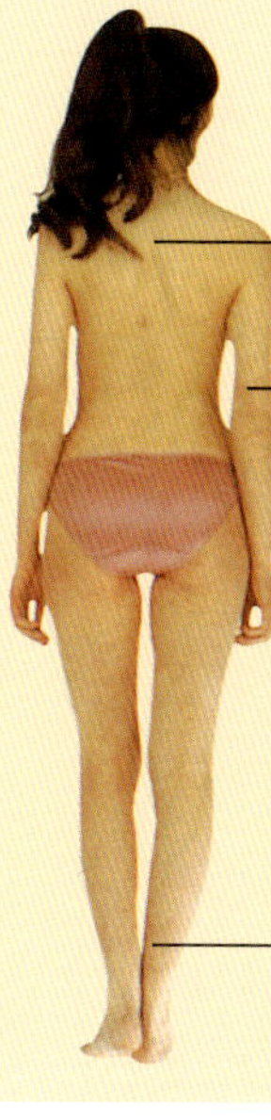

Back muscles should not be too tense

Watch for dry skin on elbows

Watch for veins in legs

From Behind
The model's back and the shape of her legs can be seen. Both are important. The back should be narrow and straight, with square shoulders, and the legs should be long and curve gracefully at the hips and calves.

THIS PAGE: An experienced model shows some of the variety of poses that can be used. This was without any prompting from the photographer; a less experienced model would certainly need guidance. The lighting and backgrounds of the beach environment dictated the type of shot possible. An elaborate studio setting would have offered additional possibilities.

70–200mm zoom lens, digital ISO 100

LEFT: Be aware that if you stand too close to the model and use a wide-angle lens, you will distort her figure. If you are working at close proximity, set the camera near the midriff in height to avoid producing a large head or overly long legs.

35–140mm zoom lens, digital ISO 80, 1/125 sec at f5.6

As a start, study as many glamour photographs as possible and note any poses that you consider particularly attractive. If you see a glamour photograph you dislike, try to figure out what you consider wrong with it.

Generally speaking, it is best to concentrate on your model's best attributes and not draw attention to any particular feature, unless it can withstand close scrutiny. Make a mental note of where the hands are, how the legs are positioned, and if the breasts are shown to the best advantage. Pay close attention to knees, elbows, collarbones, and armpits. If overprominent, they can spoil an otherwise good photograph.

Certain problems only become apparent when seen through the viewfinder. By adjusting camera angles and the model's position, it is usually possible to overcome them. Short legs, for instance, can be lengthened by a low viewpoint. If your model lies or sits down and raises her legs, the calf muscles will relax downward, creating a beautifully smooth line. If she sits on her legs or tucks them under her, it will disguise the fact that they are either too thin or too plump. By tucking one leg under another and leaning back, the whole body is stretched to produce a slimline look. Heavy hips can be corrected by asking the model to lean toward the camera—this, at the same time, reveals the cleavage.

If your model is positioned at a three-quarter angle or you take a side view, this will narrow the waist and accentuate the breasts. By crouching on all fours—a popular beach pose—the bottom is emphasized by the curvature of the back. Lying face up is not particularly flattering, since it tends to flatten the breasts.

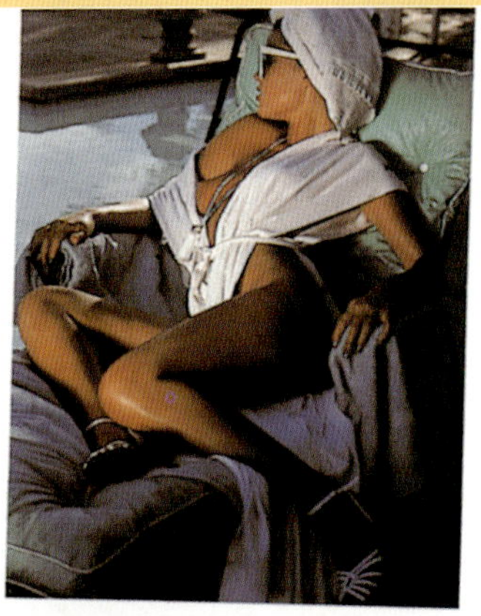

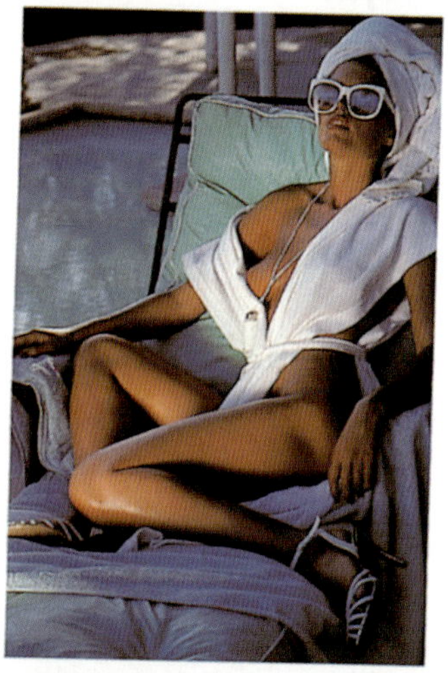

RIGHT: Even small changes to the pose can affect the way the body looks. This motor-drive sequence shows how slight movements can change the shape of the breasts and affect the apparent length and slenderness of the legs.
85mm lens, Kodachrome 25, 1/30 sec at f5.6

BELOW: This popular studio pose flatters most models, depending on the angle of the shot.
70–200mm zoom lens, digital ISO 100, 1/125 sec at f8

ABOVE: Leaning back always creates a slimming effect and can be particularly flattering to the breasts.
200mm lens, Kodachrome 25, 1/12 sec at f5.6

Expressions

A person's face is always the first point on which attention focuses; what we register in the first few seconds often determines whether or not we take a second look. Though an attractive face is virtually a prerequisite for glamour photography, beauty alone is not always enough. A face must express something. It could be a mood, a feeling, or a thought—but it must be positive.

If your model is shy or not used to projecting herself in front of the camera, she will need direction. Help her to relax by talking to her and suggesting a range of expressions she could adopt. This will not only give her something to concentrate on, but it will stimulate her own ideas, so that she can bring something positive of her own to the photography.

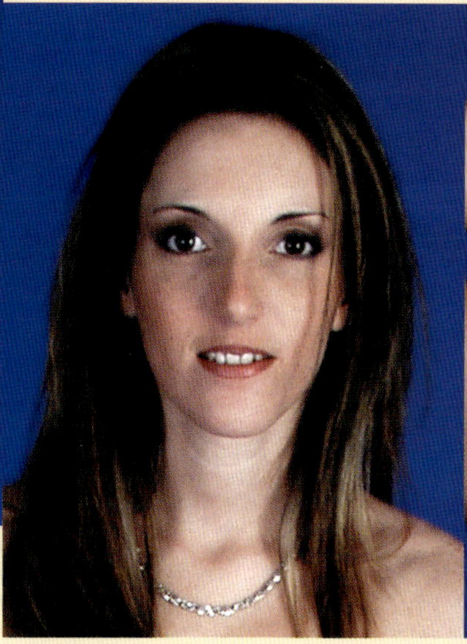

Shape, Pattern, Texture, and Color

RIGHT: The slender and delicate pose of the model contrasts with the decay and texture of the adjacent wall. The lighting concentrates on the wall and front of the model.
28–70mm zoom lens, digital ISO 100, 1/125 sec at f22

Shape, pattern, texture, and color are each vital elements of composition. One of the best ways of emphasizing the inherent quality of any object is to place it next to its opposite—rough against smooth, hard against soft, black against white are the general principles. The symmetry and coarseness of a plain brick wall, for example, will emphasize the flowing lines of your model and accentuate the softness of her skin and hair.

Background is an important factor in glamour photography: it must not dominate the model. It is often the background that creates a contrast that works best. There is no need to contrive elaborate situations. Bold, graphic lines will naturally enhance the roundness of the female form. For contrast, imagine your model reclining in a fur coat slightly parted, against an industrial backdrop, perhaps high above a freeway complex, with smokestacks belching into a gray sky.

Different shades of the same color can be exaggerated by adding a splash of color where it is unexpected. Remember that red will seem to come out of the picture, while blue appears to recede. A suntan can be accentuated by placing your model against a white background.

If you analyze the shapes, patterns, textures, and colors before you get into action, you will achieve a photograph that is more than just a picture of a woman. An eye for detail takes a photograph out of the ordinary.

Keep in mind that digital SLR cameras offer roughly half to one stop more depth of field than 35mm, but feature-rich compacts produce five times more depth of field. Using a camera like this will almost guarantee that the background is highly visible, even at the widest aperture.

RIGHT: A gritty and grainy picture, placing the model in an urban environment and emphasizing it with an angled composition. A medium power setting was used and then the aperture was taken down one f-stop to ensure that light fell off rapidly behind the model.
180mm lens, digital ISO 100, 1/125 sec at f16

RIGHT: A really distressed looking wall makes an excellent backdrop to sit your model against, particularly if she lounges against it in this aggressive pose.

35–140mm zoom lens, digital ISO 80, 1/125 sec at f8

ABOVE: Look out for the possible contrasts offered by location and props. The rough wall contrasts with the model's body, its cool white with the warm flesh tones, and the whole effect is accentuated by the addition of the bright red flower.

85mm lens, Kodachrome 25, 1/30 sec at f5.6

RIGHT: The texture of horizontal bamboo reeds provides an interesting backdrop for the model. The color of the bamboo matches that of the model's skin, resulting in the black clothing really standing out.

28–70mm zoom lens, digital ISO 100, 1/125 sec at f11

Models and Machines

Curvacious and beautiful women posed on cars and motorcycles are one of the mainstays of glamour photography, to the extent that they have become a cliché. As this sort of shot is so popular for magazines, advertisements, and calendars, the market is wide. The challenge to produce an out-of-the-ordinary picture is nevertheless there, since clichéd photos are likely to be rejected.

You should decide first of all what role the model is to play in the picture, so that the composition works. Will she be the focal point of the picture, with the machine in the background or to one side? Or will the machine be the focus, with the model simply providing added visual interest, contrast of textures, and to the male-oriented market, the illusion that both she and the machine are possessions and status symbols?

Photography with machines demands a great deal of experimentation with the camera angle and the best pose for the model. Decide first of all precisely which feature of the machine characterizes it, or alternately, in which way it makes a good prop for your model.

When deciding what your model should wear, whether clothes or accessories, take into account the age, make, and color of the machine. Status is one of the key factors in shots such as these. You can choose either to capitalize on any obvious associations or invent an unconventional one. You might decide, for example, to reverse traditional concepts by shooting a low-priced car on a lawn with castle or mansion in the background and the model relishing champagne, salmon, and peaches from a basket.

If the model is to pose against or on the automobile or motorcycle, relax her by taking a lot of test shots and discussing poses with her. Encourage her to take the initiative and to suggest the ways in which she would like to be photographed: this is the way to a lively and creative session that should result in an interesting and saleable end product.

RIGHT: Fantasy is a central element in glamour photography —a naked blonde hitch-hiking in the Mojave desert is the kind of image that could enliven any dream.

200mm lens, Kodachrome 25, 1/30 sec at f5.6

RIGHT: A vintage Rolls-Royce made a superb setting with the dark, luxurious interior contrasting well with the model. The sexy dress and shoes were chosen to match the image of opulence.

85mm lens, Kodachrome 25, 1/30 sec at f4

RIGHT: With the sun low in the sky, the metallic paint of the speedboat looked almost gold—a good match for the model's gold bikini pants. The low lighting of late afternoon also gleamed effectively from the chrome and the dark surface of the sea.
85–210mm zoom lens, Kodachrome 64, 1/30 sec at f5.6

RIGHT: The name of the truck, Miss Mary K, set the idea for this shot, suggesting that the model should look a little old-fashioned. Dress and hairstyle were chosen to fit this image.
200mm lens, Kodachrome 25, 1/60 sec at f5.6

LEFT: The only color in this shot comes from the model's red shoes and matching lipstick. The see-through jumpsuit was chosen to match the stark whiteness of the boat. Machinery often makes a fussy background, so try to keep everything else as simple as possible. The model was in the shade for this shot, with plenty of light reflected from the white surfaces and a gold reflector placed in front of her.
85–210mm zoom lens, Kodachrome 25, 1/60 sec at f5.6

The Art of Makeup

Makeup is a vital tool of the glamour trade. It is therefore important that you have a clear idea of how you want your model to look and also the expertise to advise her. You need not go as far as becoming a makeup expert, but you should certainly develop a basic knowledge of cosmetics.

To begin with, study women's faces and the way makeup is applied and used. There is no point in giving general style advice in a book like this because fashions change season by season. Instead, keep a file of photographs and magazine cuttings of styles you like for copying or improving on. Study Sunday newspaper color supplements and celebrity magazines to see the latest popular styles.

The proper use of makeup will help you overcome one of the basic problems of glamour photography, particularly if you are shooting amateur models. The problem is that, while the experienced model will know exactly how to achieve certain looks, the beginner will either apply insufficient makeup, because that is what she normally wears, or apply far too much because she thinks this is what is required for photography.

If you are shooting photos for a client who is paying well, you must employ a professional stylist to do the model's hair and makeup.

RIGHT: The bright red lipstick in this shot is dramatic and works because it picks out the red trim of the underwear and the deep red color scheme of the background.

28–70mm zoom lens, digital ISO 100, 1/125 sec at f22

Makeup Basics

The basic selection of cosmetics and equipment shown here is a useful starting point. It includes: cleanser, toner, eye makeup remover, foundation, face powder, eyedrops, mascara, blusher, eyeshadow, eyeliner, lipstick, lip gloss, and lipliner. For accurate application, a selection of different-sized brushes will be essential. You can expect your models to have their own basic makeup, but keep your own stock as well for emergencies.

Basic Rules

The basic rules of skin care and makeup technique are few and simple. Cleansing cream, for instance, is an essential part of any model's makeup kit. Before applying new makeup, all traces of the old must be removed and this may be necessary several times in a single session.

Skin tonic or freshener should be applied generously after cleansing. It removes excess grease and makes the skin come alive by stimulating the blood flow. It is also extremely effective for brightening tired skin during a session. Moisturizer prepares the skin for makeup. Allow this to soak into the skin for at least five minutes before applying foundation; otherwise the makeup may clog.

RIGHT: This theatrical shot uses bright lipstick, pale makeup, and a bright red flower in the model's hair. It is intended to harken back to the 1930s and 1940s.
50mm lens, digital ISO 100, 1/125 sec at f16

Eye Shapes

The shape of the eyes can be adjusted.

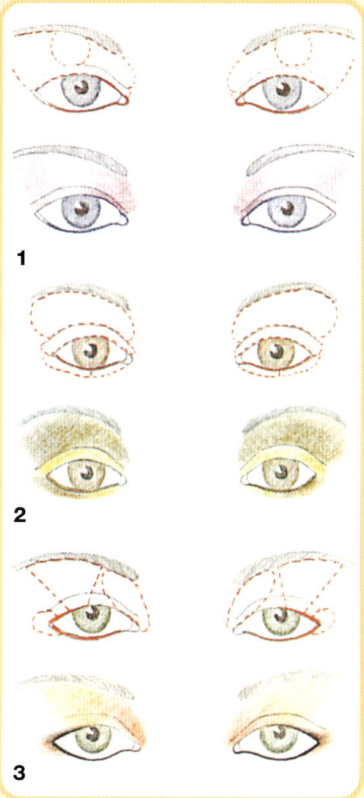

1 To make wide-set eyes appear closer together, draw a bright line inside the lower lashes and highlight the center of the lid.
2 Small eyes should not be outlined. Use a light shadow on the lid.
3 For eyes that are too close together, put pale colors on the inner half of the lid and darker on the outer.

The color of the foundation should accord with the model's skin tone. Blondes and redheads are generally suited to pale shades, though pink should be avoided; brunettes are favored by a beige tone; women with darker skins will find a slightly brown tint suitable. Most skins require only a thin film of the lighter type of foundation, though if the skin is poor, it can be evened out with a thickish one. Whatever the choice, the final effect must look natural. Smooth the foundation on the face with a moistened sponge, gradually thinning out down the neck to avoid any "tide" marks.

Blushers and shapers add depth, color, and shape to the face. They can enhance a model's good points and shift the emphasis away from weaker ones. Used effectively, shapers can slim down a round face, raise the cheekbones, and shorten a nose. Blusher is applied with a soft sable brush in sweeping strokes from the middle of the cheekbone to the ear. When the line has been defined, add a narrow, slightly darker streak of color beneath it and a lighter streak above it. Carry the blusher up to the temples, fading into the middle forehead. If the nose is too broad, brush lightly down the side of the nose; if it is too long, add a touch of blusher at the tip. Put some blusher on the end of the chin and continue it lightly down the center of the neck.

Eyes

Eyes are one of the main features of any woman's face, and mascara is generally considered to be a woman's most important item of makeup. Apply it to the upper and lower lashes, using two light coatings, rather than a single heavy one. Use a lash comb to separate the lashes before they dry.

Eyebrows also play an enormously important part in adding expression and personality to the face. If the eyebrows look right, less eye makeup is needed, so make sure that they are well plucked and shaped. Ideally, the high point should line up with the center of the eye vertically and end in line with the center of the eye horizontally. If it fails to do so, correct by penciling in tiny hair marks with an eyebrow pencil.

Lips

Lip color should always be applied last, the color being selected to match the clothes the model is wearing and not the color of the eyes. Blondes are flattered by plum shades

Full Makeup Kit

A makeup set can run to a considerable number of items. If you intend to do a lot of beauty or glamour photography, however, a full kit will be a wise investment. The materials shown here are comprehensive, although you will need many more colors to suit every occasion.

RIGHT: You can even shoot the model applying her makeup. This early morning shot is entirely natural, taken while the model was preparing for the session.

85mm lens, Kodachrome 25, 1/30 sec at f5.6

and deep pinks, while bright reds can look extremely theatrical and exciting. Redheads are suited to rich brown shades, while brunettes can wear dark oranges and deep burgundies. Any vivid color will suit a dark-haired model, though the actual shade will depend on the color of her skin. The darker the skin tone, the stronger the color that can be taken.

Always outline the lip first with a lip pencil and then fill in with lipstick applied with a brush. For very full lips, it is often sufficient just to use a lip pencil and lip gloss.

ABOVE: This model has fair, freckled skin, so pink lip gloss and pale eye makeup was used.

35–140mm zoom lens, digital ISO 80, 1/125 sec at f8

Camouflage and Precautions

There may be times when you will have to resort to camouflage. Here, cover sticks are especially useful for covering up blemishes and concealing dark circles under the eyes. Powder, on the other hand, should be used only to take the shine off the face and never to alter the color. Only use loose powder that is translucent.

Although most models will have their own makeup kit, you should have one of your own as well. Build this up gradually, because it can be an expensive investment. Above all, buy only allergy-tested products. There is nothing worse than a model developing rashes and swollen eyes seconds after applying cosmetics that do not agree with her.

Lips and Eyebrows

Lips can be reshaped quite easily with the clever application of lipstick and lipliner.

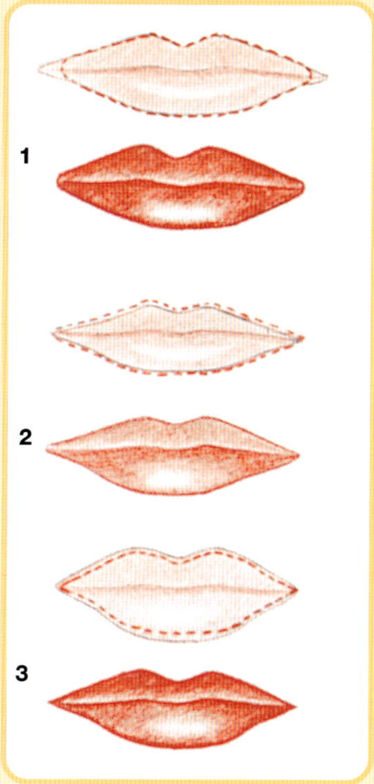

The illustrations show how to correct a wide (1), a thin (2), and a full (3) mouth.

Eyebrows can be tidied up by brushing the hair in one direction, plucking stray hairs, and penciling in the shape.

Coloring the Body

In glamour photography, makeup does not necessarily stop at the neck. Frequently, body makeup is used. This can mean anything from body oil to exotic designs painted on the body with removeable makeup. The oiled body is largely seen as passé when used with female models these days but is popular for male models, particularly for the gay market.

Body makeup has two other main purposes: camouflage and display. As most of us are only too aware, the camera mercilessly highlights any defects we may possess. Unless you want to draw attention to a birthmark, scar, or blemish, your model should camouflage it carefully before a photographic session. Any ordinary makeup that matches the skin will be suitable. While these defects can be removed digitally, you should aim to minimize the amount of work there is to do after the picture is taken.

Be particularly wary, though, of fake suntan creams. Although they are ideal for covering up sunburn marks, most of them become streaky if applied over the entire body. The texture of the skin is generally far more important than the color, although a rich suntan is unbeatable for beach shots.

It is very easy for body designs to go wrong, so do not attempt anything overcomplex unless your model knows exactly what she is doing, or you are working with a professional makeup artist. Properly executed designs can be stunning, but amateurish ones will look dreadful.

BELOW: Shapes and intricate patterns like this one can be applied with removable dye and provide extra interest in an otherwise mundane shot.
28–70mm zoom lens, digital ISO 400, 1/125 sec at f8

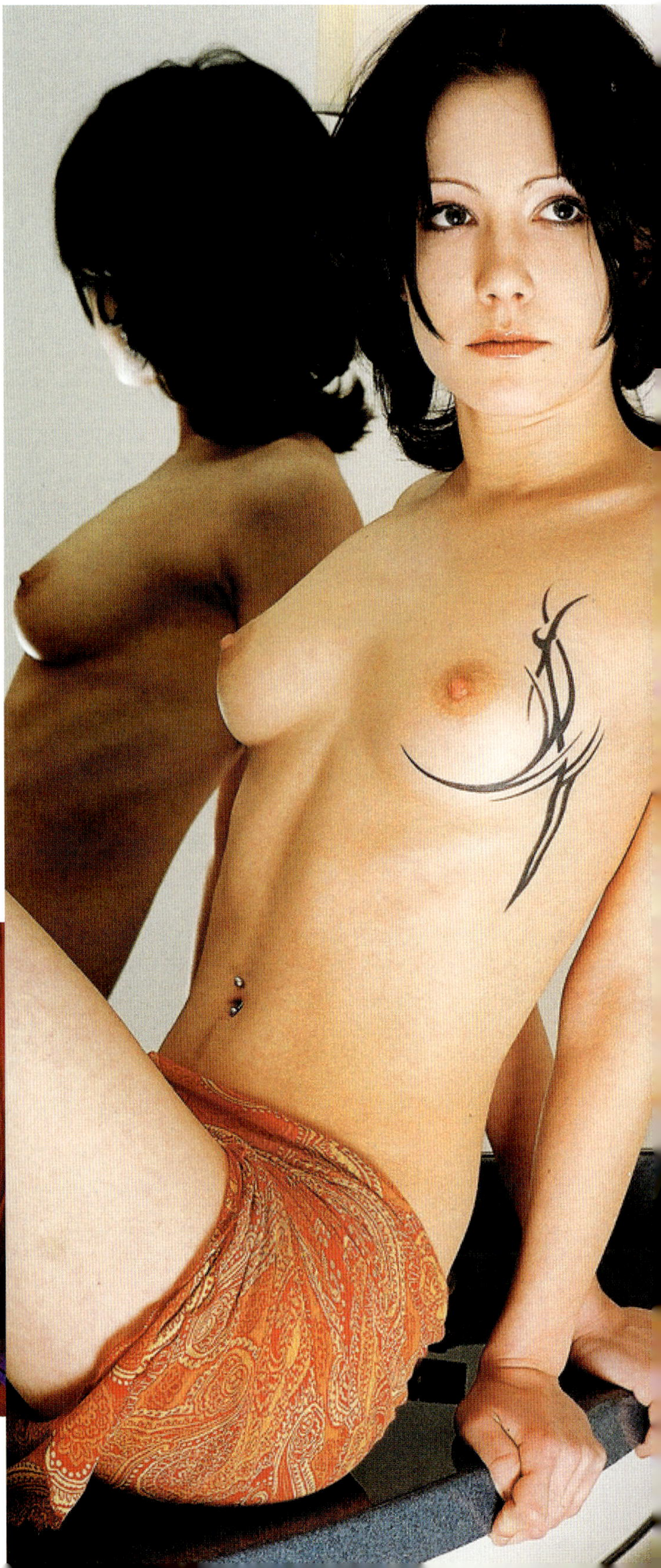

BELOW: Rather than physically plastering your model with paint, which takes up time that you are paying for, creative effects can be applied through the use of colored gels placed over flash units.
35–105mm zoom lens, Fuji 100 ISO, 1/60 sec at f11

BELOW: Mixing tungsten lights and flash, and setting the shutter speed accordingly, can produce evenly lit images with splashes of yellow.
35–140mm zoom lens, digital ISO 100, 1/125 sec at f8

RIGHT: The effect here is subtle. The model has been lit by a flash unit to the left, but a blue rim effect has been added from a secondary flash unit fitted with a blue gel on the right.
28–70mm zoom lens, digital ISO 100, 1/30 sec at f5.6

Special Body Designs

Body makeup can be used to produce exciting designs, creating a startling impact if well executed. Be careful, however, not to be overconfident, because such designs will look disappointing in a photograph if they are less than perfect. Just as the camera will exaggerate skin blemishes, it will also show up any slight mistakes in a body makeup design.

The first precaution is to make sure you are fully prepared, with the right equipment and a clear plan. It may be wise to find a good reference for your design rather than relying entirely on imagination—you could try adapting from a magazine photograph or material catalog, for example. The best designs are simple—a bold conception with a limited range of colors and without unnecessary elaboration. Look for humorous ideas—adding a makeup suspender belt, for example—or designs with an implication of mystery and exotic allure. Choose props and the setting to match your makeup idea.

RIGHT: The snake is a good example of the success of uncomplicated ideas when using special-effects body makeup. It was drawn with a brush using dark kohl. A little glitter was added, with sequins for the snake's eyes. The sunglasses were chosen to echo the design, which was well suited to the jungle vegetation of the setting.

55mm lens, Ektachrome 64, 1/60 sec at f4

LEFT: Sunburn is unlikely to be attractive in photographs. The obvious discomfort of the model can communicate itself to the viewer of the photograph. First of all, take precautions against it. Do not, for example, have a fair-skinned model working in hot sun immediately. Instead, allow her to develop a tan at her own pace if on assignment, or for short jobs keep her out of the sun when not shooting.

70–200mm zoom lens, digital ISO 100, 1/60 sec at f8

RIGHT: The white outline of swimsuits in suntan are best avoided, so either book a model with an all-over tan if shooting for long periods in the sun, or one with no tan at all for short ones.

28–105mm zoom lens, digital ISO 200, 1/250 sec at f5.6

Props and Accessories

Props and accessories can create a mood, enhance a feeling, and make the difference between a sensational and a mediocre photograph. There are no guidelines for what and what not to use, just the dictates of good taste and sex appeal. This is nearly always subjective. You should discuss with your model beforehand the kind of shots you are going to take so that she can bring her own accessories. In addition, the glamour photographer should possess a wide range of props and a well-stocked wardrobe. Not only will this allow greater freedom to accommodate a change in mood during a session, but it may also inspire your model to think of new ideas about how she would like to look.

Think of props and accessories for photography as you would for the theater. Glamour photography is about dressing up and acting a part. If your model sees something that captures her imagination, it will be easier for her to act in front of the camera. Develop a magpie instinct and keep anything that could be useful as a photographic prop.

In more ways than one, a good rule to follow in glamour photography is "less is more." Nothing in your photograph should be superfluous. Props and clothes must be there for a purpose. In real life, for instance, it is extremely unlikely that a woman would go swimming wearing a blouse. In the world of glamour, however, one of the classic shots is of a model emerging from the sea with a wet, translucent garment clinging to every curve. Sunglasses may hide the eyes, but they make a devastating point about nudity when they are the only thing your model is wearing. This is true of any accessory—scarves, shoes, stockings, for instance—on an otherwise nude model. Soft and luxurious fabrics, especially silks and furs, have instant sex appeal. So, too, does leather and particularly PVC, with its overtly fetish associations.

The more you put into a photographic session, the more you will get out of it. A model will know if you have gone to a good deal of trouble and will repay your efforts. Dress her up in an elaborate costume, provide her with an unusual or exotic prop, and she will invariably play her part.

RIGHT: While a tennis skirt and racket set the scene, it is the model's glance that involves the viewer.
85mm lens, Kodachrome 25, 1/60 sec at f5.6

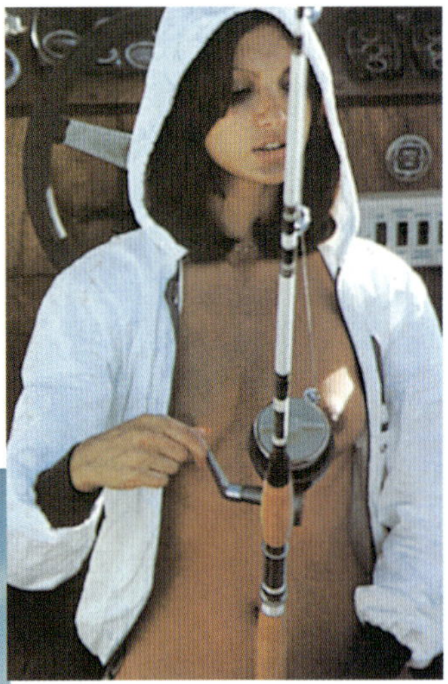

ABOVE: Letting her try her hand at fishing helped to relax the model on this boat trip session.
85mm lens, Kodachrome 25, 1/60 sec at f5.6

RIGHT: The feather boa is a classic prop, here matching the white underwear and rounded off with a mirror for the model to pose in front of.
28–105mm zoom lens, Jessops ISO 100, 1/60 sec at f16

LEFT: This is a fabulous set—an old Western town, with the model placed on a bench with a large wheel as backdrop, and ornate lingerie to complete the image.
35–70mm zoom lens, digital ISO 100, 1/250 sec at f16

RGHT: The outdoor healthy look of the model is created by adding simple props—a sporty cap and an exercise machine.
85mm lens with polarizing filter, Kodachrome 25, 1/30 sec at f5.6

BELOW: A broken cup in a color that suits the model's skin is enough to add interest to an intimate close-up.
85mm lens, Kodachrome 64, 1/30 sec at f5.6

LEFT: The most unlikely props can help. This model even looks stunning brushing her teeth.
85mm lens, Kodachrome 64, 1/15 sec at f4, with fill-in light from a household light

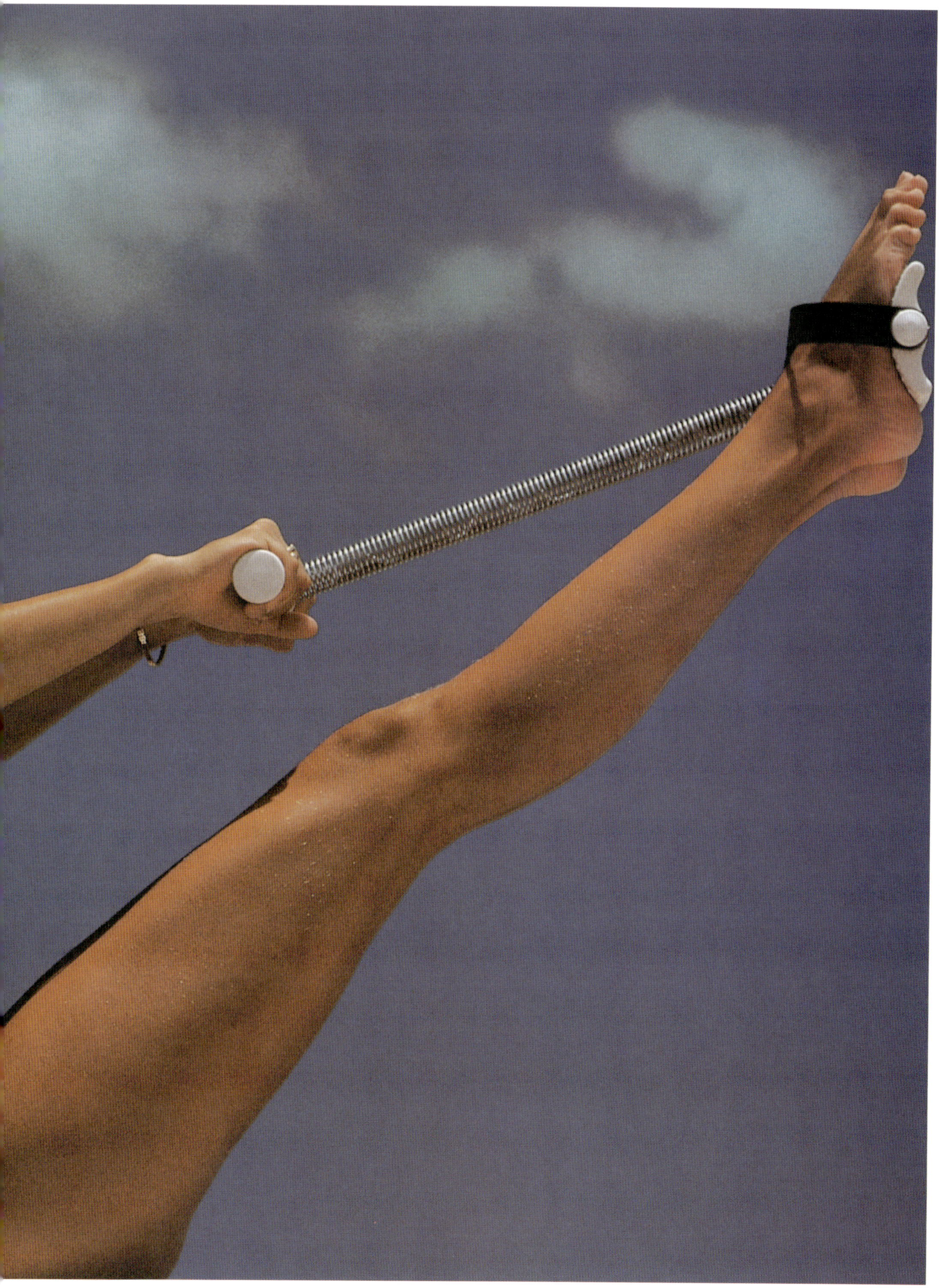

Selecting a Wardrobe

Not all your models will be the same size, so stock a selection of garments to fit different builds. This, obviously, is less important for clothes that are meant to be loose fitting or can be tucked up at the back with safety pins (you can never have too many safety pins in the dressing room).

Try to develop contacts with owners or managers of local dress and shoe stores. They may either give you, or sell at a reduced cost, rejected items that cannot be sold because of minor flaws, but would be quite suitable for photographs. Some stores will even lend items in exchange for free photographs, or a credit in whatever publication the photograph appears. Either you as a photographer or the publication will have to be well known for them to agree to this and incur the risk of lost merchandise. One practical alternative is to use the services of a fancy dress hire shop where you can hire a variety of costumes for a particular themed session.

If you do borrow clothes that have to be returned, warn your model to be careful not to get makeup or other marks on them. Ask her to wear a sweat shield with dresses or blouses, unless they are see-through. Wherever possible, select garments that are washable or at least easy to keep clean. Your model will feel a hundred times better wearing well-laundered and fresh-smelling garments. It is also a good idea to have an iron and ironing board at hand, so that any creased clothes that are to be used at the last minute can be pressed.

Often models will have their own supply of clothes so it is worth discussing options with them beforehand, particularly for shoots that are only a couple of hours long. Be aware, though, that particularly amateur, beginner, or semipro models may claim to have just what you want, but in all likelihood either the clothes may not look as good as you want or the lingerie will not be as expensive. Until a model's career really has brought in the money, she is unlikely to invest a small fortune in dazzling lingerie.

Underwear This is an obvious glamour accessory. There is a wide choice available, from flimsy, next-to-nothing bras and panties to elaborate 19th-century corsets. Not surprisingly, your model will normally want to wear her own underwear and is likely to have a wide selection herself. Neverthless, be on the look out for especially pretty or unusual items that a model is unlikely to have in her own kit.

Stockings and Socks Stockings are an indispensable part of a glamour wardrobe. Any color or type of stocking can look sensational if used in the right way. Very sheer or silk stockings are perhaps the sexiest of all, because their texture is readily conveyed in a photograph. Dark stockings can slim down heavy legs, while patterned or light-colored stockings will fill out very thin ones.

Garters or suspenders certainly can be attractive, but they can also clutter a picture. Try stockings without the garter and vice versa.

Socks are a popular accessory. Consider all the varieties, from men's thick woolen football socks to plain white tennis nylons.

LEFT: If you can invest in more expensive lingerie, it does pay off as can be seen with this model in a black basque with prominent red flowers. Combined with a dark background, it achieves a deep sensuality.
35–70mm zoom lens, digital ISO 100, 1/125 sec at f4

LEFT: In this studio shot the model wears a thick wool sweater, and nothing else. The color coordinates with the background, while the model looks relaxed as she holds a cup of coffee.
35mm lens, Fuji ISO 100, 1/125 sec at f8

Making the Most of Small Spaces

Taken in the restricted space of a small room, the mirror image is a useful means for overcoming the shortcomings of a close-up view.

RIGHT: White lace underwear accentuates the softness and femininity of a woman's body. Fill-in light was provided partly by the mirror acting as a reflector and partly by a gold reflector placed in front of the model.
85mm lens, Kodachrome 64, 1/30 sec at f5.6

ABOVE: The setting with the mirror suggests a hallway where an upmarket fancy dress ball in progress. The mask and black party dress add to the suggestion.
28–70mm zoom lens, digital ISO 400, 1/30 sec at f5.6

RIGHT: Pale pink bedding provides a soft and romantic erotic photo opportunity. The model is lounging in the bed and the pink lipstick and blonde hair, carefully arranged to frame her head and face, complement the color scheme rather than contrast with it. A jaunty angle gives the photo some dynamism.
28mm lens, digital ISO 400, 1/60 sec at f8

Shirts, Blouses, and T-shirts How a model wears shirts and T-shirts is as important as the garment itself. T-shirts should be worn without a bra, and blouses must allow cleavage at the very least (unless the intention is to emphasize the lower regions that are not covered at all). Selecting a specific size is not important, because oversize blouses can be pinned at the back to seem smaller, while very loose shirts (such as men's shirts) can sometimes look extremely seductive. It is often not a bad thing if a blouse is too small.

Swimwear Like underwear, your model is likely to have her own swimwear and she will prefer to wear it, unless you have some amazing designer swimsuits in your wardrobe. Select small to medium size garments when buying them because larger models are generally not ideal for swimwear photos.

Shoes and Boots Uncovered, your model's feet should be pretty, smooth, and unobtrusive. Dressed up with style, your model may not need any other accessory at all. Decorative shoes should generally have high heels and be dainty and light. Even if the current fashion is for big wedge sandals and these suit certain types of photo, remember that they are a distinctive fashion statement and will date the photo quickly. Boots often dominate a picture even more than shoes and should only be worn with a view to the overall effect.

Possibly the worst thing about footwear you can possibly do is shoot a model wearing shoes that look tatty or have scuff marks. If you can't correct the flaws digitally, your photo may as well go in the trash.

RIGHT: A blonde model always combines well with light, semi-transparent material like these curtains. You can shoot from the front to highlight the model herself, or have lights around the back to provide glare on the curtains, framing the model. To get the focus to fall off away from the model and add to the dreamy feel, a wide aperture and low flash power were used.
70–200mm zoom lens, digital ISO 100, 1/125 sec at f4

LEFT: Coordinating the colors of the swimsuit and the background, plus the flower garland around the model's neck, gives a beach-type image direct from the studio.
50mm lens, Fuji ISO 100, 1/125 sec at f8

RIGHT: Taken on a Hollywood film set, the old-fashioned corset and stocking combination matches the period feel of the wagon.
80–210mm zoom lens, Kodachrome 25, 1/30 sec at f8

LEFT: Something as simple as colored shorts can be very effective in glamour shots.
35–140mm zoom lens, digital ISO 80, 1/125 sec at f8

LEFT: Tennis shoes give a sporty look. Make sure they are clean and perfectly white; even slight marks will ruin the shot. The same is true for the white towel, chosen with the white coffee set to complete a unified color scheme. No reflectors or extra lights were needed to augment the late afternoon Jamaican sun.

85–210mm zoom lens, Kodachrome 25, 1/30 sec at f5.6

RIGHT: Set in an old-fashioned train carriage on a film set, the Western ankle boots add to the nostalgic charm of this scene. The lighting was provided by a spotlight behind the windows and flash bounced off a white reflector to the side of the model.

85mm lens, Kodachrome 25, 1/60 sec at f8

RIGHT: Clumsy rubber boots, wet to suggest rain in this fishing shot, contrast appealingly with the model's body. This is, in fact, a studio shot, with backlighting from a flash unit bounced through the umbrella and back to the model from a reflector in front.

85mm lens, Kodachrome 25, 1/60 sec at f5.6

ABOVE: These are the kind of shoes that may be popular with models but, as fashions can change rapidly, it is best to employ them in an extreme pose like this where the emphasis is not just on the shoes but also the length of the model's legs.

35mm lens, digital ISO 100, 1/125 sec at f8

RIGHT: Shoes are often best used as a single prop without the addition of unnecessary elaboration. The simple act of putting on a pair of shoes gives this shot a real intimacy. The lighting, too, was kept simple—unmodified daylight.
85mm lens, Kodachrome 25, 1/30 sec at f6

Trousers Trousers must be well fitting; in most cases, your model will and ought to provide her own. If you do want some in your wardrobe, select the smaller sizes and buy the unusual styles that a model is unlikely to possess—leather or suede, for example. Most women's trousers fasten in the front and in glamour photography are usually better left unfastened.

Headgear Any sort of headgear should be used with caution. This is especially true with hats, since psychologists say that these have strong associations with formal occasions. Use headgear with panache and style, or for a specific purpose,

LEFT: A jaunty hat and pose work well with the summer feel of the photo. Summer hats make ideal accessories because they give a casual and relaxed attitude.
28–105mm zoom lens, digital ISO 100, 1/250 sec at f5.6

ABOVE: A jungle hat, green combat jacket, and a green miniskirt complement the model's aggressive stance and attitude.
35–105mm zoom lens, Fuji ISO 100, 1/125 sec at f8

LEFT: A stylish combination of white trousers and red bra plus red hat creates a distinct look to this photo.

28–70mm zoom lens, Fuji 100 ISO, 1/125 sec at f11

BELOW: The model's red top is matched by red panties and red shoes in this teasing studio shot.
28–135mm zoom lens, Fuji ISO 100, 1/125 sec at f16

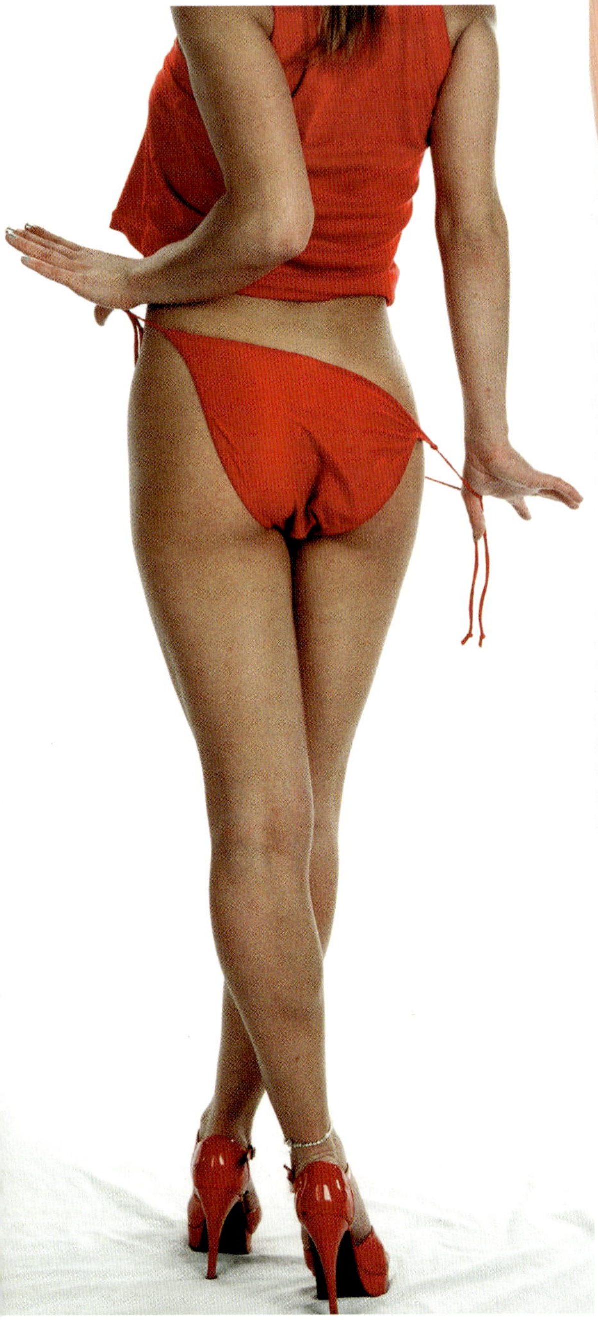

ABOVE: The tartan miniskirt is teamed with a scarf tied around the breasts to give an erotic matching outfit.
28–200mm zoom lens, digital ISO 100, 1/125 sec at f11

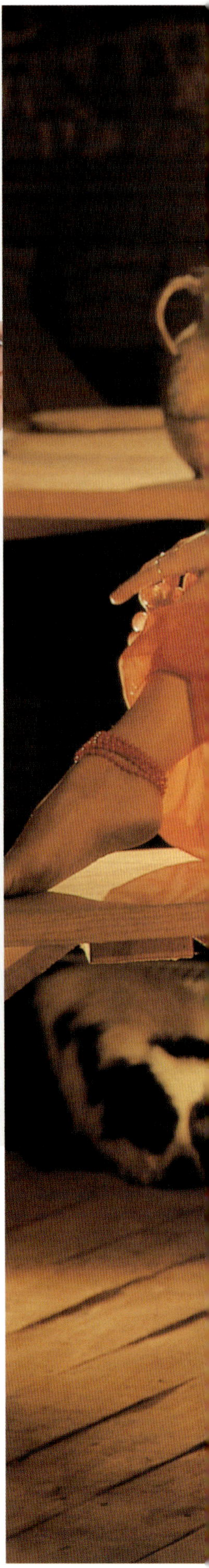

RIGHT: See-through trousers are part of this elaborately staged scene, helping to create the fantasy of a slave girl in a medieval banqueting hall. Studio lighting was used.
50mm lens, Ektachrome 64, 1/30 sec at f8

BELOW: Short shorts make an excellent costume for glamour photography, here seen at a poolside. **85mm lens, Kodachrome 25, 1/30 sec at f5.6**

ABOVE: A deep tan contrasts with the white of the blouse, made transparent by the swimming pool water. Always choose shirts and blouses to make the most of the model's strong features—a white blouse will emphasize a tan, for example. **85mm lens with polarizing filter, Kodachrome 25, 1/60 sec at f5.6**

such as protection from the sun. Caps, vizors, and sunhats all fall into this category. In photography, they are also useful for providing extra shade for the face.

Brightly colored scarves can give your model a gypsy or ethnic look, but do not overlook the charm and simplicity of ribbons, bows, colorful hair grips, and flowers in the hair.

Sunglasses Sunglasses are always associated with glamour. They evoke thoughts of the rich and the famous incognito, or expensive beaches on sun-drenched islands. They hide the eyes—the mirror to the soul—and keep the observer guessing. Take fashion trends for sunglasses seriously because they can look ludicrous when outdated. Consider your model as well. If her eyes are her best feature, it may be better for her to push the sunglasses on top of her head, or use them as something to hold rather than to wear. Whichever type of sunglasses you select, make a point. It could be humorous, as with the exaggerated plastic variety, or about sport—ski sunglasses, for instance. Remember that sunglasses can be worn indoors as well as outdoors, often with more impact for being incongruous.

ABOVE: An elegant turban establishes the atmosphere of late afternoon on a sultry day on a beach in the Middle East, with the desert coming right down to the cool sea. A telephoto lens was used to close in on the model some distance out in the shallow water.
300mm lens, Kodachrome 25, 1/30 sec at f4

LEFT: A captain's hat worn at a jaunty angle contributes to the obvious enjoyment in this shot of the model at the wheel of a yacht.
85mm lens, Kodachrome 25, 1/30 sec at f4

RIGHT: A straw hat is used to draw attention to the model's perfect mouth and flared nostrils by hiding the eyes. Sunlight provided the main lighting, with a natural and warm fill-in provided by a yellow blanket acting as a reflector on the floor.
85mm lens, Kodachrome 25, 1/30 sec at f5.6

LEFT: A workman's hard hat adds interest to the shot by its incongruity, but also throws a soft red glow on the model's face. No reflectors or extra lights were required for this effect; the model just had to be carefully placed to use a shaft of sunlight.
85mm lens, Kodachrome 25, 1/30 sec at f5.6

LEFT: A straw hat to match the model's blonde hair creates a very simple color composition, with only the bright red lips standing out.
85mm lens, Kodachrome 25, 1/60 sec at f5.6

RIGHT: Use hats as props cautiously, choosing them to look natural and informal unless you are attempting to create a special period atmosphere. The headgear on this model fits in with the blouse and offers an ethnic look.
70–200mm zoom lens, digital ISO 100, 1/125 sec at f5.6

RIGHT & OPPOSITE PAGE, ABOVE LEFT: Sunglasses stop the model from screwing up her eyes in strong sunshine. With a tough urban background, the viewer does not need to make eye contact. The color version has been hand-tinted in Photoshop to give it a different, graphic art feel.

28–105mm zoom lens, digital ISO 100, 1/250 sec at f8

LEFT: Looking over the sunglasses directly at the camera gives the model a provocative look.
85mm lens, Kodachrome 25, 1/60 sec at f8

RIGHT: A model in the same setting looks quite different with and without sunglasses. With them (right), she is in a world of her own; without them (far right), she looks directly at the viewer in a challenging way. Daylight lit the patio on which the shot was taken, with a single reflector on the left.
85mm lens, Kodachrome 25, 1/30 sec at f4

BELOW LEFT: In very strong sun, the model will need dark glasses to protect her eyes.
85mm lens, Kodachrome 25, 1/60 sec at f.8

BELOW: Sunglasses add mystery to this simple shot of a model at the wheel of a car.
85–210mm zoom lens, Kodachrome 25, 1/30 sec at f5.6

RIGHT: It may be an old standby, but a nurse's uniform, and in particular the exaggerated style found in costume stores, continues to find favor. The fact that this one is made of white PVC and has a matching hat gives a modern, fresh appeal instead of a clichéd look.
35–140mm zoom lens, digital ISO 100, 1/125 sec at f8

BELOW: The model's "tough guy" costume, with stetson hat, 1930s suit, gaudy tie, and cigar serve to emphasize her provocative femininity. The shot was used for a jigsaw puzzle.
85mm lens, Kodachrome 64, 1/60 sec at f5.6

LEFT: Single color costumes often make the best shots, but be careful that strong colors do not create unattractive color casts. Here, a green light was shone on the venetian blind to achieve backlighting to silhouette the model's body through the plastic, but the front lighting was white flash bounced off a reflector.
85–210mm zoom lens, Ektachrome 64, 1/60 sec at f5.6

LEFT: More elaborate costumes set a definite mood in a photograph. Here, the sequinned evening dress and telephone suggest sophistication and wealth. Keep color schemes simple—note how background vegetation, dress, telephone, and eyeshadow are all in matched greens, and how the single note of color contrast is given by the complementary bright red of the lipstick.

85–210mm zoom lens, Kodachrome 25, 1/30 sec at f5.6

RIGHT: This is a simple but effective shot. The model is one of Santa's helpers, putting the decorations on the tree.
70–200mm zoom lens, digital ISO 200, 1/30 sec at f5.6

ABOVE: Diving gear makes an attractive beach costume. The headgear sheltered the model's eyes from the strong sun, allowing her to look openly toward the camera and keeping all her face in the shadow rather than just parts of it. A polarizing filter controlled the glare from the sea behind.
85mm lens, Kodachrome 25, 1/30 sec at f4

LEFT & BELOW: PVC is very popular, largely thanks to the shiny, reflective nature that shows up under studio flash photography. In these examples, the almost lurid pink works well with a blonde model (below), while the addition of black underwear and PVC boots (left) increases the effect.

35–105mm zoom lens, digital ISO 100, 1/125 sec at f11

Costumes If your model dresses up in some weird and wonderful costume and acts out the role, you will have an interesting time and some first-rate photographs. Pick on any theme—a movie star or a historical character, for example. The choice does not matter, provided your model can relate to it.

Most towns have a theatrical costumier or costume store, so if you do have a specific idea, get your model kitted out there. It is a good idea to have certain standard items in your wardrobe in any case, such as a gypsy outfit, gymslips, skin-diving gear, grass skirts, and plenty of net and lace petticoats. Keep a file on costumes you have seen and liked and may be able to copy or improvise on.

Jewelry Jewelry can be used to stunning effect and does not need to be expensive to look good. A cheap dimestore badge, placed strategically and with humor, can sometimes work far better than million-dollar diamonds worn self-consciously.

Jewelry should adorn and decorate, but not dominate. One earring may be better than two, for instance, while you should never encourage your model to wear lots of rings, unless her hands can warrant the extra attention. A neckchain may look better around the ankle, while a double or single chain wrapped around the waist can look devastating against a suntan. Put jewelry where you would least expect to see it—a gemstone in the belly button, for instance. Use your imagination—and the model's.

ABOVE: The simple necklace is a key element in this shot, providing a focus of interest at the center of the frame.
85mm lens, Kodachrome 25, 1/60 sec at f5.6

ABOVE: On location, keep an eye out for locally made craft jewelry. The model here is wearing a bead necklace bought from a nearby market stall.
85mm lens, Kodachrome 25, 1/60 sec at f5.6

LEFT: This piece of jewelry around the head gives the model a hippy or new age appeal. This could have been accentuated by using shawls or appropriate clothing.
35–135mm zoom lens, Fuji ISO 100, 1/60 sec at f8

BELOW: A toy deputy sheriff's badge is the focal point of this humorous shot. Use your imagination in choosing and placing jewelry. Sunlight was used with reflectors on either side.
55mm macro lens, Kodachrome 25, 1/15 sec at f5.6

RIGHT: The depth of field is shallow in this extreme close-up, and the star of David necklace in the model's mouth is the point of focus.
55mm macro lens, Kodachrome 25, 1/60 sec at f5.6

The range of outdoor locations is vast. It is this that makes the open air so good for glamour photography. The techniques are often simpler, too, but

Outdoor Glamour

success depends on the ability to spot and use locations and an understanding of how to use natural light.

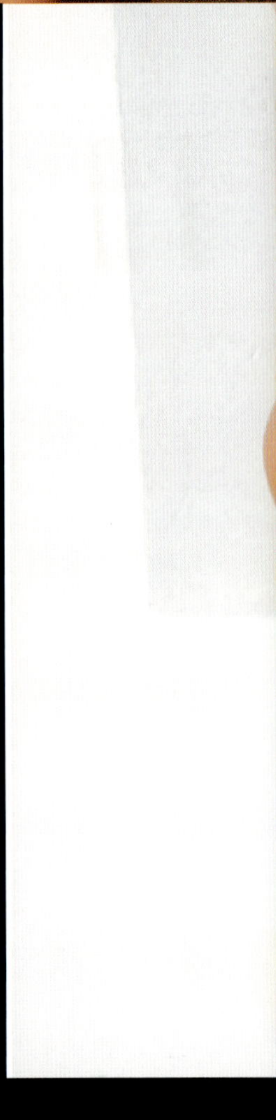

Lighting Conditions

The one constant aim in glamour photography is to make your model look her best. Shooting outdoors in natural daylight is often the best way of achieving this, provided, of course, that the light, location, and the weather in general are favorable to the end result. Consider the requirements of your photographs carefully. If a special background is essential, your starting point must be the location. If, however, your aim is simply to suggest a certain mood or situation, you can go as far as your creative imagination will take you in your own backyard.

One particular factor you must consider is the question of privacy. A combination of beautiful models and a photographer laden with equipment invariably attracts attention. If you intend taking nude shots, it is safe to say that you will need total seclusion. Even if nudity does not bother you or your model, there is a fair chance it will bother someone else.

Weather and Light

Weather and light are vital factors in all outdoor photography. Both are constantly changing, either for climatic reasons or because of the time of day, and it is important to cultivate an awareness of this in order to adjust your techniques accordingly.

On a clear, cloudless day, for instance, the sunlight is strong and will cast sharply defined shadows; on a slightly overcast or hazy day, the sunlight will be less intense and the shadows correspondingly softer. If the weather becomes progressively more overcast, the proportion of direct light is reduced even more and the shadows will be light in tone and indistinct in outline. When the weather is heavily overcast, the sunlight is diffused and therefore there are no real shadows.

Light also changes in quality according to the time of day. The early morning sun is low, throwing a warm, soft light and casting long, ill-defined shadows. The light at this time of day changes rapidly, becoming stronger and more constant as the sun rises, eventually reaching its zenith at midday. At this point, the light is flat and formless, with hard, deep shadows.

The light becomes softer as the sun starts to set, and the light conditions at dusk are much the same as at dawn. Although moonlight appears to possess a different quality to sunlight, it is no more than weak reflected sunlight.

Choosing the Time of Day

The best time of day for photography depends on the effect you want to produce. Many photographers, for instance, try to avoid light at high noon whenever possible and utilize the magical and beautiful quality of light reflected at dawn or dusk instead. Low sun is highly directional and permits a variety of

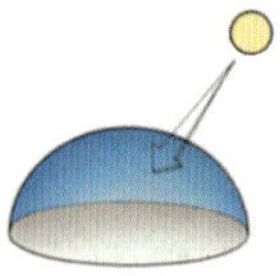

ABOVE: Some of the best photographs are taken without strong sunlight. All the elements in this shot contribute to its soft unity and quiet mood. The light, late in the afternoon, was cool, veiled by the trees, but still created a beautiful warm halo for the model's hair and down the curve of her back. The purple scarf and blue shoes match the quality of the light perfectly. Finally, a long telephoto lens was used to compress the perspective, making the cool gray of the mountains into a complete backdrop, almost like a studio curtain.

300mm lens, Kodachrome 25, 1/30 sec at f5.6

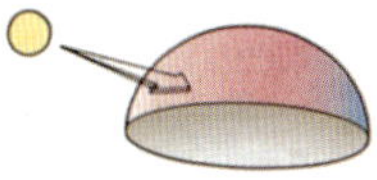

LEFT: Early morning is one of the best times of day for photography; this shot was taken at 7am. The sun is low in the sky, bathing the subject in bright but softened light from one direction, emphasizing the rounded forms of the body.

70–200mm zoom lens, digital ISO 100, 1/60 sec at f4

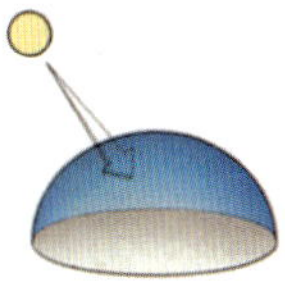

BELOW LEFT: During the morning, before the sun has risen too high in the sky, the model can be silhouetted against it effectively. The main difficulty is flare, where light reflects off the surfaces of the lens and degrades the image. Here, the photographer waited until the sun was just coming out from behind a cloud and this reduced its glare. The controlled amount of flare over the model's shoulder adds to the impact of the shot.

28mm lens, Kodachrome 25, 1/60 sec at f8

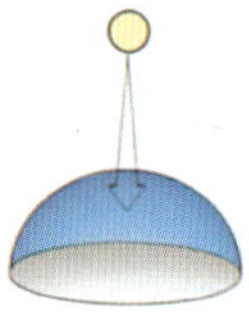

LEFT: The bright sky in the middle of the day can be used for graphic effect if the photographer takes up a position lower than the model.
70–200mm zoom lens, digital ISO 100, 1/250 sec at f5.6

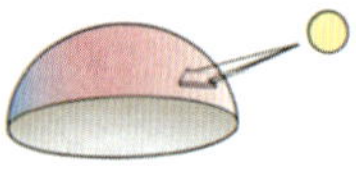

RIGHT: Sunsets make superb backdrops for glamour photography. Their warm light creates a mood of romantic fantasy, particularly on a beautiful beach with the sun going down behind the sea. It is difficult to judge the exposure for this type of silhouette. Bracket over two or three stops.
300mm lens, Kodachrome 25, 1/30 sec at f8

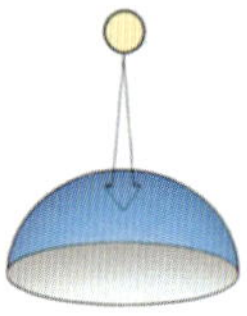

RIGHT: In the strongest midday sun, the shade may be the best place for the model. The bamboo umbrella threw attractive patterns of light and the blue water provided some color in the background.
85mm lens, Kodachrome 25, 1/30 sec at f5.6

lighting effects, from flat, full-face light to back lighting. Pose your model in various positions until you find the most suitable angle. In addition to a normal light meter reading, you should also take a reading with a spot meter. This type of light can be very deceptive.

Back lighting can also present a problem in these conditions, since it is easy to create unwanted silhouettes. Avoid this by exposing for the darkest areas. If, however, your intention is to produce a silhouette, this is the time of day when results will be the most successful.

Shoot into the sun, or use it as side lighting for portraiture; if, however, you choose the latter method, be sure to take a meter reading in the shadows. If shadows are underexposed, the end product will be dark, with loss of detail and subtlety. If the face is brightly lit, try to balance this with use of shadow to soften the effect.

There are also instances when the bright overhead light of the midday sun can be used extremely effectively. Colors are exaggerated against the background of a dark blue sky to appear richer. If, for instance, your model has a suntan, the skin will photograph darker than it actually is. A single, brightly colored accessory or carefully arranged garment can be used to good dramatic effect to create contrasts. This particularly applies to sunglasses and sports vizors. Not only do they give real protection against the sun, when used correctly they can also create attractive shadows on your model's face.

Always be aware of shadows and where they fall, taking advantage of any that can be used effectively. It is easy to capture a variety of tones in the shade if you calculate exposure correctly. If necessary, brighten the shadows with a reflector or a fill-in flash.

A reflector positioned just out of the picture area seen through the viewfinder will fill in shadow without adding more light. A hand mirror can be used but the effect will not usually be very subtle. Weaker reflections can be achieved by using crumpled foil glued to cardboard. The most unobtrusive reflections require plain white cardboard or even black cardboard.

Most photographers agree that it is difficult to preserve a natural feeling in the picture when flash is used. If you keep the maximum output of the flash to one-half or even less of the recommended setting, the flash output will not dominate.

Night Lighting

This shot used photographic lights but in such a way as to keep the effect of night.

ABOVE: Cables were run from the house out to the pool to power two spotlamps. One lamp was placed in front and to the right, shining directly on the model; the other behind to give stronger backlighting and create the long shadows that are a key feature of the shot. It was a dark night and all other lights were switched off.
85mm lens, Kodachrome 64, 1/15 sec at f5.6

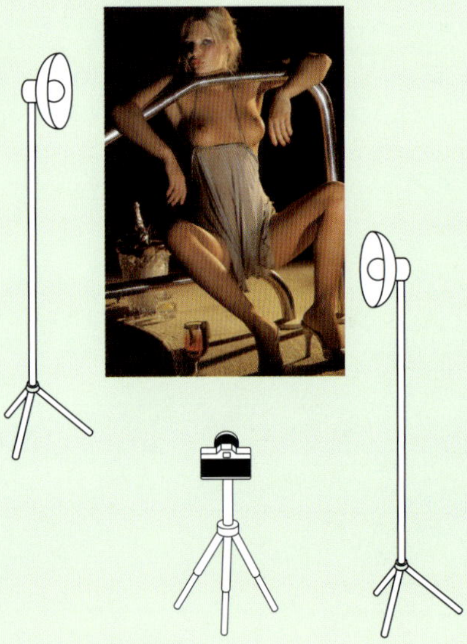

Shooting at Night

You can achieve stunning and unusual effects when shooting at night by using the available light and capitalizing on shapes and patterns. The country by moonlight assumes velvety tones that would be spoiled by using flash. Floodlit areas and pools of light from lamps or electric signs in towns can sometimes throw enough light to produce some startling results, especially if you capture the essential excitement of nightlife.

Look for special features when you are shooting at night, such as silhouettes and patterns in iron constructions. Bridges and piers, for example, take on completely new dimensions at night. When you are composing your picture, take account of the horizon—a tree that looks ordinary in daylight may possess different qualities at night, for example. Reflections at night can often be dramatic, whether they are the bright flashes of a neon light or moonlight reflected on the water.

If you decide to shoot on location, study the available light before you use flash. You are unlikely to find yourself in a situation where it is pitch-black. Make use of a full moon on the beach or in the country; in towns you will often find adequate light thrown out by restaurants, stores, streetlights, and car headlamps.

A high-speed film and a large lens aperture (f2.8 or larger) should be used for such shots. For digital, you can crank up the ISO rating on the camera, but anything beyond 400 may start to incur digital noise that is simply unpleasant in color photography. In this case, a tripod for you and a good sense of balance and keeping still for the model are essential. Do not rely upon a through-the-lens meter too much because it may be fooled. Switch to center-weighted metering for a more accurate exposure. Film users should bracket their shots, whereas digital users can at least check exposures and make

Night Shoots

As evening falls, the sun goes down rapidly and the light changes can be dramatic. The first three shots in this sequence were taken over only about 10 minutes. An 85mm lens was used, with Kodachrome 64 film.

1 Note how the daylight reflecting off the walls of the verandah at first covers the whole model, with the light from the candle looking insignificant.
1/15 sec at f5.6

2 The reflected light is much reduced, the shadows are deeper, and the candlelight is more prominent.
1/15 sec at f5.6

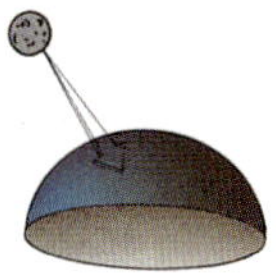

LEFT: Shooting by available light in cities at night is not commonly possible in glamour photography. The model aroused a lot of attention from passersby even before shooting began because it was obvious some form of photography was about to take place. The whole operation had to be completed very quickly, so the camera was prefocused and the model instructed to walk toward the camera and pose at various points. The neon lights have registered wonderfully, while the model has a light cast from the low light level. The shutter speed was so low that an almost dreamlike effect was created by the movement of the model and people, while the camera was on a tripod to ensure the buildings and pavement remained sharp.
35–140mm zoom lens, digital ISO 80, 1/4 sec at f2.8

3 After only a few minutes, the sun began to go down and the reflected light disappeared. The sun's light is directional and has a higher color temperature, giving an orange glow to the subject. The candlelight is now strong enough to contribute to the shot, filling in the shadow on the model's cheek. It, too, has a high color temperature.
1/8 sec at f5.6

4 Half an hour later, the evening light is barely adequate. Most of the light now comes from the candle.
1/8 sec at f4

Shooting in Pitch-black

This "lady of the night" shot was tricky to do because it was virtually pitch-black. There was no illumination other than that which came from the flash when it fired.

RIGHT: This photo balances an exposure for flash with that of the evening sky outside to produce a memorable image. The aperture of the camera was set to the power of the flash unit. Using that aperture, the background sky was then metered and the resulting shutter speed entered. In order to do a combined shoot like this, your camera must be capable of syncing with the flash at all speeds.
28–70mm zoom lens, digital ISO 100, 1/4 sec at f8

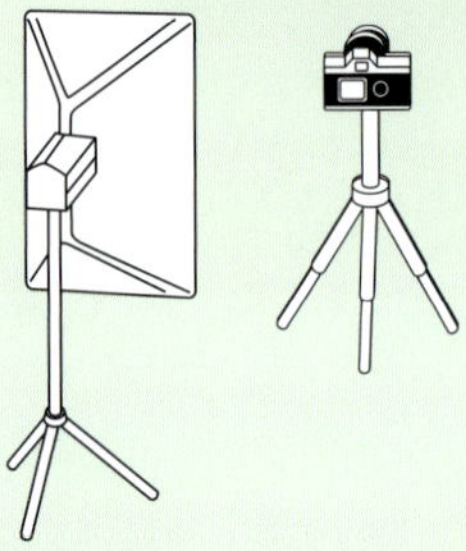

LEFT: The model was lit by a flash head and softbox, connected to the main power of a nearby cottage via a long extension lead. The focusing was done manually because autofocus simply does not work in the dark unless you have a spotter or infrared focus assist beam on your camera. The camera was set up and the model framed by guesswork; it was only by checking the LCD after each picture that the model was correctly framed after three attempts.
35–105mm zoom lens, digital ISO 100, 1/125 sec at f8

adjustments if necessary. Keep your model in the foreground as much as possible because focusing may be difficult in these conditions.

If flash is used, it is best separated from the camera. You can choose between a flashbar that fastens the flash unit to the camera, or, ideally, a handheld unit or a separate stand. You will need to experiment if you are handholding the flash. Generally, however, remember that the higher you hold the unit, the more the shadows will resemble those created by sunlight or ceiling lights. The farther to the left you hold the unit, the more shadow will be formed on the right of the subject, and vice versa.

Direct flash tends to give a hard light and create dark shadows. A natural look can be preserved in flash photography in the studio by bouncing the light of the flash unit off the ceiling. A bounced flash will eliminate shadow and give a softer light. You can either direct the flash at the ceiling or invest in an automatic flash unit with a tilt head.

RIGHT: The model was lit by a portable flash unit, leaving the cityscape behind her in the deepening dusk to create an attractive blue background. The f-stop is set to the power of the flash. The shutter speed is the ambient light reading at that f-stop.
28–70mm zoom lens, digital ISO 100, 1/4 sec at f8

Location Shooting

When the model arrives, be as friendly and welcoming as you can. Remember that this is glamour photography and it is essential for your pictures that she looks as relaxed as possible. Keep in mind, too, that most human beings feel vulnerable when they take off all or some of their clothes. If you are doing a beach shot, for example, try to make sure that you have not selected the busiest part of the promenade.

The model should take off her clothes as soon as she arrives and slip on a loose robe. Unsightly marks caused by underclothes will not enhance any picture. If you are shooting in a hot climate, try to pick a suntanned model to avoid the risk of your model being sunburned on the first day. (Never risk using a model whom you have not seen: ask for her portfolio or "Z" card first. Even if the model is shapely and healthy, she may not be the type of woman you had in mind.)

Do make sure that the model is warm enough; apart from the fact that it is difficult to relax if you are shivering, goose pimples are not attractive. Once in front of the camera, explain to the model what sort of shot you envision and discuss poses and arrangement of the props.

Some professional models are easy and relaxed in front of the camera. They will know straightaway what you are trying to achieve and make positive suggestions for a successful end product. Some models, however, have all the potential for successful glamour photography but need to be relaxed and coaxed into the session. It is the photographer's job to generate enthusiasm and persuade the model to respond to the camera. It is not always enough to instruct her to "look haughty": tell her she is a medieval tyrant queen faced with a traitor.

Apart from judging composition and lighting, test shots are an invaluable part of relaxing and directing the model. Take as many as you need to show the model what you want to achieve, and encourage her to take the initiative. You should try to be sensitive to the model's mood: if she is obviously getting tired, break and have some refreshment. If you treat your model well, you will probably be surprised and pleased with the results.

Choosing the Location

Finding the best location demands an anticipation of practical matters just as much as an eye for a picture. A day will have been lost if, for example, you find that you are not allowed to shoot in the selected spot.

When you have chosen a potential location, first check that there are no unusual hazards and that no one objects to your shooting. Visit the location at different times of day and make notes on a record card about any lighting problems, the

THIS PAGE: Locations should offer visual interest and some sort of special atmosphere. These examples show the kind of thing you could look out for. A car showroom, specializing in classic cars (above), a luxurious boat (left), a fountain in Beverley Hills (below left), and a restaurant decorated in the style of the 1900s (below) are good examples.

LEFT: The model stands on a waterfront with the New York skyline in the background. She was lit by a portable flash unit.
70–200mm zoom lens, digital ISO 100, 1/125 sec at f8

horizon, special features (such as hedges, trees, ponds, buildings), and features that you consider undesirable. These may include pylons, hoardings, or smoke stacks, for example. Take test shots and attach them to the record card.

Your record cards can be built up into an indispensable source of reference if you note details of locations not only for a particular assignment, but each time that you discover a potential location.

This sort of record keeping will not only reinforce your interest and commitment to good photography, but also play a part in developing a good eye for a picture. When you are actually shooting, training of this nature helps you to make quick decisions.

As the model will be the focal point of your picture, check before you make your final choice that the location is not too "lively"—too many points of interest will tend to dominate the picture, so that the composition will appear muddled.

You may not always have to go too far afield for the right location. Your own house or backyard may offer possibilities for good photography. Keep a lookout for the houses and gardens of friends and note particularly balconies and swimming pools, both of which make excellent locations for glamour photographs.

If you know anyone with an airplane, motorcycle, or automobile that has strong visual impact, ask them if it can be used in one of your photographs. They will probably be happy to offer it.

Having selected your location, assessed any problems, and resolved practical questions, try to use the site to the full. Consider natural framing devices such as doorframes, arches, or the curve of a bridge. Any feature should be used to best advantage, so experiment with unusual camera angles and exploit reflections and silhouettes.

Think out the shot in advance and define the mood that you wish to create. The session should be planned in as much detail as possible, so that any hitch is not compounded by bad organization. You should keep in mind particularly the props and accessories and what you would like the model to wear.

RIGHT: Having found this beautiful mansion as a location, all that was necessary was to think of suitable ideas for the individual shots. The model dressed as a bizarre and sexy chauffeuse was a good solution.
35mm lens, Kodachrome 25, 1/60 sec at f5.6

RIGHT: Keep your eye open for good backgrounds in a location. This was shot on a dirt road, for example. Why is the model there? Where is she going? These are questions that will be asked by the viewer.
70–200mm zoom lens, digital ISO 100, 1/250 sec at f5.6

LEFT: A tennis club was a good location. The model sitting in the umpire's chair was shot from below to achieve a simple sky background. It was important that the floodlights were on, not for illumination but to add interest.
35mm lens with polarizing filter, Kodachrome 25, 1/30 sec at f5.6

LEFT: Spontaneous shots of the model behaving naturally in an ordinary location can be very effective. Here, she has emerged from a hotel room onto a balcony covered with plants, while the early morning light streams in.

28–70mm zoom lens, digital ISO 100, 1/250 sec at f8

Exotic Locations

Locations that are truly exotic will probably require considerable time and expense to reach, but it is worth keeping in mind that there may be several beauty spots near you that look far from ordinary. It does not matter where you are in reality if the picture succeeds in evoking the mood you wish to create.

When you are looking for this sort of location within a reasonable radius of your home, look out for any stretch of water—sea, river, or lake—that has inlets, coves, or secluded corners.

As few of us live in really exotic places, the information concerning such locations is in the chapter on professional glamour photography (see page 130).

ABOVE: A coconut plantation provided this surreal location. A long-focus lens was used to keep the crowds of onlookers out of the shot, but the dust they stirred contributes to the weird quality of the location.

300mm lens, Kodachrome 25, 1/125 sec at f5.6

LEFT: Shooting through the foliage of a Jamaican forest created the required jungle effect.

85mm lens, Kodachrome 64, 1/60 sec at f4

In the Backyard

Although beautiful and exotic locations can provide stunning backdrops for your pictures, glamour photography is primarily about women. If you couple a sound knowledge of your subject with enthusiasm, you will find that it is possible to take good photographs under most circumstances. You will find it helpful if you start in familiar surroundings with a model you know. You will then have fewer unforeseen problems.

One of the easiest locations to consider for a first photographic session is your own backyard. If you do not have one or it is not suitable, perhaps that of a friend, who will leave you to get on with the assignment, will do equally well.

When you are selecting the location, look for any details that will provide an interesting background. Remember that your model could be standing, sitting, or lying down, so remember to check details other than those at eye level. Consider as many camera angles as possible, using as many different lenses as you have access to. When taking a portrait, it is often preferable to have a very shallow depth of field, focusing on your model so that the background is blurred. If you use this method, almost any background will prove satisfactory, provided that the colors are neutral.

When shooting pictures in your own backyard, make sure that any domestic or suburban elements that would detract from the glamour of the picture are excluded. Examples of these include fences, common flowers, and clotheslines. The trees and shrubs in your backyard may be rather ordinary, too, so it would be preferable to use a shallow depth of field so that they are blurred. Tropical pot plants, provided that the pot is not within the picture area, give a feeling of the exotic and can be placed in the foreground around the model.

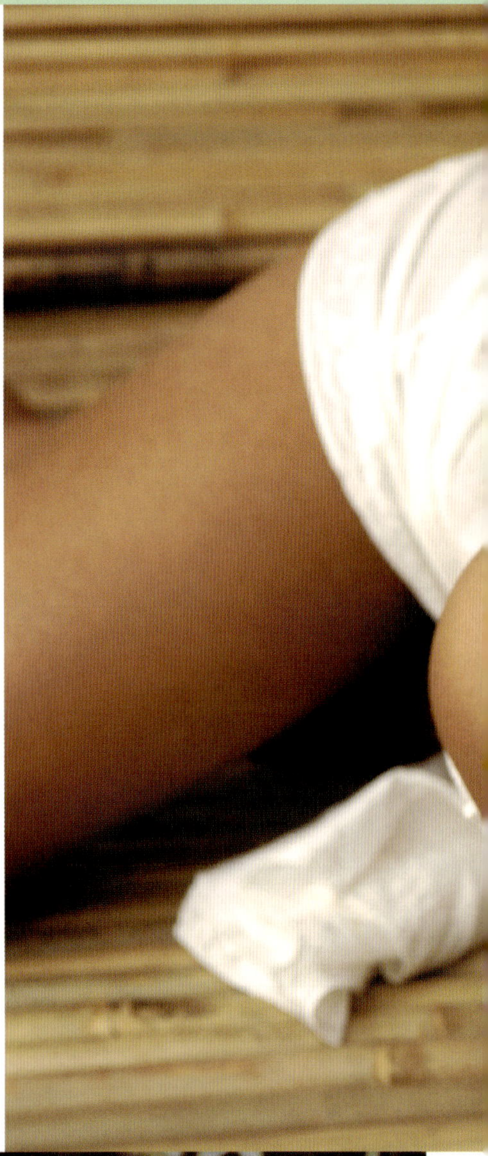

RIGHT: The model lies on a bed of reeds that complements her skin color. Simply add some light and have the model crawl into the camera for an effective outdoor shot.

70–200mm zoom lens, digital ISO 100, 1/250 sec at f4

BELOW: The backyard is all you need for a location, particularly with an attractive balustrade and leafy plants. A shaft of sun coming through the trees lit the model.

85mm lens, Kodachrome 25, 1/30 sec at f5.6

ABOVE: An early morning shot on a patio strikes a pleasantly informal note, with the model drying her hair. If the chairs and woodwork had not been all white, the setting might have looked confused.
85mm lens, Kodachrome 25, 1/60 sec at f5.6

LEFT: Behind this house is a courtyard patio with extensive gardens in the background. The model is close enough to the house to be able to use studio flash gear to light her.
28–70mm zoom lens, digital ISO 100, 1/125 sec at f8

RIGHT: The strong diagonal and horizontal lines of the stairs at the back of this house make an effective frame for the model.
28–70mm zoom lens, digital ISO 100, 1/60 sec at f8

Closing in on a beautiful model's face can produce results every bit as alluring as the whole figure.

TOP LEFT: Lighting is the most important element. Avoid hard shadows.

TOP RIGHT: Look for unusual angles. Here, the model is lying down, with her face right into the camera.

CENTER: The rich blue of the pool provides an ideally simple background for this shot. Backlighting with natural fill-in from reflections off the surface of the water contribute to the effect.

ABOVE: A close-up shot with the model looking into the camera can have a restful, romantic feel.

BOTTOM LEFT: To get close to the model, without being right in her face and risking distortion from a wide-angle lens, use a 200mm setting.

BOTTOM CENTER: Backlighting gives an attractive halo effect to the hair.

Portraits

Lighting is the single most important factor in portrait photography. When used correctly, daylight can prove the kindest and most flattering light to the face. This is especially true if you wish to project a strong sense of natural beauty.

Even the most professional of models may find the camera inhibiting at first, so do everything you can to make her feel comfortable. You may find it helpful to use a long lens so that you can work at a distance; working in this way, the model will probably feel more relaxed and therefore more likely to vary her expressions and poses. Any tension in the model's face is nowhere so apparent as in a portrait.

The camera tends to magnify any tension, just as it does the elements that make every face individual. Build on these elements so that you draw out each model's particular characteristics and personality. It is worth studying the model's face carefully and deciding which side is the most photogenic. If she has well-balanced features, she may be able to take a straight-on shot. If she does not, and you nevertheless want a full-faced portrait, draw in as close as possible, so that the picture is tightly framed. You will discover that this method will produce some very dramatic photographs, particularly if the model has beautiful eyes or a sensuous mouth.

If you find that the model tends to narrow her eyes when she looks directly into the camera, suggest that she lowers her head slightly and looks up. A slightly low camera viewpoint will shorten a longish nose, and will also improve the appearance of a narrow chin or prominent forehead.

ABOVE & RIGHT: This superbly toned model goes through a series of athletic dance moves, set inside a rundown warehouse. The evening light complements the colors of the walls and gives the model herself a lovely golden cast. The role you ask of your model should fit in with her physique; this model was ideal, but a more rounded figure would have looked out of place.

28–70mm zoom lens, digital ISO 100, 1/30 sec at f5.6

The other advantage of using a long lens for portraiture is that it will soften forward projections, such as the nose. By focusing on the eyes, the viewer finds himself drawn into the picture. Focusing on the lips enhances the sensual quality of the model.

The essential factor to remember in choosing the background is that it should be a neutral color. The background in a portrait must not detract from or dominate the model.

Choosing a Theme

A theme gives a framework to work within and you will probably find this helpful at first so that you can concentrate on the more technical aspects of glamour photography. As time goes by, you may find this method of working a little restricting, but at least you will be able to focus on one idea and explore all the possibilities.

Your model will be an essential factor in determining the theme, so discuss different ideas with her and find out what she enjoys doing. If she is the sporty type, she may look good in tennis or riding clothes. Alternately, she may enjoy water or playing around on a trampoline. If you discover that she naturally inclines to being more passive, try her playing cards, reading a book, or simply sunbathing.

Designing the Set

A shot taken in your backyard will obviously not require such elaborate set design as, for instance, a shot in a studio would. The main points to keep in mind are the disguise or elimination of any undesirable features, such as the domestic surburban elements mentioned previously, the best use of anything intrinsic to the landscape, and the addition of furniture and props.

Realism in a photograph is achieved by capitalizing on the existing features, which might include a tree, porch, steps, arches, or windows. A porch or an arch, for example, often works well as a natural framing device.

Before you add furniture or props, think out the type of shot you are taking and, in particular, the feeling or mood you wish to create. It is worth discussing it with your model in advance and asking her to dress accordingly.

Close-ups

A close-up can be of any part of the anatomy, but, as with portraits, it should fill the frame and possess a single component that draws the viewer into the picture. The visual impact can be created by adding a single item, such as a piece of jewelry or a flower, or by the juxtaposition of one part of the body with another: the hands could be placed on the knees, for example, or the arms folded across the breasts.

Some very striking photographs can result from drawing attention to one particular aspect of your model. The important thing to remember when photographing close-ups is that by isolating a detail, you are conveying texture and the feeling of touch. Ensure that your model has the sort of skin that bears the scrutiny of a close-up. It must be soft and smooth, without blemishes or goose pimples. Color is not significant, although it would be difficult, for example, to convey a healthy, natural look with a really pale model.

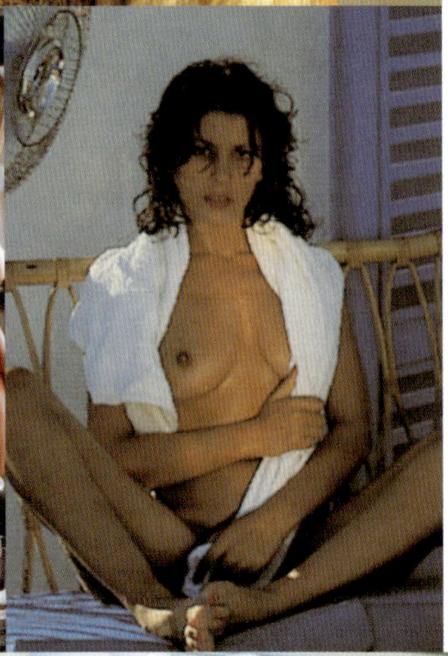

The key factor when designing sets is to keep them simple.

TOP: A bale of hay was all that was needed, with the background plain and out of focus. The golden hair and feather boa complete the unified color and textural scheme.

MIDDLE LEFT: The bathroom makes a great location, whether water is being employed or not. Make sure it is clean and relatively tidy, though.

MIDDLE RIGHT: Well-designed rooms or balconies make good sets. Here, the cushions match the walls and shutters.

ABOVE: Posing on a balcony is given some comic effect by the fact that a narrow aperture has ensured the pole in the background is in reasonably sharp focus, almost as if the model is being impaled as a sacrifice.

LEFT: You cannot go far wrong having an attractive model posing in front of a mirror. Focusing on her reflection in the mirror rather than on the model herself is often effective.

Never neglect close-ups. Make them a part of every session, to balance shots of the whole model, portraits, and wider frames that include the setting.

ABOVE LEFT: This spontaneous shot was taken during a break in photography, when the model was absorbed in a book. Closing in on the face, arm, and knee created an interesting composition.

ABOVE: The dark tones of the model stand out well against the light sky background and the white sheepskin rug.

LEFT: The tight crop draws the viewer right into the overtly sexual pose and the direct stare from the model.

On the Balcony

Private balconies with a view can often prove to be interesting locations for glamour photographs. The position of the camera will obviously be restricted, but you can experiment with different lenses, shooting from all angles until you have found the most suitable combination. If you are shooting the model on a low balcony, you could experiment with shooting from the ground using a zoom lens.

The landscape will tend to dominate the photograph unless you are concentrating on a close-up, so it is important to assess it. Height usually suggests danger and will also lend the model an aura of aloofness, so do exploit these factors if the balcony is a high one. If the backdrop is a busy street with a lot of detail, your model will appear to be part of the scene, which in nude shots can be particularly dramatic. Balconies in hotels or blocks of flats often provide enough privacy, while creating an intimate atmosphere.

In Public

The need for privacy when taking glamour shots cannot be overemphasized. You have to contend with the reactions of the public as well as reassuring the model. However, a photograph that has obviously been taken in a public place, suggesting everyday activity, has an essential excitement. Main streets, promenades, motels, and car parks are all locations that can convey such a feeling if they are used imaginatively.

The best results when taking glamour shots in a public place are usually achieved without much planning. By attempting to control a situation that is unpredictable, some of the immediacy is lost. Successful shots are often the result of photographer and model setting out with little preconceived idea of the session; if the feeling is right, almost any location will work.

A sense of intimacy or fantasy is essential to a glamour shot and this is often achieved not by a naked model but by one who has loosened her buttons or zippers. In any case, it is only on beaches where topless bathing is allowed that naked or semi-naked pictures can be shot in public. You will otherwise have to choose a very secluded beach or country area.

Fantasy can also be conveyed by overdressing or underdressing the model for the setting. Fur coats under a blazing sun or just a slip in the snow, for instance, make an unlikely, but sensual, combination.

Spontaneity often works well for glamour shots in public places, but it is worth being prepared for the foreseeable eventualities. You should take as wide a range as possible of equipment as well as several changes of clothes and accessories for your model.

ABOVE: Beautiful old buildings sometimes have good balconies on which to pose the model when shooting from below. Here, a warm glow from the late afternoon sun highlights the model's face.
85–210mm zoom lens, Kodachrome 64, 1/30 sec at f5.6

RIGHT: The sense of drama on a high balcony can be very effective. Here, the model seems poised above an immense drop to the streets below.
85–210mm zoom lens, Kodachrome 25, 1/125 sec at f5.6

RIGHT: Almost any balcony will offer the viewer a sense of mystery, even if it is only above the car park at the side of the hotel, as in this shot.
28–105mm zoom lens, digital ISO 100, 1/250 sec at f8

ABOVE: The regular balconies of a modern hotel make a stunning backdrop for this early morning shot. The concrete reflects plenty of light around the model—a useful advantage on many modern balconies.

85mm lens, Kodachrome 25, 1/60 sec at f5.6

RIGHT: Drama again with the model's seemingly dangerous pose silhouetted against the sky, stressing the sense of height. In reality, there was a ledge below the wall on which the model was leaning.

85mm lens with polarizing filter, Kodachrome 25, 1/30 sec at f5.6

Glamour on the Beach

A woman sunning herself on an exotic beach spells glamour and pleasure. Beware, however, of too ordinary a shot. Look for interesting natural features, such as a curved coastline or one with coves and cliffs. Trees provide a focal point in beach photography, particularly if caught at an imaginative angle or in an interesting light. A moonlit beach must be one of the most evocative locations.

Beach photography needs to be planned in as much detail as possible since the difficulties can be magnified by the inaccessibility of the location. The ideal location, of course, is a secluded beach close enough to a road to allow access for your car. This combination often proves difficult to find, so take with you as wide a range of equipment as possible.

Your preparation should include necessities such as a couple of large umbrellas to provide shade for the model and the equipment; suntan cream and skin protection, food and refreshments, and a first-aid box. Possible props and accessories would be beach robes for the model, straw and cotton beach hats, sunglasses, beach balls, a beach bed, deckchairs, diving gear, fishing equipment, and perhaps a picnic basket with wine, salads, and fruit.

It is important that the beach is secluded because otherwise you will be beset by onlookers and the model may well find it difficult to make it a successful session.

Do ascertain from your model that she can withstand the heat if you intend spending a day photographing on the beach. It is best to take a model who is already suntanned, so that the risk of unsightly sunburn is minimized. You must take into account for glamour photography the question of the model's bikini marks. It is for you to decide whether it is more or less attractive to choose a model who is completely suntanned. Finally, remember that even when the sun is at its weakest,

LEFT: Use props that are suited to the beach location, such as this inflatable boat.
85mm lens, Kodachrome 25, 1/125 sec at f5.76

ABOVE: A background such as this reed windbreaker can provide both security from prying eyes and also an interesting and effective backdrop to the model.
28–200mm zoom lens, digital ISO 100, 1/500 sec at f8

ABOVE: Look around for interesting features of the location, such as this fallen tree, to achieve variety in beach shots. There is no point in taking 20 or 30 identical shots.
85mm lens, Kodachrome 25, 1/30 sec at f5.6

LEFT: The late afternoon sun provided soft, directional lighting for this shot, taken in the hotel swimming pool.
70–200mm zoom lens, digital ISO 100, 1/250 sec at f4

Spicing Up Your Beach Shots

Look for interesting natural features to spice up your beach shots.

Rocks

A beach landscape broken up by rocks can provide an interesting background to a glamour shot. Rockpools and seaweed can lend points of interest, too. Rocks near water can be treacherously slippery and it is not worth taking chances with your model.

Wind

There is usually a wind or breeze on the beach even on a hot day. You can .and even the passivity of the model. Long hair, lightweight clothing, or palm trees are all sensitive even to a light breeze.

A beach offers more opportunities than most locations to conjure up a world of fantasy. Warmth and indolence means luxury and a freedom that can only be delightful.

Examine the landscape and the relationship between land, sea, and sky. If it is windy or cloudy, anticipate the changes in the light and the weather and use to best effect the action of the wind on the waves.

Waves

The power and movement suggested by waves are invaluable to a glamour shot. Try shooting the model jumping in and out of the waves or resting on a beach bed.

As waves are usually accompanied by wind, be sure to protect the camera lens from spray and sand. Watch how the waves break for a while so that you understand their pattern. If they are strong, ensure that the model can cope.

If your model has her back to a rogue wave, warn her, but try to keep things lighthearted or the shot will suffer. A long lens is required for this type of shot, combined with a fast shutter speed and wide aperture.

RIGHT: Two models on a rocky beach. One model is slowly taking down her trousers to add eroticism to a scene that already features the dangerous elements of rocks and a mystery observer in the distance.
35–140mm zoom lens, digital ISO 80, 1/64 sec at f8

either early in the morning or when it is hidden behind clouds, it can still be powerful. Have plenty of suntan cream available, as well as beach robes, hats, and sunglasses for the model, and remind her that the effect of the sun is even greater when she is in the water although she may not feel it.

Sun, sand, wind, and waves are the natural hazards of beach photography. Everything that needs protection from the sun should be kept under a beach umbrella, on top of large white towels weighed down at the corners. Not only will this reflect the sun, but it will also reduce the possibility of sand creeping into everything. Your equipment should be kept in white or silver containers, and should only be taken out when you need it. Film should be kept in refrigerated cartons because excessive heat would damage it. Padded thermal bags are ideal for this purpose. Digital memory cards are more heat-resistant but should still be kept out of the sun's glare.

Above all, remember to safeguard your equipment from the sand. If there is no protected area in which to change film, always do it sitting down, with the wind behind you so that your body acts as a shield. Check that no sand has got into the back of your camera and that the lenses are clear of spray. The same applies when changing lenses on digital SLRs—the bane of these cameras is getting dirt onto the sensor. If sand gets in, it can wreck the camera. You are strongly advised to fit a big zoom lens before getting on the beach, and not to change it while you are there.

You will probably find it easier to handhold your camera rather than use a tripod on the beach, since sand does not usually provide a stable base.

With well-organized advance planning and preparation, you will be free once you have reached the site to take full advantage of an evocative and sexy location.

LEFT: Wet sand will stick to the model's skin. In some cases this adds an extra dimension of texture to the shot. The luxurious pose makes use of the location to the full.

85mm lens, Ektachrome 64, 1/60 sec at f5.6

ABOVE: Waves breaking over the model can make exciting shots. Take care to protect the camera from the corrosive spray. A slow shutter speed gave the sense of movement.

85mm lens, Kodachrome 25, 1/15 sec at f5.6

The Wet Look

Water provides a natural environment for nudity. In glamour shots women in, around, or simply soaked in water make an unbeatable combination. Water adds spontaneity to any session because it immediately gives your model something to respond to. She can float in it, paddle in it, jump and splash around in it, or be sprayed by it.

The previous section on beach photography will have given you some ideas on how to use water, but this section describes ways to photograph women and water under the more controlled conditions found in swimming pools, jacuzzis, and showers.

Swimming Pools Private swimming pools make an ideal location. If you do not have access to a private pool, you may find that a hotel or club will be prepared to negotiate for the hire of theirs, particularly if you can offer some sort of credit or other publicity.

Consider all possible camera angles the pool possesses before actually shooting, making a mental note of the best positions. If the background is uninteresting, build a set with garden furniture or tropical plants. By drawing in close to your subject, using water as the only background, you will create an impression of a vast expanse of water.

Successful swimming pool shots demand a sunny day, so artificial lighting will not be required. Reflectors, however, will be useful because water creates glare. Polarizing filters reduce glare, but these should only be used when necessary because they tend to deaden textures and reduce shutter speeds.

Jacuzzis Relaxing in a jacuzzi is a pleasurable experience and one that your model will certainly enjoy. Jacuzzis tend to be small and functional, so it is best to concentrate on close-ups or to shoot the model from a downward angle.

Showers, Fountains, and Sprinklers Such simple props used with a model who enjoys playing with water can create some evocative photographs. Showers, particularly, convey a sense of intimacy. Timing is crucial and you will get most of the action shots in the first few minutes. Not only will the sensations from the water be novel and exciting to the model, but she is likely to get cold quicker than in a swimming pool, where the body temperature remains relatively constant.

When photographing in fountains or powerful showers, it is practically impossible to give directions to your model. It will be noisy and she will probably get water in her ears. The best thing to do is to let your model enjoy the situation for as long as she wants, encouraging her with gestures if possible. Remember to take frequent breaks and make sure the model keeps warm.

ABOVE: In this jacuzzi shot, the model is looking slightly apprehensive, but the painted background adds extra interest and the bubbling, foamy water looks inviting.
70–200mm zoom lens, digital ISO 400, 1/60 sec at f5.6

ABOVE & RIGHT: These two shots were taken during the same session set in a jacuzzi with the evening sun low in the sky and warm in color. The jacuzzi was small, so the shots had to frame closely on the model to exclude the distracting surroundings. At first the model was tentative about the new experience, but she soon began to enjoy the rushing water (right). The shutter speed was too slow to freeze the movement of the water, with a really effective result—the ecstatic model in sharp focus against turbulent water (above).

85mm lens, Kodachrome 25, 1/30 sec at f5.6 (right), 1/15 sec at f4 (above)

RIGHT: Portable photographic lights achieved the shot of the model in a fountain at Caesar's Palace, Las Vegas. A blue color-correction filter balanced the light to the film. The champagne bottle added to the uninhibited atmosphere.

28mm lens, Kodachrome 64, 1/30 sec at f5.6

LEFT: This spectacular shot was achieved with a simple shower and minimal props—a see-through jumpsuit and a large glass. The secret is the backlight from a powerful spotlamp that picked out the drops of water as a rain of bright streaks. It also lit up the jumpsuit and outlined the model's body. Another spotlamp, bounced off a reflector, provided softer frontal lighting. This shot took careful planning in the studio—remember that it is extremely dangerous to allow water near photographic lamps.

85mm lens, Kodachrome 64, 1/15 sec at f5.6

RIGHT: This dramatic and dynamic swimming pool shot was taken from a distance in order to show the water and hair flying through the air, but also to ensure that none of it went over the camera. Prefocusing and then switching to manual focus will help you get the shot in circumstances like this, particularly for digital users. A fast shutter speed will totally freeze the action, with water droplets in the air, but a slower one will give a more creative effect where the hair is blurred.

28–105mm zoom lens, digital ISO 100, 1/15 sec at f8

ABOVE: Blue is the predominant color of swimming pools, and here it is used to advantage with an airbed of the same color providing a single, undistracting backdrop for the model's tanned body. A polarizing filter was needed to control the reflections from the surface of the water.
85mm lens, Kodachrome 64, 1/30 sec at f5.6

LEFT: A close-up shot shows the model enjoying the water in this swimming pool and gives the photo a feeling of intimacy.
70–200mm zoom lens, digital ISO 100, 1/250 sec at f5.6

LEFT: The model appears oblivious to the camera as she relaxes under a rushing waterfall. Thanks to the low light level and lack of direct sunlight, a fast ISO rating had to be used.

70–200mm zoom lens, digital ISO 800, 1/60 sec at f4

BELOW: By framing tightly on the model, the impression of a large expanse of water can be achieved in a small pool. The obvious pleasure of the model gives this shot its impact. The swimming pool is a good setting because it can distract the model from the photographer's presence and lead to really natural shots.

85mm lens with polarizing filter, Kodachrome 25, 1/30 sec at f5.6

ABOVE: Swimming pools make excellent backdrops. The strong clear blue of the water works well with the warmer flesh tones of the model. For the best effects, avoid intrusively colored props in the foreground—here, the white chair is no distraction—and keep everything else out of the shot. A polarizing filter may be needed to control the reflected light from the water's surface, although the flesh colors will be better, as in this example, without one.

85mm lens, Kodachrome 25, 1/60 sec at f5.6

BELOW: Close-up shots of the model emerging from the water can be very effective, especially if eye contact is made with the camera.
70–200mm zoom lens, digital ISO 100, 1/125 sec at f4

RIGHT: Encourage the model to display her enjoyment of the sun and water. Such pleasure is one of the strong points of a pool as location, but be careful of hot sun, for concentration plus the cool of the water may distract from the dangers of sunburn.
85mm lens, Kodachrome 25, 1/60 sec at f5.6

Indoor photography uses both available light and photographic lamps, and the range of effects is as extensive as your imagination. Indoor photography is by no means as difficult as you expect.

Indoor Glamour

On the contrary, these conditions enable you to achieve the highest quality because you can control the light and are not at the mercy of the elements.

Natural and Available Light

Every glamour photographer should be aware of the virtues of indoor photography. Not only can working indoors be just as satisfying as working on location, but if approached methodically and with patience, it is often the preferable location for certain types of glamour shot.

Indoors, for instance, you will frequently find that you are able to build up a closer working relationship with your model than is possible on location. In addition, once you have mastered the use of available, mixed, and studio lighting, your photography itself may well display a greater sense of freedom, since you will have far better overall control of the situation. Most importantly, you will no longer be dependent on the weather; dull light or bad weather will no longer be a reason for putting your camera away for a sunny day.

Without a Studio

At the start, you may decide not to go to the expense of setting up a studio, but, instead, to use your own house or apartment as the setting for your photographs. There are obvious advantages to this; working on ground you know well, for instance, means that you can quickly size up its atmosphere and create the mood for your shots. Second, close acquaintance means that you will quickly realize the disadvantages, particularly where space and lighting are concerned.

In most interiors, lack of space is usually coupled with poor lighting conditions. There is no denying that the former can present considerable technical problems, but these can usually be overcome by careful planning. Remember, too, that, for certain glamour shots, the very intimacy of the environment can be a considerable advantage. An alternative to shooting at home—which can put some models off—is to hire a studio for a couple of hours. If you scout around, this can be done fairly cheaply, with the added bonus that the studio will usually have a full set of flash heads and diffusers for you to use at the time.

Natural Light

If you are fortunate enough to be able to rely on a good source of daylight, your photographs will benefit as a result. Though it is always possible to set up studio lighting, nothing can duplicate the delicate and subtle qualities of good natural light. Because it can be unpredictable, using it successfully requires skill and imagination; however, used to best advantage, it will lend realism and charm—both extremely important ingredients in glamour photography—to the end result.

Working with daylight has its problems. The most important thing to remember is to assess the best time of day at which to shoot, though this, of course, depends to a certain extent on the result you wish to obtain. The ideal position for shooting indoors is under a traditional studio skylight that gives a large, direct source of soft light, without harsh shadows or unpleasant contrasts. Otherwise, make do with the light provided by windows, glass or open doors, and sunrooms. Study where and how the light falls at different times of day and decide accordingly on the best positions from which to take your photographs. If shooting on location inside, it pays to visit at the same time, the day before, to check out the light and general ambience.

ABOVE: A circular reflector bounces light from an outside window back onto the model. The advantage of using lower levels of light is that it makes it easier to use maximum apertures, thereby throwing the cluttered background out of focus.

140mm lens, digital ISO 80, 1/60 sec at f2.2

LEFT: Natural window light at midday filters into the room. As the exterior conditions were cloudy, it resulted in very diffused light.
105mm lens, digital ISO 80, 1/30 sec at f5.6

BELOW: A doorframe to the outside of a cottage is utilized to frame the model. With the light much brighter outside than in, the interior descends into gloom, leaving attention on the model.
150mm lens, digital ISO 100, 1/60 sec at f2.8

LEFT: Overcast days are excellent times to shoot indoors because they offer an even spread of diffused light. Here, the natural light is supplemented by the tungsten lamp on the wall, adding a pleasing glow to the orange wall.
45mm lens, digital ISO 800, 1/90 sec at f4.5

RIGHT: Window daylight through sheer curtains creates a soft and romantic light that suited the image content. Sheers are useful devices for acting as diffusers.
90mm lens, digital ISO 100, 1/60 sec at f5.6

LEFT: These two shots show how light from outside can either be ignored to create a glowing aspect lacking detail (far left), or have contrast and detail and throw the model into shadow (left).
14–30mm zoom lens, digital ISO 100, 1/125 sec at f5.6

Available Light

Not every house or apartment possesses an acceptable source of natural light, or the right amount of it for top-quality photography. Assuming that you do not want to use flash or studio lighting, the trick is to use the available light to its best advantage.

Photographs taken with available light must create mood and atmosphere. Though you have less control over the final quality of the shot, you still have plenty of scope to create a subtle and sensitive picture. Remember that, in most rooms, the general level of illumination will be low and the contrasts high, with localized pools of light around the lamps or windows. Multiple shadows are common, so note where and how they fall, particularly if they fall directly onto the model, or obscure an object to which you would like to draw attention.

Under such conditions, the film you choose is vital. Many daylight color films are not fast enough to be used. Choose one rated at 400 ISO that still has fine grain.

You may also find it necessary to use a fast lens and a slow shutter speed. Unless precautions are taken, the results are often grainy, with a shallow depth of field and image blur from subject or camera movement. Deal with the last by always using a tripod for indoor shooting, unless lack of space prohibits its use; in such a circumstance, bracing the camera against a wall will reduce the risk of camera movement.

Remember, too, that you can use reflectors to improve light availability. Though most domestic interiors are only moderately reflective, light-colored surfaces on walls, furniture, fabrics, and so on produce natural reflections that will reduce the contrasts to some extent. Place the reflectors in direct line with your light source and at right angles to the point on which you want the light to fall. If this still is not sufficient, experiment with ordinary center and side lights, standard lamps, or bedside lamps.

ABOVE: The window silhouette contributes a great deal to the shot. By exposing for the outside, furniture in the room remained in the dark and did not clutter the shot. A spotlamp lit the model's back.
35mm lens, Kodachrome 25, 1/15 sec at f5.6

LEFT & BELOW: This pair of shots in a New York loft apartment use natural light from the windows and reflectors to bounce light back into the darker areas of the model. In both cases, the effect is completely natural, light, and effective.
70mm lens, digital ISO 100, 1/30 sec at f5.6

LEFT: This shot had to be carefully posed and several exposures taken to get hand and ball in the right positions. Some daylight and the lights of the pool table lit the model, although flash was used for the table in the foreground.
85mm lens, Kodachrome 25, 1/60 sec at f5.6

RIGHT: With good daylight reflecting off the light-colored walls, this room was well lit throughout. The overhead lights and table lamps also helped. Three large reflectors concentrate light onto the model to focus the composition.
85mm lens, Kodachrome 25, 1/15 sec at f4

LEFT: The daylight was sufficient for this shot taken from a stairway, but for a dramatic effect a single spotlamp was bounced from a gold reflector onto the model, leaving the surroundings darker.
28mm lens, Kodachrome 25, 1/30 sec at f5.6

ABOVE: Late evening sun casts a golden light onto the model and plaster walls. The translucent fabric virtually shimmers with the soft, pleasing light.
50mm lens, digital ISO 100, 1/60 sec at f4

LEFT: Daylight comes from the window on the left and is diffused by the gold fabric the model is holding. A gold reflector to the right adds extra warmth to the scene.
70mm lens, digital ISO 100, 1/60 sec at f5.6

A Studio of Your Own

A studio is the only answer if your aim is to have the ability to manipulate every step in the picture-taking process, just as professionals photographers do. Taking photographs with daylight or available light presents its own challenges, but invariably the final results are dependent to a certain extent on factors beyond your direct control. In the studio, on the other hand, you have almost complete freedom; you can design a set to your own specification and adjust the lighting until it is exactly the way you want it. For better or worse, the end product is entirely your own responsibility.

However, while studio photography offers more freedom, it also requires a greater initial commitment. Whereas outdoors you have an abundance of natural light and possible backgrounds, a studio is a dark, confined space within four walls until you transform it into something else.

Setting up a studio requires space, money, time, and effort. You will have to learn new techniques and how to design a set. You will also have the additional task of discovering how your model reacts under studio conditions.

Studio Layout

A permanent studio for glamour photography will need to be fairly large—you will have to be able to include furniture and even whole sets in the shot. Space can be expensive, so make sure you really need this facility before taking it on. The studio can also, of course, be taken to mean an ordinary room temporarily converted for the purpose, with the windows blacked out and photographic light introduced.

If you do decide to design a permanent studio, make sure there is enough space. You should also be able to cut out all daylight with light-tight blinds. Ordinary room power may not be sufficient for photographic lights, so check and install extra power lines if necessary.

A changing room will be essential, ideally with a well-lit mirror for the model to apply makeup. Adequate storage space for equipment and props is also important.

ABOVE: If you cannot afford the expense of a dedicated studio, converting a room in your house is the next best thing. Paint all the walls white to ensure there are no color casts reflected onto the subject, add some backgrounds, and install your equipment. Use a bathroom for a changing room and you are ready to shoot.

35mm lens, digital ISO 80, 1/60 sec at f4

Studio Equipment

A well-equipped studio will have many items of equipment as well as the photographic gear.

Background Rolls
These rolls of thick paper are available in different sizes and colors. The type illustrated is supported on two expanding poles that fit between floor and ceiling. Make sure the roll is wide enough.

Stepladders
These will help when putting up the set and when using a high camera position.

Folding Flats
These large freestanding screens act as reflectors.

Planning Your Studio

When you decide to set up your own studio, the most important thing is to ensure that you have sufficient space in which to work. For glamour photography, your space requirements will be greater than, say, for still life or portraiture, so try to get as large a room as possible. The minimum requirement is about 12 x 18ft (3.5 x 5.5m); this will allow you to take a full-length figure shot with a normal lens. For digital SLRs with a focal-length shift, possibly even more room is required, otherwise a wider angle lens will need to be used with resulting danger of distortion. A high ceiling is also an advantage; it facilitates a greater range of camera positions and can be used to "bounce" lighting.

The walls and ceiling should be painted with a matte, washable white finish; colored paint is the enemy of good photography, since it will produce a cast on the pictures. Paint over existing windows, or black them out with purpose-designed roller blinds, to ensure the studio is light-tight. You will need to install an extractor fan or air conditioning; sealed windows coupled with the heat built up by camera lights will make the studio impossible to work in, unless there is adequate ventilation.

In the beginning, it is not necessary to invest in a great deal of expensive paraphernalia. Build up your equipment slowly, buying only items for which there is a specific need. Wind machines, for instance, are used in quite a few glamour shots, but, unless you are going to specialize in such subjects, it makes far more sense to hire a machine when it is required. In all studios, space is at a premium; an excess of unwanted or underused equipment means precious workspace wasted.

Dressing Room There is one additional facility that all glamour photographers should provide: a dressing room for their models. Make sure that this is well lit and that it has a large enough mirror. It must have adequate hanging space for clothes, plus storage room for shoes and other accessories. Provide an emergency supply of face and body makeup, creams, towels, a hairdryer, and heated rollers.

Studio Equipment Normal set furniture includes folding flats, a stepladder (useful for high-angle camera shots), trestles, and backgrounds. One of the most useful forms of backgrounds are seamless paper rolls, aptly known as hanging rolls. These are ideal for portraiture or for whenever you require a plain

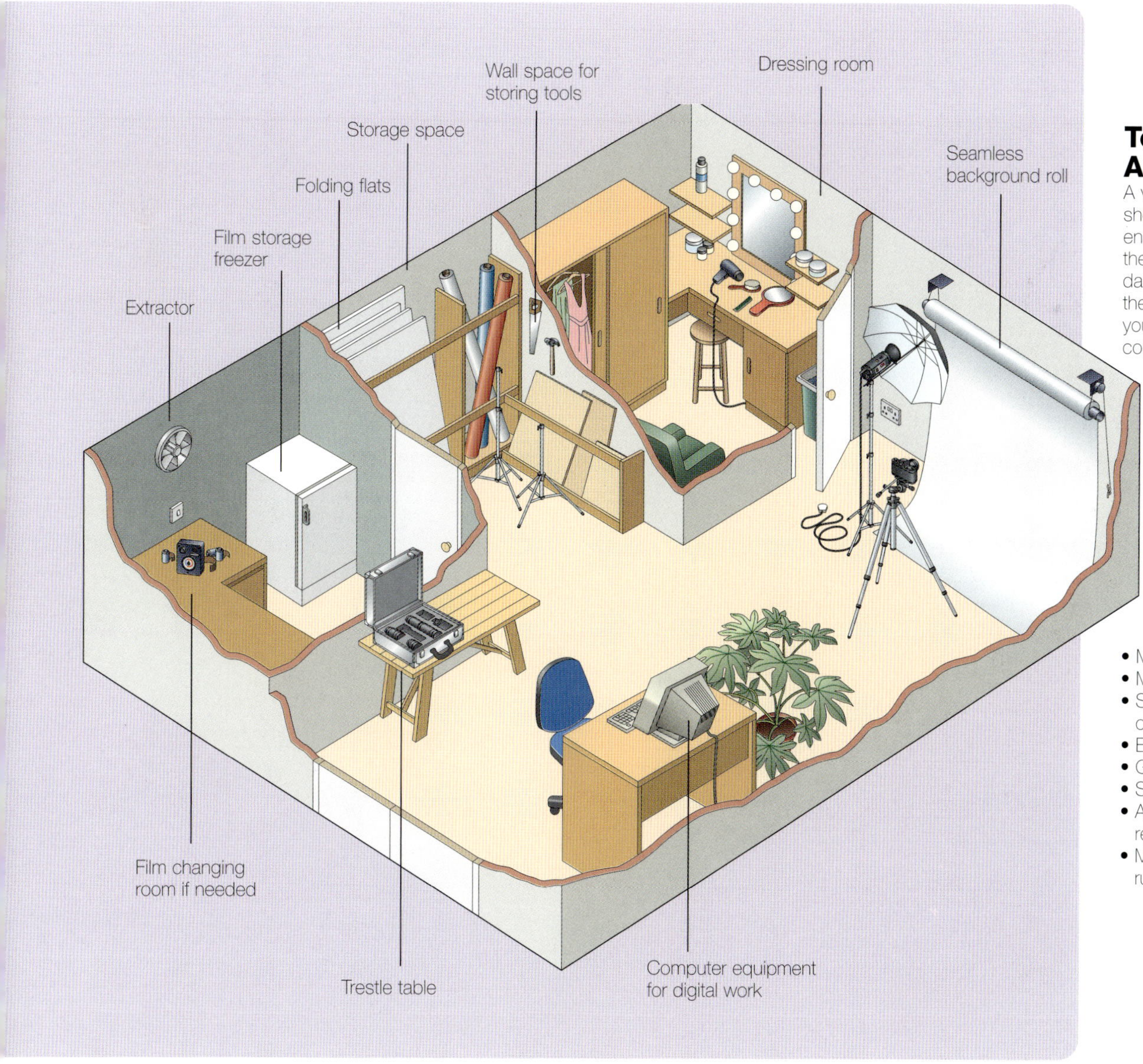

Tools and Accessories

A variety of items should be built up to enable you to build the set and repair damage. Choose them according to your needs. They could include:

- Modeling tools
- Miniature drill
- Scissors and cutting tools
- Eraser
- Glue
- Staple gun
- Antistatic gun for removing dust
- Metal and plastic rulers

background. The rolls, usually 9ft (3m) long and available in several colors, can be hung on a cross bar, supported between expanding poles.

When it comes to complex set construction, however, the requirements are obviously as complex or as simple as the idea you have in mind. In addition to the usual do-it-yourself equipment for the actual business of construction, you should also have a basic kit for emergency on-the-spot repairs during shooting. This should consist of some basic modeling tools, small drills, fixing agents, and an antistatic gun for removing dust from the set.

Studio Lighting

Artificial light is more consistent and generally easier to deal with than daylight, but only if you understand how to use it. One of the chief faults of beginners is to place lights randomly, correcting mistakes by using additional lamps, rather than by diffusing or changing the position of the main light source. The result is often harsh, uneven illumination, with the effect of a shallow, crowded space.

Always remember that it is the area of a light source that counts. A large source, such as strip lighting or a reflector, will produce soft light, characterized by indistinct shadows or low contrasts. A point source, such as a flood or quartz halogen lamp, will produce sharp-edged shadows, with high contrast. The closer a light source is positioned to a subject, the softer the shadows will be; the farther away it is, the more distinct the shadows will be. The overall lighting effect, however, becomes more uniform and diffused as the distance increases.

There are two main types of studio lighting available: tungsten and electronic flash. The latter is more expensive, but preferable to the former. Electronic flash is more reliable, has a longer life, is heat-free, and unsurpassed for stopping motion. Tungsten bulbs heat up a studio uncomfortably and normally require fairly slow shutter speeds.

Lighting Techniques

Lighting techniques depend as much on the personal taste of the photographer as on the technical requirements. Although any lighting arrangement can be used, provided the desired results are obtained, it is best to follow a few basic rules until you are completely familiar with studio lighting. Above all, remember that you should constantly refer back to the camera and be guided by what it sees. No matter how skilled the photographer, the human eye cannot match the camera lens for objectivity. Always assess your lighting through the viewfinder and, as a final check, take test shots with a Polaroid or a digital camera set to lo-res capture before embarking on the actual session.

One of the main techniques used by professionals is "bounced" light. This is the next best thing to natural light; if the technique is used skillfully, it is barely possible to tell the

RIGHT & OPPOSITE PAGE: This sequence of shots was taken within the same set environment, starting with a bed for the model to lie on. The main light illuminates the model but a secondary one bounces light up the back of the set. The idea was a nautical theme with moody lighting. The next two shots in the series swapped the bed for a chair, and then simply standing space. The standing shot moves the model light even farther around to the right-hand side to cast shadows across her back.

35–140mm zoom lens, digital ISO 80, 1/125 sec at f4

difference between the two in the end photograph. The trick is to direct the light against a flat wall at an angle; the light bounces back, producing a diffused result, without strong shadows. If you want to light one side of the model, aim a lamp directly at the wall nearest the point you want to light.

Light can be bounced off the ceiling as well as walls. The use of this effect means that you can achieve a soft, uniform illumination of your subject. Build up the light until it is sufficiently intense to make an exposure and then direct one main light at the model. Adjust the position and strength of the light source until you are satisfied with the overall effect.

By placing your subject between a pair of strong floods or strip lighting, you will produce flat, overall illumination that is rarely flattering to a model. To bring out shapes and textures, you must create shadows and highlights. Omit one of the floods and add a spotlight. Place a reflector behind the model to provide some backlighting and give a sharper definition to the outline. If you want to emphasize a specific area, add another spotlight.

If you want to soften the borderline between light and shadow, cover the light source with suitable diffusing material. For trimming down or controlling the beam of a flood or spot, attach barn doors to the light.

Studio Lighting Control

With a fully equipped studio, a great variety of lighting effects are possible. Moving the lights and using more or fewer light sources radically alters the appearances of the shot and its atmosphere.

One light is used here, placed just above eye level and slightly to the right of the camera. It gives an even finish to the lighting and is a standard position.
35–140mm zoom lens, digital ISO 80, 1/125 sec at f8

The key light is now positioned to the right, above the model, and aimed down at around 45 degrees. This puts plenty of light onto the hair. A fill-in light is positioned on the other side, below the eye level, pointing upward to fill in any shadows.
35–140mm zoom lens, digital ISO 80, 1/125 sec at f8

This is the same lighting setup as the last shot, but now a large reflector has been added to the side of the model. If she had dark hair, this would have put plenty of detail into it.
35–140mm zoom lens, digital ISO 80, 1/125 sec at f9

Moody and dramatic, both the key light and fill-in light have been moved around the sides of the model, illuminating the hair and the odd piece of face, but leaving the torso mainly in shadow.
35–140mm zoom lens, digital ISO 80, 1/125 sec at f4

One key light at 45 degrees to the right and above the model gives plenty of highlights, but also shadows for more atmospheric shots.
35–140mm zoom lens, digital ISO 80, 1/125 sec at f8

One key light is placed to the right, just below eye level, giving upward-slanting shadows. This creates a menacing effect that normally is not suitable for glamour, but could be employed for a special setup such as a gangster or spoof horror set.
35–140mm zoom lens, digital ISO 80, 1/125 sec at f8

Lighting Equipment

Lighting equipment is divided into several categories: the lights themselves, their supports, and various accessories, such as reflectors and diffusers. Although professionals almost always prefer electronic flash, tungsten floods are still used, mainly now by digital users on a tight budget because the lower light temperature can be more accurately controlled on a digital camera.

There are many reasons for the use of electronic flash by professionals, but one of the most important is that the color quality closely approaches that of daylight. The only significant disadvantage is that the exact effect of the light cannot always be judged before exposure. However, many designs now have built-in tungsten modeling lamps to give representative lighting. A simple unit will have a modeling lamp that works at full power; a more expensive unit will have variable power lighting that can be set to match the power of the main electronic flash to give a much more accurate preview.

The principles of studio flash equipment are similar to those of handheld units, but the handling characteristics are different. Studio flash is operated by main voltage, with sufficient output to meet the needs of small aperture work. It is possible to adjust the output, so that fractions of the total can be used—the more expensive the unit, the more control it offers.

There are two main types available: the power pack can be a separate unit, connected to several heads, or the pack and head can be combined. In the first case, a good unit should be able to handle up to four separate lights from its power pack. Although designed to enable each power head to be individually adjusted, the unit should also be able to deliver 300 watts to each head when operating at full power.

LEFT: This shot makes use of the all-around light in a studio apartment. The model is posed so that light patterns fall across her face and a reflector provides fill-in light.
50mm lens, digital ISO 100, 1/125 sec at f11

RIGHT: This bedroom shot had two lights—one beyond the model's head and a secondary light at 45 degrees to her legs. A reflector on the side of the camera ensured that there was plenty of light bounced back to fill in.
50mm lens, digital ISO 100, 1/180 sec at f16

The integrated unit is becoming increasingly popular. It is convenient and highly portable. Although the power output is limited, it is usually sufficient for most 35mm lenses, since these do not stop down as much as large-format lenses.

If you are planning to use studio flash frequently, an incident light meter is an essential and not particularly expensive investment. The meter is connected to the lights by either a wire or an infrared trigger. When the fire button on the meter is pressed, the lights are activated and the meter records the result. This result can then be entered into the camera in manual mode, and the camera connected to the lights.

Stands and Supports For most purposes, lights can be mounted on simple tripod stands. These are available in different heights and sizes. If space is at a premium, an expanding pole can be used. Expanding poles are held by tension against the floor and ceiling, but are awkward to move once they are set up. For extra mobility, use a boom stand.

Spotlights and Strip Lights If you need to highlight specific areas, small spotlights are essential. These can be handily attached to super-clamps that are specifically designed to be attached to doors, stepladders, chair backs, and so on.

Studio Lights

Modern lights are both powerful and versatile, and a variety of diffusing and reflecting devices will modify the quality of the light. Studio flash has none of the drawbacks of small portable flash units. In combination with diffusers and reflectors, the light from studio flash units can be broad and soft, and can be closely controlled. Such units now usually have modeling lights to show the effects they will have.

Stands
Tripods with extendable center columns are the standard lighting support. Expanding poles can be fixed between floor and ceiling for heavier lamps and extending, counterweighted boom arms will support lamps over the set.

Umbrellas
These are often used with flash heads to soften the effect. They can diffuse the light if white and translucent (with the light shone through the umbrella) or they can reflect it. For reflection, white, silver, or gold umbrellas are often used. Here, the light is pointed away from the subject and reflected back by the umbrella.

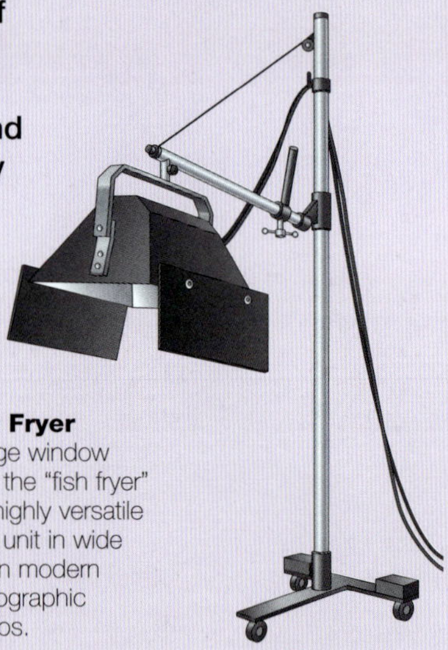

Fish Fryer
A large window light, the "fish fryer" is a highly versatile flash unit in wide use in modern photographic studios.

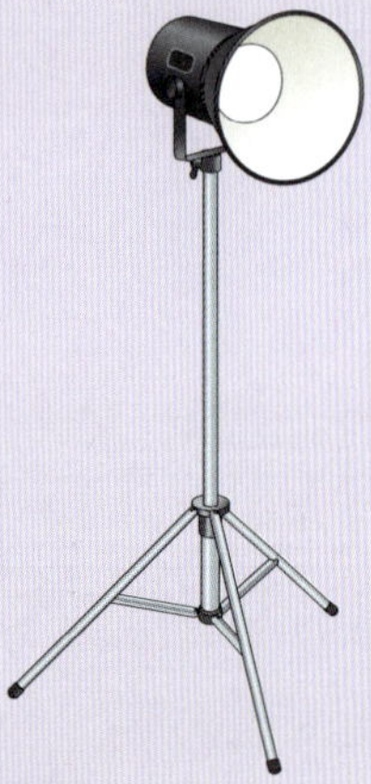

Diffuser Attachment
For a more gentle and broad-spread type of light, opal and gauze disks can be fitted to the front of the flash heads. Alternately, a shallow bowl reflector with a blocked center will have a similar result.

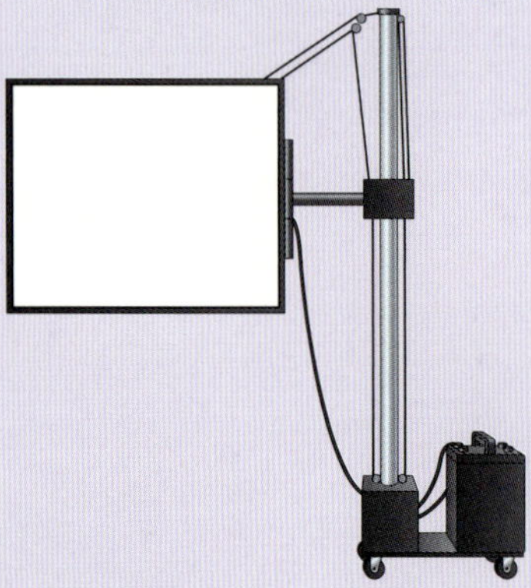

Swimming Pool
This large flash unit provides a broad spread of diffused light, giving flattering, shadowless results.

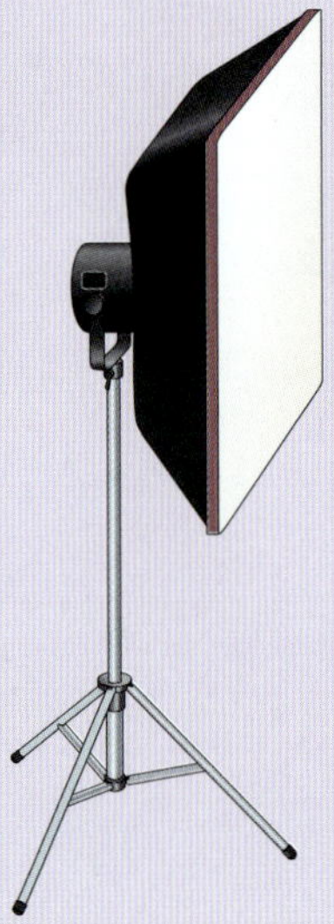

Softbox
The most popular and modern flash head attachment is the softbox, which provides an excellent level of diffusion for light. The larger the softbox, the more diffuse the light.

Power Packs
A 5000-joule (watt per second) power unit will be sufficient to power a number of flash heads through separate cables. Smaller units have lower capabilities.

The best way to light backgrounds evenly is with two purpose-built strip lights. These are trough-shaped and fitted inside with flash tubes. Though they are an expensive investment, they vastly improve the result if a large area has to be illuminated.

Reflectors and Diffusers Reflectors and diffusers are an essential part of any studio equipment list. Mirrors are extremely effective reflectors and can

RIGHT: A tungsten lamp to the left mixes with light from a large window to provide lots of illumination. A reflector just in front of the model bounces light up onto her body as she comes down the stairs in an old cottage.
45mm lens, digital ISO 100, 1/180 sec at f13

Reflector Attachments
This flash tube with an integrated modeling light can be fitted with general-purpose or wide dish reflectors to direct the light. A barn door can be fitted for precise control (as shown on tungsten lamp below right) or, as here, different shapes of snoot to concentrate the beam of light.

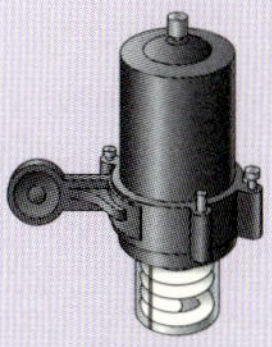

Flash Heads
Modern heads usually have two parts: the coiled filament and a modeling lamp.

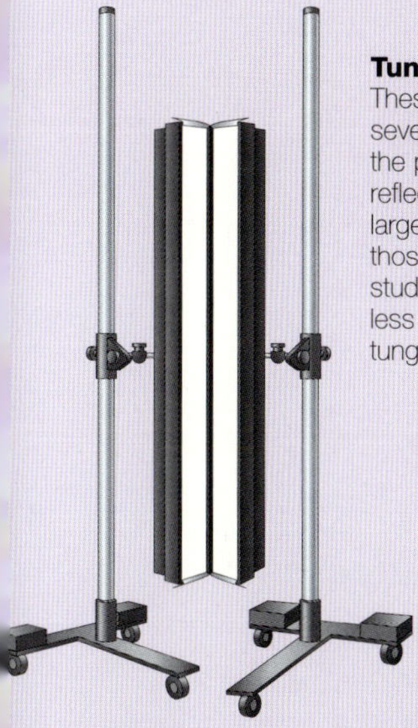

Tungsten Lamps
These are available in several forms, from the portable unit with reflecting head to larger models like those in movie studios. Bulbs for less sophisticated tungsten lamps vary.

Striplights
Two long lights are often used at either side of the set to light the background.

Integrated Window Lights
With their own power packs, these window lights on mobile stands can be used in numerous positions and freely moved around the studio.

RIGHT: Lights are positioned to the left and right of the model, while a reflector fills in the middle area.
70mm lens, digital ISO 100, 1/125 sec at f8

Mirrors and Screens

Interesting effects can be obtained with the inclusion of glass or other materials in the shot—either between the lens and the subject, or reflecting the subject. Screens in front of the camera distort the image. The effect is much greater when the screen is close to the subject (and therefore in focus) than when it is close to the camera. A gauze or muslin sheet in front of the lens, for example, may become almost invisible.

RIGHT: Gauze can be used to create a hazy, romantic atmosphere. It also reduces harsh lighting and cuts out obtrusive backgrounds.
85mm lens, digital ISO 800, 1/180 sec at f4

BELOW: A mosaic effect can be added to any photo after the event, if you do it digitally. This was done in Photoshop using a separate layer for the effect, which was then blended into the original.
50mm lens, digital ISO 80, 1/125 sec at f5.6

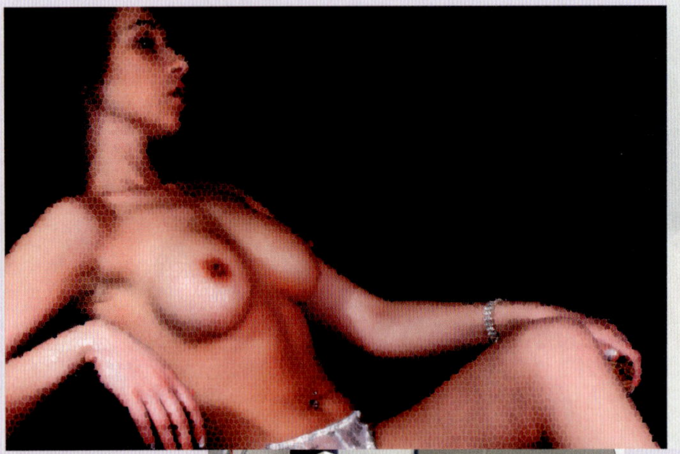

RIGHT: Mirrors can be included in glamour photographs very effectively. Focus on the model rather than the reflection, and be careful to position camera and lights so that neither photographer nor equipment appears in the shot by mistake.
70mm lens, digital ISO 100, 1/125 sec at f8

be especially useful for selectively filling in dense shadows. Cooking foil is also strongly reflective. It is easier to control if it is first crumpled and then pasted down onto a piece of cardboard. Freestanding folding flats are used as reflectors for lighting large areas.

Spotlights and floods can usually be controlled with reflector attachments, such as snoots, barn doors, or wide-angle or general-purpose reflectors. Their principal purpose is to direct the light to where it is wanted and to keep it away from areas, such as the camera lens or large reflective surfaces, where it is not required.

As the name implies, diffusers are used to diffuse light. Umbrellas and softboxes are invaluable for studio glamour photography. A white finish throws a soft light and shadows, a gold finish casts a warm glow, a silver finish increases light intensity but produces harder shadows, while a translucent umbrella diffuses a flash. Black umbrellas absorb extraneous light that might otherwise cause harsh contrasts of light and shadow.

ABOVE: The main flash was fired through a golden-colored umbrella, helping to give the model the golden hue. The white balance for the camera was set on manual to stop it from trying to turn the gold into white. A reflector on the other side of the model provided bounce-back side lighting.
70mm lens, digital ISO 100, 1/125 sec at f5.6

Color in the Studio

In studio photography, satisfactory color organization is rarely accidental. If you do not pay attention to color combinations when composing your photographs, any errors will probably scream out from the transparency or color print. At the very least, you will feel dissatisfied, even if you are unable to identify the precise reason for the failure of the picture.

Teach yourself to be aware of colors, shades, and tones in everything around you. Examine the color changes that take place in artificial and natural light and experiment by placing the same object against backgrounds of different colors. Analyze the results and identify what does and does not work and why.

Naturally, your decisions will be subjective, but remember the guiding rule in glamour photography—everything around your model must complement her. Avoid clashing and discordant colors and tones that compete for attention with the subject of the picture. Anything that detracts from this should be eliminated from the set.

ABOVE: It is not necessary to create elaborate sets in the studio—a plain seamless backdrop will sometimes produce the best results. Choose props to complement the background color or contrast with it; concentrate on simple schemes rather than elaborate combinations. Notice in these shots how dark- and fair-haired models look different against different toned backgrounds. One of the most popular combinations is a white background with black underwear. However, take note that this has been done to death and, unless your model is stop-the-traffic gorgeous, one of the other variations will be better.

RIGHT: A good location can be turned into a studio for a session with portable studio lights. Here, flash heads with blue gels were fired at a model wearing shiny black fetish gear, against a backdrop of industrial metal and a warehouse environment. The camera needed to be set on manual white balance to record the blue color faithfully.

28–70mm zoom lens, digital ISO 100, 1/125 sec at f11

You should first take into account the hair and skin color of your model. Very pale skin often absorbs colors; while this may occasionally create an effect you desire, it tends to be unflattering in general. This is especially true if you are using solid blocks of strong colors. The darker the model's coloring, the more you can afford to use brilliant colors and bright contrasts.

Soft blues and pinks create an intimate, cozy atmosphere; bold reds and yellows are aggressive colors that demand action. Your model will naturally respond to the environment you create for her, so do not expect her to look or feel demure and sensitive if she is surrounded by vibrant colors that call for a more positive response.

Once you have found the right color combination for your photography, use lights of the precise color temperature to match your film. Unless you are able to reproduce on film what you see through the lens, all your careful preparations will have been wasted. Try to avoid using filters whenever possible.

Choose a film that gives maximum color saturation. If you select a brand that can be developed individually, you can sometimes ask for the film to be pushed a couple of stops in the development. This will increase the color saturation of photographs that have been evenly lit; however, it will give excessively hard results if you have used high-contrast lighting.

RIGHT: Who needs to go to the beach when you can add sunglasses, a blue backdrop, and a surfboard in the studio?
50mm lens, Ektachrome 64, 1/125 sec at f8

LEFT: A mock fitness club setup can easily be created by adding a weights machine against a neutral wooden background and covering the model with spray to suggest sweat.
28mm lens, digital ISO 100, 1/125 sec at f8

Good professional glamour photographers are in great demand, but they have to combine photographic skill with the ability to work well with

Professional Glamour

models. Photographs can be undertaken to commission, for magazines or advertising purposes, or done on spec.

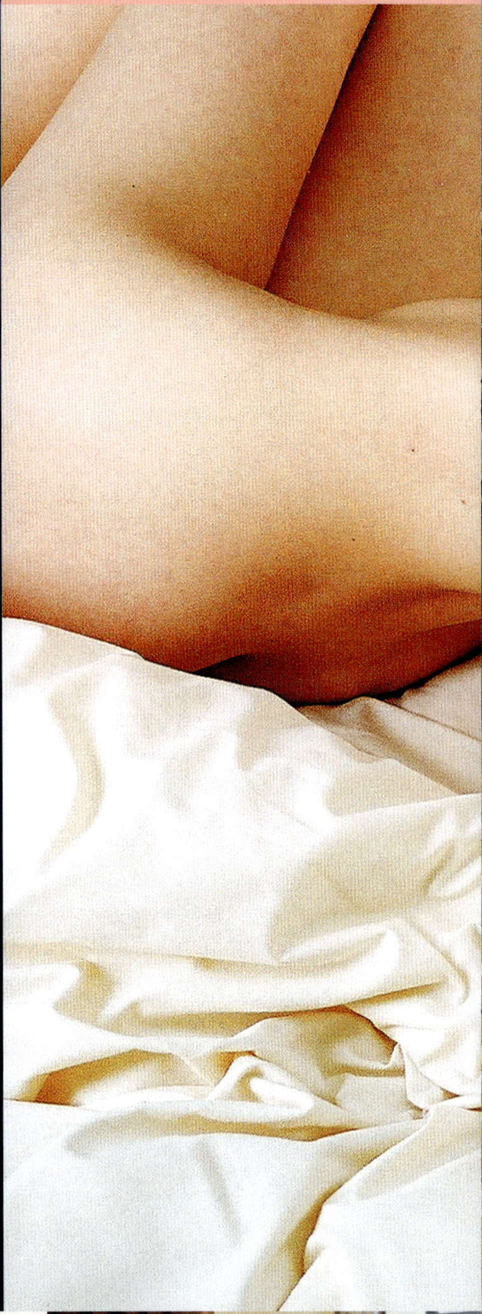

THE CLASSIC PHOTOGRAPHERS

(Above) An interior personal project shot, featuring a dress by Pigalle. As the dress is glossy rubber, flash heads were used both to light the model and to create the shiny reflections on the dress.
90mm lens, Fuji NPS 160, 1/30th sec, f11

(Right) This was shot as part of a series for Glamour Girl catalogue. The lighting was fairly sophisticated with a twin flash head and softbox combination providing flattering and even lighting, as well as a flash head with an umbrella offering fill-in flash.
180mm lens, Fuji Provia 100, 1/125th sec, f11

Newton, Bill Brandt, André Kertez, Madam Yvonde, Julia Margeret Cameron, Norman Parkinson, and Man Ray. I enjoy looking at lots of types of photography, and used to go to galleries a lot, although I don't get much of a chance to go now. Bath has lost two of its main galleries, the RPS and F.Stop, which is a great shame."

Though increasingly busy, she still has time for her own photographic interests. She remarks, "I'm always working on my own projects. A lot of the work on my website is personal projects. I see it as a way to improve myself, meet new models, have fun, and work without having the pressure and deadlines."

Does this mean she continues to use herself as a model in her photos, as she did in her early days? "I still do that and I enjoy it. In fact, most requests that I get from people who want to buy my photographs are for the self-portraits. I've never really thought of myself as a model so I find it quite flattering really." Being a woman in a predominantly male world has other advantages too. "Being a woman, and photographing women, is great, as we already have an understanding—I know how to make them look good and they can feel comfortable with me. There are no hidden agendas. Some of my models have the odd incident where the male photographer can make them feel really uncomfortable, which isn't a great situation to be in, and gives those, who do what I do, a bad name."

Currently Emma is negotiating with a book publisher to have a collection of her work published and aims to travel more and photograph people while on the road. She has recently been to Los Angeles and spent her time snapping new faces. In amongst the commercial assignments Emma is also working on a series of catsuit images—"Katwoman" being one of her early and most successful photos. She explains, "I'm using a mixture of models with their own outfits, plus some catsuits from various latex designers." So whether it's for her own designs or for commercial application, you can be sure of seeing plenty more of Emma Delves-Broughton and her sassy and stunning photography in the future.

28

(Above) This is a composite photograph, which began with the figure shot of the model being rim lit from behind by three flash heads—one each side and one at the top against a black background. The background effect was created by firing the focusing spot down onto silver mirror foil and then photographing the resultant reflection that formed on the wall. The reflection was then rotated by 90 degrees and a copy made and pasted in reverse next to the original. The burst of purple light on the background was created using Micrografx Picture Publisher.
Figure shot: 28–80mm lens, Fuji S1 digital, 1/125th sec, f16
Background: 28–80mm lens, Fuji S1 digital, 1/90th sec, f5.6

His studio is called Kaz Studio and the web address is www.kaz-studio.co.uk.

Clive shoots a lot of ideas with Sarah, his assistant, who is also a superb figure model. She keeps toned by aerobic kick boxing and was a competitive Latin dancer from the age of six. Sarah and Clive work well together; as soon as one of them has a new idea for a shot, they immediately begin planning and organizing, and even after working together for three years, they still maintain that professional distance when working on figure shots. Clive professes that many amateur photographers have the wrong approach with naked models—in his studio a model is only naked for a few seconds to do the actual shot—at all other times she is covered. That way Sarah, or whoever is modeling, feels completely comfortable and at ease. Shooting digitally means that they can see the image straight away, making any modifications if required. Many such ideas then go on to the website and become the subject of a tutorial session.

Future ideas include figure shots in a cathedral, although Clive has his concerns that this may be construed as blasphemous. In addition, he thinks Yosemite Park and Monument Valley would be an exciting project and he is also trying to work out how to achieve outdoor figure shots in the concrete canyons of London. As far as digital photography is concerned, Clive is a convert. "Digital is the way forward—ease-of-use and no chemical impact on the environment has to be a good thing. However, it does mean that nowadays we need to always be aware that every image has been retouched and therefore is not in its true form. This can have a huge effect when misused." But ultimately it is creativity that counts, so, as long as he can keep coming up with ideas he will be shooting models for a long time yet.

Glamour on Location

An overseas assignment makes a welcome break from routine for any photographer, but particularly for a glamour specialist. Here, John Kelly details the events of one of his overseas trips and explains why he feels that they are an essential part of his work.

"On a well-organized overseas trip, I can often shoot more good work in three weeks than I could operating in my studio for three months. There are many reasons for this, the chief one being that a new environment can do wonders for both the photographer's and the models' morale. There is an urgency that creates an exciting momentum and this is invariably reflected in the photographs that result.

"Things can go dreadfully wrong, of course. I once arranged a two-week shoot in the Mediterranean to be faced only with nonstop rain, homesick models, and my own bad light. The next important consideration is variety in the surroundings that, ideally, should include a coastal resort, distinctive landscapes, and some interesting architecture. Good hotel facilities are important, too, so that, in the event of bad weather, interior shots are also possible.

"A couple of years ago I decided to make a working trip to Haiti in the Caribbean. I had been there once before on a calendar assignment and, although I hadn't explored the island much, I felt instinctively that it had enormous photographic potential. Any reservations I might have had were overcome by my agent, who had been back to the island several times. He returned with hundreds of location shots that illustrated its potential, plus a well-stocked address book that guaranteed us help and cooperation from the residents.

"The importance of this last point cannot be overemphasized. Working in another country may be exciting, but it can also throw up all sorts of problems for the glamour photographer. Local customs, for instance, may be against photographing seminude models. The reaction can be anything from complete outrage, to the entire community wanting to get in on the action and be photographed as well. It is essential to know what to expect."

Preparing for the Trip

"Like all my trips, this one emerged as a matter of necessity. I had a couple of pressing magazine and calendar assignments. I also wanted to boost my library stocks.

"My first step was to discuss in detail with the magazine editors what their requirements were. These presented no problems. The calendar assignment, on the other hand, was to feature trucks and trucking. I quickly decided to stop over in Miami for a couple of days to take advantage of Florida locations for this.

"From this, you can see the importance of systematic preplanning, particularly where commissioned work is concerned. As far as my library shots were concerned, I simply informed the library to expect a consignment of pictures over the next few weeks. To shoot speculative work successfully, it is vital to have the courage of your own convictions and take the photographs you think are good. If this is supported by a feel for the marketplace, you are likely to accomplish a great deal on a two- to three-week trip.

"The most important initial decision was to decide how many and which models I should work with. I usually prefer models who have traveled before and are happy working on location. They are generally more self-sufficient and able to cope with the strains and stresses that arise on a two- or three-week job. I also like to have worked with them on a couple of occasions before hiring them for an overseas assignment. On this occasion, however, I broke both of these rules. The final party consisted of six models, two of them twins and only two with overseas experience.

LEFT, ABOVE & RIGHT: The Haiti assignment produced numerous superb locations, from deserted beaches to fine modern hotels surrounded by tropical vegetation and old buildings steeped in character. Research the possibilities before you set off—plan to be at the best places in the best light and weather conditions.

"It was crucial before leaving that the models all knew exactly what would be expected of them in work terms and fees. They had to provide a model release and their own up-to-date passports and visas. I also asked them to bring along a basic summer-vacation wardrobe and to prepare their skins for a suntan. The makeup artist and hairdresser were given the same detailed briefing. Insurance, covering personal and public liability as well as equipment, also had to be arranged, plus accommodation, air tickets, car hire, and so on. The basic team at any one time was to consist of myself, my agent, makeup artist, hairdresser, and at least two of the six models.

"A first-aid kit is essential, particularly for the tropics. Ours consisted of salt tablets, suntan lotion and sunburn cream, plasters, bandages and surgical tape, germicidal cream, and headache and indigestion tablets. For myself, I took comfortable clothing both for location hunting and for photographic shoots. The right shoes and sufficient protection from the sun are particularly important. Hot days generally mean cool nights, so extra sweaters are necessary."

RIGHT: A calendar commission for truckers was dealt with in a stopover in Miami. A good range of props had to be taken to ensure that effective color combinations with the trucks would be possible.

35–80mm zoom lens, Kodachrome 25, 1/60 sec at f5.6

Props, Clothes, and Accessories

"Unless I've been commissioned to take a photograph to an exact specification, I rarely predesign a shot unless I am sure of the location. Thus, I tend to take very few props with me overseas, unless they are absolutely necessary. For Haiti, although I had collected a couple of outfits I particularly wanted to feature in some of my shots, I decided to honor my tradition of relying on luck and innovation to provide on-the-spot props. The models had already been asked to bring a basic summer wardrobe; I supplied some extras, such as sunglasses, summer hats, scarves, shawls, designer shoes, and some jewelry."

Into the Sun

"It took roughly three weeks from the day I decided to go to Haiti to boarding the airplane. Normally, I would take longer to prepare for a trip like this, but my agent was fulsome in his guarantees that Haiti was the only place on earth where I could be sure of getting good weather, plus beautiful surroundings, in March. I never pass up a certainty.

"After two days of successful shooting in Miami, we boarded the airplane for Haiti. For the next four days we admired the island through a haze of torrential rain from our hotel windows. Nevertheless, I was anxious to capitalize on the momentum that had built up in Florida and lost no time in getting behind the camera. The hotel proprietor was extremely helpful and gave us a free rein to photograph wherever we wanted. There were no problems with the power supply—we only used tungsten lighting—and the models were keen to work hard. It transpired that those few days of rain were, in fact, a blessing in disguise. One of the twins later suffered from severe sunburn and was unable to work. Had this happened at the start, we would not have had any pictures of the two twins together. This would have been a great loss.

"The two-and-a-half weeks of sunshine that followed ensured the success of the trip. The agent contacted some old acquaintances and, with their help, was able to come up with some extraordinary beauty spots. In all, we must have covered about 30 interior and exterior locations and they all looked entirely different. As well as the luscious tropical island shots, some of the pictures could have been taken in East Africa and others in the American desert. Several locations that would have made stunning backdrops had to be abandoned for a variety of reasons—inaccessibility, no power supply—but I have filed them away for next time.

"Once I had decided on the location, the right model had to be selected for the photographs. One of the advantages of long trips is that a photographer can get to know the models very well and is therefore able to judge almost instinctively how they will photograph to the best advantage. In Haiti, for instance, I found that one girl worked extremely well indoors, but was uncomfortable in many outdoor locations. The surviving twin was extremely extrovert and excelled herself in outdoor shots.

"It is crucial that the photographer/model relationship is good at all times during a long overseas assignment, though, people being what they are, this is not always possible. I usually try to keep abreast of what is going on without actually getting involved. This way, I can be sensitive to the model's feelings without having to comment on them. This approach seems to suit everyone, since most models are anxious to project a positive, professional image, especially to their photographer.

"But problems do arise—never more quickly than when people are forced to live and work closely together without a break. I tend to fire on all cylinders when I am abroad and I expect the models to do likewise. Since there is only one of me and six of them, it's improbable that I will push any of them to their limits, but the strain of being in another country, often for the first time, is sometimes overwhelming for many of the younger, less experienced models. Modeling is also an extremely competitive profession and it occasionally happens that the models do not mix well among themselves.

"In Haiti, we had a few crises of confidence and one nasty accident, in addition to the sunburn. By and large, our problems were well distributed over the three weeks and I was able to work satisfactorily on every single day we were on the island, come rain or shine."

The Models

Janet, at 24 years old, was an experienced model. It was known that she could be relied on, both for professionalism in front of the camera and as a mature influence on the others models.

Toni was only 18, but a really attractive model coming to be in great demand. It was her first trip abroad, but it was clear that she would handle it well.

The twins, Suzie and Sally, had just had their 22nd birthday. It was really fortunate that these busy models were available for the trip.

Lynn was only 16 when she came for an interview a few weeks before the trip. A real professionalism was soon revealed, however, and her sense of humor was invaluable.

Carole-Ann was also a newcomer to modeling at 17 years old, but she was a quick learner and worked hard, despite initial nerves.

LEFT: Late afternoon and early evening offer some of the best lighting for glamour photography, with a calm and mellow atmosphere that can give great mood to the shot. The exposure for this example was set for the landscape rather than the model, with the fading light shimmering off the ripples in the bay. The reflections from water were used to achieve a partial silhouette effect.

300mm lens, Kodachrome 64, 1/60 sec at f5.6

Assignment Technique

"The main reason I make overseas trips is to follow the sun. For me—and I am sure many other photographers—nothing can beat working with good natural sunlight. The sun is unpredictable, of course, but, in the course of a day, its movements can transform the mood and atmosphere of a scene several times over. To keep pace with and take advantage of these changes is one of the greatest challenges for any photographer.

"Learning to work quickly is one of the fundamental requirements of good photography. You must be acutely aware of everything you see and able to make instant decisions. Move an inch, wait five seconds, and you have a completely different picture. On location, therefore, I try to be constantly alert and never like to be far away from camera or model. Photography is about capturing moments in time and when time is limited, as on assignment, everything takes on greater significance.

"Trimming my needs—as far as equipment is concerned—is an important part of being able to work spontaneously. My equipment checklist for Haiti shows that, by comparison to what I could have taken, my requirements were modest—no handheld meters, for instance, and only two filters. Nor did I bother with a wide range of film stock or lighting equipment. I simply took what I believed would see me through a three-week trip. Of course, it would be inadequate for other branches of photography, but, for my purposes as a glamour photographer, I had all I needed.

"If the light and model look good, it only takes a moment to pick up a camera (already loaded), compose a picture (each camera is fitted with a zoom lens, the three combining to give a 28–300mm range), select the aperture and shutter speed (reliable TTL on all cameras), and shoot. Of course, I could take half an hour to set up the same shot, but this is no guarantee that the results would be better. What often happens is that the model, the main focus of the picture, becomes bored and self-conscious.

"This is not to say that I constantly take gambles and shoot at breakneck speed. On the contrary, I merely cover myself as far as possible against creating an inhibiting atmosphere of high technology for the model.

"I like simple solutions to the problems of indoor photography, too. During our first four days, the rain forced me to take all my pictures indoors. I spent a lot of time searching for pools of light around the hotel that could be either warmed up or amplified by tungsten lamps and gold reflectors. By mixing my own light sources with the natural light available, I could create what appeared to be brilliant sunbursts coming in through the windows, even in overcast conditions. I boosted the low light with reflectors and spotlights, mounted the camera on a tripod, and used a cable release for any shots under 1/30 second.

"The whole point of being on location is lost if you feel the need to duplicate studio conditions. If you do not feel confident enough to take the risks inherent in such a shoot, you are probably better off spending your money in the studio and not on an airplane fare."

Equipment Checklist

"The golden rule of photography is to be prepared for any eventuality. Nevertheless, I try to keep my equipment down to a practical minimum on overseas assignments. For Haiti, I took the following equipment."

Camera Bodies Three Nikon bodies.
Lenses 28–45mm zoom, 85mm, 70–210mm zoom, 50–300mm zoom.
Camera and Lens Accessories Lens hoods, lens cap (front and back), camera body caps, star filter, polarizing filter, filter holders, cable release, spare batteries.
Camera Supports Two tripods suitable for indoor and outdoor work.
Lighting Four tungsten lamps with stands, six 120-watt bulbs, gold fabric for four 5x5in (12.5 x 12.5cm) reflectors, hand mirror, handheld flash gun, batteries.
Film 125 rolls of Kodachrome 25, 125 of Kodachrome 64.
Cases Metal case for equipment transport and for use in exposed outdoor areas, shoulder bag for indoor shoots, refrigerated film containers.

LEFT: It is a mistake to think that the strong midday sun is essential for successful glamour photography. Evening light is soft yet directional, and is flattering to model and color film alike. The warm glow of the low sun gives a natural appearance to skin, with good highlights showing off the rounded shapes of the body, but without deep shadows that can cause ugly distractions. However, you have to work fast because the light changes quickly.
85mm lens, Kodachrome 25, 1/30 sec at f5.6

ABOVE: A polarizing filter had to be used for this shot in a boat to cancel out the glare from the surface of the sea that was interfering with the light reading. The boat was pulled up next to the jetty to allow the photographer a firm base from which to work. The towel was chosen to match the color of the boat.
85mm lens, Kodachrome 25, 1/30sec at f5.6

RIGHT: On an overcast day, a large gold reflector was used close to the model to add to the level of illumination.
85mm lens, Kodachrome 64, 1/30 sec at f5.6

LEFT: Sometimes effective shots are possible even when the light is almost gone. By placing the model high up to catch the last rays of sun, and against a dark canopy of leaves, a dramatic shot with a steamy, jungle atmosphere was achieved.
85–210mm zoom lens, Kodachrome 25, 1/30 sec at f5.6

RIGHT: The sun provided plenty of light for this beach bar shot, although a reflector facing upward on the floor softened the shadows. Note how the black swimsuit is flattering to the fuller figure.
85–210mm zoom lens, Kodachrome 64, 1/15 sec at f5.6

RIGHT: There was only limited light available for this shot against a brick wall, with little being reflected from the dark surroundings. A white sheet was placed on the ground to reflect light back into the shadows.
55mm lens, Kodachrome 25, 1/15 sec at f4

ABOVE: The dark surroundings and poor daylight necessitated the use of artificial light for this shot. A spotlight was placed to the right of the model and bounced across from a gold reflector for directional lighting, with a main spotlight placed at the front to light her face, arm, and breast. A second gold reflector to the left softened the shadows even more.

85mm lens, Kodachrome 64, 1/60 sec at f5.6

LEFT: Taken on the same spot on the balcony as the shot on the far left, a wide-angle zoom was set here at a longer focal length to close in on the model and exclude much of the background. The background should play a major part in the shot or be kept to a minimum to avoid unwanted distraction.

35–80mm zoom lens, Kodachrome 25, 1/60 sec at f5.6

RIGHT: A particularly beautiful model will be a sufficient subject for even the most straightforward shots, such as this impromptu portrait. With the model relaxed and ignoring the camera, this has some of the informal qualities of candid photography. Be prepared to take advantage of simple moments like these.

85mm lens, Kodachrome 25, 1/60 sec at f4

LEFT: The large mirror was ideal for photography. It was just a question of waiting for the time of day when the most sun poured through the windows—in this case, at midday. All the room lights were switched on, with the bulbs around the mirror adding to the illumination and an extra glow coming from a concealed light. These tungsten lights add an orange glow on daylight-balanced film.

35–80mm zoom lens, Kodachrome 64, 1/15 sec at f8

ABOVE: Early morning on the balcony allowed a shot that took full advantage of the fantastic Haiti location, with rich tropical vegetation covering the mountains surrounding the hotel. The limited space made the shot difficult and a wide-angle lens had to be used. It had the advantage, however, of great depth of field, so that the plant in the foreground, the model, and the palm trees in the distance are all in sharp focus.

28mm lens, Kodachrome 25, 1/30 sec at f5.6

ABOVE: This shot was the first of the day, showing how quickly and well a good model can become used to the camera. Early morning daylight, reflecting from the white walls and filling in the shadows, was sufficient for an entirely natural view as the model dried her hair in the sun on the balcony.

85–210mm zoom lens, Kodachrome 25, 1/30 sec at f5.6

RIGHT: The assignment produced some additional work when a Haitian brewery asked for some shots of the models with their products for use in a calendar. When on location, it is always a good idea to contact local businesses that may want some pictures.
85–210mm zoom lens, Kodachrome 25, 1/60 sec at f5.6

LEFT: A classic glamour pose in an exotic location made an effective photograph. Reflectors placed quite close to the model softened the shadows and lit the face.
80–210mm zoom lens, Kodachrome 25, 1/60 sec at f5.6

ABOVE: A beautiful Haitian summerhouse of graceful metal filigree provided an excellent location. The shot was taken from about 10ft (3m) below in a courtyard, with the sun fading rapidly in the evening.
35–80mm zoom lens, Kodachrome 64, 1/30 sec at f5.6

Redirecting Sunlight

The sun behind the model provided the main light for this leopardskin swimsuit shot.

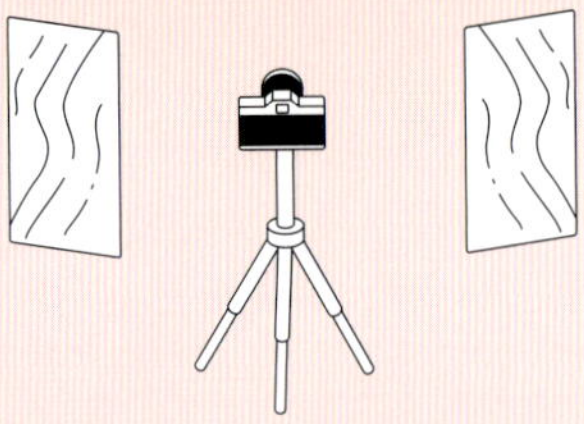

RIGHT: Two reflectors were placed on either side of the camera to provide adequate illumination for the front of the model.
80–210mm zoom lens, Kodachrome 25, 1/30 sec at f5.6

LEFT: The late afternoon sun shining through a yellow blind created this special color effect, with no additional lighting. The red top was ideally suited to the warm color scheme.
85mm lens, Kodachrome 64, 1/30 sec at f5.6

RIGHT: This shot of a model in a pensive mood was taken on an overcast day. The poor light made the use of a spotlight necessary, placed to the left of the camera and aimed approximately at her right hand.
85mm lens, Kodachrome 64, 1/30 sec at f4

BELOW: On a warm day, a sunny mood prevailed. In fact, the sun was hidden behind clouds, which allowed this shot to be taken at midday without hard shadows appearing in the shot.
85–210mm zoom lens, Kodachrome 64, 1/30 sec at f5.6

RIGHT: The wide-angle zoom lens set at its shortest focal length of 35mm was needed to include the extensive view of the beautiful bay. Notice how the high viewpoint raises the horizon in the frame, allowing the blue sea to provide an uncluttered background and keeping the moored yacht from interfering with the main area of interest in the foreground. Hazy sun is sufficient to create an image of blissful warmth without harsh shadows.
35–80mm zoom lens, Kodachrome 25, 1/15 sec at f5.6

RIGHT: The Haiti location offered a few settings with an almost Mexican feel, such as this superb window. The costumes were chosen to enhance this mood. The conditions were particularly difficult, with a weak and unpredictable sun. Two spotlights inside the room were responsible for the attractive halo on the models' hair.
85mm lens, Kodachrome 64, 1/30 sec at f5.6

ABOVE: The hotel corridor provided a fine location, with the clean lines of the arches and an attractive tiled floor. For this shot, sunlight from the alcove on the left was bounced back with a gold reflector placed to the right. The twins' makeup, hairstyles, and props (the shoes and the flowers) were matched to increase the illusion of double vision.

85mm lens, Kodachrome 25, 1/15 sec at f5.6

Long Shots

For a long shot of the twins in a hotel corridor, photographic lights were needed.

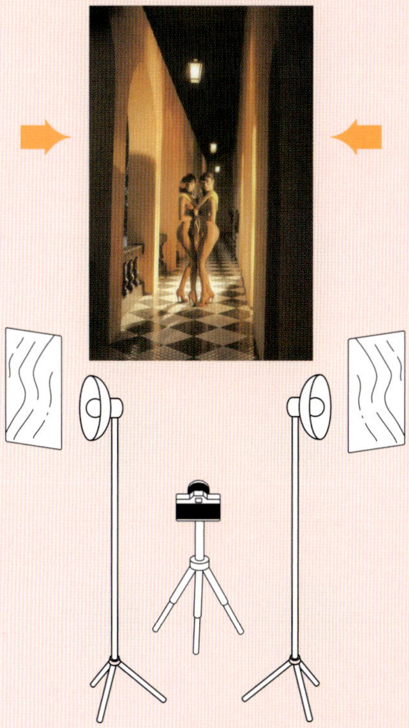

RIGHT: Two spotlamps were placed in the doorways and pointed away from the models to be bounced back by reflectors. Here, the pose was chosen for a mirror-image effect.

35–80mm zoom lens, Kodachrome 64, 1/30 sec at f5.6

LEFT: Using daylight film with tungsten spotlights alone gives a rich orange color cast. With other types of photography, the results would be unacceptable, but for glamour work, the effect is flattering to the body. One light was placed to the side, and another behind the model.

85mm lens, Kodachrome 64, 1/15 sec at f4

On Location Digitally

While shooting digitally does not affect your choice of location, the location itself can determine what equipment you take. Digital is all about power. If it runs out, you are in trouble. The first consideration, therefore, is the voltage of the local electricity supply. If it is different from what you normally use, you will need to take a voltage converter. Take more than one in case of emergencies. Some digital cameras use proprietary power packs, but most SLRs use batteries. Rechargeable batteries are essential, whether they are Ni-Cad (Nickel Cadmium) or the more common Ni-Mh (Nickel Metal Hydride), because digital cameras guzzle power. While you should certainly take numerous sets of batteries with you, and ensure they are charged before you go, of equal importance are battery chargers so that you can recharge your batteries at the hotel. The number of batteries/chargers you need will depend on how many photographs you will be taking each day, but the advantage of having extra is that the spares can be recharging while you are out shooting.

The next essential digital accessory is the memory card. Rather than having lots of small-capacity cards, take fewer, higher capacity cards because it makes them easier to manage.

RIGHT: The texture of an old sawn-off tree trunk and a background of lush greenery provide an attractive natural setting for this glamour shot. A reflector was used to bounce light into the body of the model.
70–210mm zoom lens, digital ISO 100, 1/1000 sec at f2.8

ABOVE: Potted plants on the windowsill combine with views of greenery through the window to give a natural backdrop to this photograph, even though it is actually inside.
35–70mm zoom lens, digital ISO 100, 1/125 sec at f11

How much memory do you need? Per day, you need a bare minimum of 1Gb storage. Using a 6Mp SLR camera and shooting in TIFF format, you will get fewer than 60 photos on a 1GB card. Shooting in maximum-quality JPEG format will give nearer 250 photographs, but you would not want to compromise quality by reducing resolution or increasing compression. So, take plenty of 1 or 2Gb memory cards. CompactFlash and MicroDrives are resilient, so these cards are excellent storage choices for overseas.

Even with this amount of storage, you are still likely to fill all your memory cards, and the last thing you want to have to do is start reducing the quality of images so that you can squeeze a few more on the card, or have to delete ones to make room. Instead, take a laptop computer with a portable CD or DVD writer and transfer the pictures from your storage cards to CD or DVD every night. An alternative is to take a portable storage device that combines hard drive space with a memory card interface.

That will cover your basic digital shooting needs, but you will still need all the other paraphernalia, such as filters, reflectors, flashguns, and so on. If you are taking a laptop, it is also worth investing in AutoRoute Express if it covers the country you are shooting in; this software package provides the best route to your destination. In addition, a portable printer will allow you to generate proofs on location, while a larger, main-powered printer allows prints up to letter (A4) size to be generated at the hotel. This is not essential, but can be useful if you are trying to sell pictures to local businesses while you are there.

RIGHT: A hint of sunshine, some greenery, a wooden bench, and the texture of an old hut—as long as the model is pretty and you light her properly, the most innocuous of locations can be employed for photography.

28–70mm zoom lens, digital ISO 100, 1/125 sec at f5.6

LEFT: Posing the model in front of a wooden summer house in a garden creates interesting contrasts between the rough texture of the wood and the model's smooth skin.

50mm lens, digital ISO 100, 1/250 sec at f5.6

Digital Basics

- Main digital SLR body
- Backup bodies if you can afford them, hi-res compacts if you can't
- Range of lenses
- 16 batteries
- 1Gb memory card, though five 1Gb cards would be better
- Local voltage converters
- Battery chargers
- Laptop computer
- PCMCIA card for the laptop
- Portable CD or DVD writer

Presenting a Portfolio

So far, this book has explored the practical business of taking glamour photographs. Whoever you take pictures of—your wife or girlfriend, an amateur, or professional model—the same photographic rules apply. The only variable is the standard of photography that is produced in the end, a definition that applies equally to amateur and professional work.

By definition, professional standards are higher than those set by amateurs. Nevertheless, many amateurs produce stunning work and nowhere is this more apparent than in the glamour field. It will likely become obvious if you have an instinct for this kind of photography. How you respond to your subject and vice versa is of prime importance, but the acid test is naturally the quality of the end product. If this is high, you may well consider turning professional.

Before taking such a step, however, you should consider that the world of professional glamour photography does not stop at good photography—it starts there. Much of it has very little to do with photography as such. One important thing to remember is that you will have to work with and depend on a lot of other people. These include clients, art directors, set designers, models, makeup artists, stylists, laboratory technicians, and agents. The list is endless.

Another necessary requirement is either to develop a thick skin or to find an agent who has one already. Competing with other photographers you think are better than yourself can be tough, but losing work to those who are not is even tougher. You will have to select the right model for the job and will meet some beautiful women, but you will also have the tricky task of explaining to some that they fall short of the necessary standards of physical beauty for the glamour world.

There is often traveling to be done. One day, you may find yourself working in one of the world's most expensive vacation resorts; the next day, you may have to transform your own backyard into an equatorial jungle with half a dozen rubber plants.

In short, professional glamour photography has its peaks and troughs, but, if you are able to stay the course, it is a very enjoyable way of earning a living. It can also be lucrative.

This section of the book discusses the logistics of turning professional and introduces you to some of the people professionals work with in the glamour field. It is intended to give you an insight into how and how not to approach the business of making glamour photography a full-time career—but in the end, success will depend on your own talent.

Presentation and Portfolio

Every glamour photographer is something of a salesperson. If you want to sell yourself and your work, you must project a professional image. You must have a working address and get business cards and letterheads printed. Ensure you have an email address, possibly a website, and a cellphone. If your telephone is unattended during the working day, install an answering machine so that messages can be left for you. The missed contact rarely comes back. Any meeting you attend should be planned carefully; above all, make sure you have some tangible ideas to present.

First and foremost, however, you must create an impressive portfolio. A first-rate portfolio is the foundation of any professional career. It must contain the best possible selection of your work to date, though, in certain instances, you should select work you know is suited to the taste of the particular client you are meeting. If you are presenting work to a magazine, for example, it is often possible to get a clear idea of the kind of pictures it is in the market for by studying back issues closely.

Your portfolio must combine two qualities—it must be stimulating and memorable. Remember that, in every presentation you make, your work will be competing against rivals. You should enlarge, or at least alter, the contents at intervals. If you have a changing flow of work, your portfolio will always have something fresh and new in it. There is nothing worse than returning again and again to the same editor, with exactly the same work to show.

The comments that potential clients make on your pictures will naturally vary; if nothing else, different reactions to the same photographs will confirm the subjectivity of art direction.

RIGHT: A good portfolio is the basis of every professional photographer's working career. As transparencies are the preferred medium, black cardboard window mounts are an ideal solution.

Presentation and Display

Attractive presentation of your work is vital if you hope to make any sales. Choose your best pictures and organize them to show the full range of your work—indoor and outdoor shots, close-ups, and full figures. A portfolio with a ring binder system will present them easily and attractively to your potential clients. Any published material—pages from magazines and so on—should be neatly presented. Some of your very best shots could be made into laminated prints. These are of high quality and can look very good, although they are expensive.

Do not necessarily take every comment to heart, but, if comments made at several presentations warrant it, you should decide whether to add or discard photographs from your presentation.

Displaying Your Work

Although content is the most important element in the portfolio, you should go to maximum lengths to ensure that your pictures are displayed to the best possible effect.

Published work should play a special part in any presentation. It shows that you have an established track record; this will make a new client feel confident about commissioning you. Always collect printed copies of your work; if possible, obtain final proofs from the publisher as well, since these are sometimes of higher quality than the printed version. Have such material laminated professionally (a number of companies provide a laminating service specifically for presentations and portfolios, with a choice of backing materials, borders, and finishes). The final product not only looks professional, but it also protects your work at the same time.

As many publishers now produce material in an entirely digital format, right up to sending it to the printers, it can be worthwhile asking for Adobe Portable Document Format (PDF) files so that you can either email them to potential clients or have them printed out at a later date.

The normal way of presenting work is in the form of color transparencies that are viewed on a lightbox. The best way to present transparencies is mounted in sets. Black cardboard mounting, available from any photographic store, shows off color to its best advantage. Print your name and telephone number on the mount cards.

Color prints are more useful in the initial stages of presentation. Make a selection of your best transparencies and have them enlarged, printed, and laminated. Such prints can illustrate more clearly the quality of your work. Small prints can be used to demonstrate the broad range and style of the stock of pictures you have built up, but a few really high-quality, large prints of your very best shots will give a more appealing impression of how good your pictures will look enlarged—particularly if you do not have published work to show.

A website will showcase your work on a full-time basis without you needing to be there, so ensure that only your best images are represented. Many website authoring packages include a gallery function that will create a virtual arrangement of thumbnails in the form of slides. Once clicked on, each image is then displayed at a higher resolution. This is far preferable to a page full of slowly loading, high-resolution pictures. As a general point, if you cannot afford to have a website professionally designed and maintained, use a web authoring package with plenty of templates so that the design has a slick look.

Creating a Calendar

A calendar is one of the most rewarding commissions for any glamour photographer. Not only are you able to convey a theme or message in a series of pictures, but it is also extremely satisfying to see your photographs on display, rather than between the covers of a magazine. Even for a top professional, though, there is no sure way of securing a calendar assignment or even guaranteeing that you will hold the account from one year to the next.

Glamour calendars are big business. Because many companies use them as major advertising vehicles, budgets are usually fairly high. You will be working with top models and a first-rate design team. In return, you must deliver a high-quality product to the client. If you get it right, the calendar will grace the walls of homes, bars, offices, and factories for a full year and the company will be delighted with the promotion. If you get it wrong, the calendar will quickly end up in the trashcan and you can cross that client off your books.

Most large organizations are usually willing to see an established photographer for a presentation. If the meeting goes well, the photographer is invited to show some concrete ideas and designs for the calendar. The photographer who gets the jobs is the one who, in the opinion of the art director and marketing manager, has offered the best idea for the concept.

Obviously, not all calendar assignments fall into the league of big budgets, expert art direction, top models, and exotic locations. As in all glamour photography, there are different levels to which to aspire. Nevertheless, if you are persistent, have good ideas, and the ability to carry them through, you will probably be able to break into some area of the calendar market. Remember that working within the limits of a tight budget should never be inhibiting; it should be a challenge and incentive to find the right creative solution for the right price.

The Tricks of Retouching

It is a fact of life that on the day of the shoot your model will suddenly burst into spots, or reveal a blemish or scar that she had not revealed previously. Sometimes it can simply be that underwear marks have not faded when the shot was taken. By careful research in the first place, retouching the model because she has basic flaws should be kept to a minimum. However, there are two circumstances that invariably involve lots of retouching, which is now done

Calendar Commission

For an important calendar commission, considerable backup may be available from the clients. Here, the agency's art department produced roughs of the types of shot they wanted—all contributing to the careful planning.

ABOVE: One shot used an old MG sports car in the California desert. In the afternoon there were interruptions from traffic and the light offered llittle atmosphere.
85–210mm zoom lens, Kodachrome 25, 1/60 sec at f5.6

ABOVE: When the sun was going down over the mountains in the evening, a more interesting light was achieved. Reflectors added light to the model.
85–210mm zoom lens, Kodachrome 25, 1/15 sec at f5.6

ABOVE: As the darkness increased, another shot was tried using car headlamps for the illumination. The desert can no longer be seen.
85–210mm zoom lens, Kodachrome 25, 1/4 sec at f5.6

ABOVE: A typical modern calendar-style image with the main flash causing reflections on the sequinned skirt and a blue gel light adding extra interest.
28–70mm zoom lens, digital ISO 100, 1/125 sec at f11

on computer rather than on negatives. The first is for the amateur using would-be or inexperienced models. The model can be working for free so standards are not as high and retouching may be needed to make her look really special. The other instance is that at the professional end, particularly using celebrity models, their image is their fortune so retouching is de rigueur. All flaws must be removed and the model made thinner, curvier, and the image given a glossy finish that is impossible to create directly on film. Learning to use Photoshop may help your image presentation but it is important to realize that getting a good model in the first place will cut down on your time spent retouching, which is time you are not getting paid for.

ABOVE: Even after carefully researching your choice of model, there are times when the reality does not quite match up. Whether the promo photos were five years old or the model has had a late night, the only alternative to canceling the shoot is to go ahead anyway and improve the photographs digitally later. The first headshot (top) is unretouched, while the second one (above) has been substantially improved through digital editing in Photoshop.
35–105mm zoom lens, digital ISO 100, 1/15 sec at f8

Agents and Agencies

When you first turn professional, you should remember that there are considerably more photographers looking for agents than there are agents looking for photographers. Finding an agent at all, therefore, is not necessarily easy, while finding the right agent for you as an individual can be even harder. In the first place, you must have attained a certain professional standard before an agent will generally agree to represent you. In normal circumstances, agents are interested only in representing photographers commanding high fees; otherwise, it is not worth their time and effort trying to find you work. Equally, it is hardly worth your while to pay large commissions to an agent who rarely gets you assignments.

If, however, you start to find that administration, paperwork, and knocking on doors are using up valuable time that could be better spent behind a camera, the chances are that you are ready to join forces with an agent. Usually, agents work for a commission of around 50 percent if the material is from stock, and approximately 25 percent if the photographs are commissioned. The relationship between photographer and agent can vary from a formal arrangement to handle your stock shots, with little or no personal contact, to close involvement with all aspects of your career.

The most important requirement between agent and photographer is mutual trust. Before you sign any agreement with an agent, it is important to get a number of issues clear to avoid the possibility of any misunderstanding. The following are the basic questions that any professional glamour photographer should ask before coming to such an agreement.

What exactly is the agent's commission and does it apply to all work you do, or just the jobs the agent secures for you? Is he or she your sole agent, or can you be represented by someone else in countries where the agent has no representation? How and when will you be paid for the work you have done? Will you or the agent be responsible for the cost of presentations? If the agency changes ownership or closes down, do you have a contractual right to immediate return of your material?

Unless you are well established, it is unlikely that you will be lucky enough to have an agent who is able to work solely on your behalf, assuming responsibility for almost everything except the actual taking of photographs. Indeed, it is probably unwise for a photographer to relinquish all administrative involvement. Apart from enhancing the commitment to a job, it can also be extremely exciting to see an assignment through from beginning to end.

Stock Agencies

Far more likely for the photographer who is making progress is the option to use stock agencies. This means that you remain a free agent, able to select your own models, deciding for yourself what photographs to take of whom and when.

To register with such an agency, you will probably have to submit at least 200 photographs representative of a large selection of your work. Once accepted by the agency, you can send additional batches at regular intervals. Such libraries are not only extremely efficient, they are also in regular contact with buyers all over the world. They know whom to approach with which photographs and can often be more successful in securing high fees. In addition, a library with a good reputation will be used regularly by picture researchers for top-quality publications.

However, relying on stock agencies does have its drawbacks. The initial expenses—model and location fees, cost of film stock, and so on—are the photographer's alone; unless you are confident that your pictures will sell, you will find yourself heavily out of pocket. A stock agency can charge anything between 20 and 90 percent commission and will pay you only after it has been paid by the people buying your photographs. It can therefore sometimes take several months before you see any financial return on your work. Obviously, if you are placing images with an agency that charges a high commission rate, it is important that they are able to charge top-rate fees for them for it to be worth your time.

The best policy is probably to forget about the photographs the minute you lodge them with an agency. Though you may find this to be a regular source of income, the acid test, as always, is whether your work is good or commercial enough to sell. If, however, you intend to invest in expensive model fees or location work abroad, it is worth checking beforehand to ensure that the agency is interested in and will distribute your work. There is never any guarantee that an agency will take all your photographs, so it is important that you are familiar with the marketplace and are able to judge its requirements as much as possible. With experience, you will soon get to know what is acceptable and what is not. On the other hand, you are always better off relying on your own standards and taste, because this is the only way of developing your own style. Compromise will only win you a reputation for mediocrity that will be hard to shake off.

All stock library material is now scanned so that originals or poor-quality duplicates no longer have to be sent out to clients. The good news for digital photographers is that a lot of agencies are now accepting digital photos, not just scanned film, because they cut down on overheads enormously.

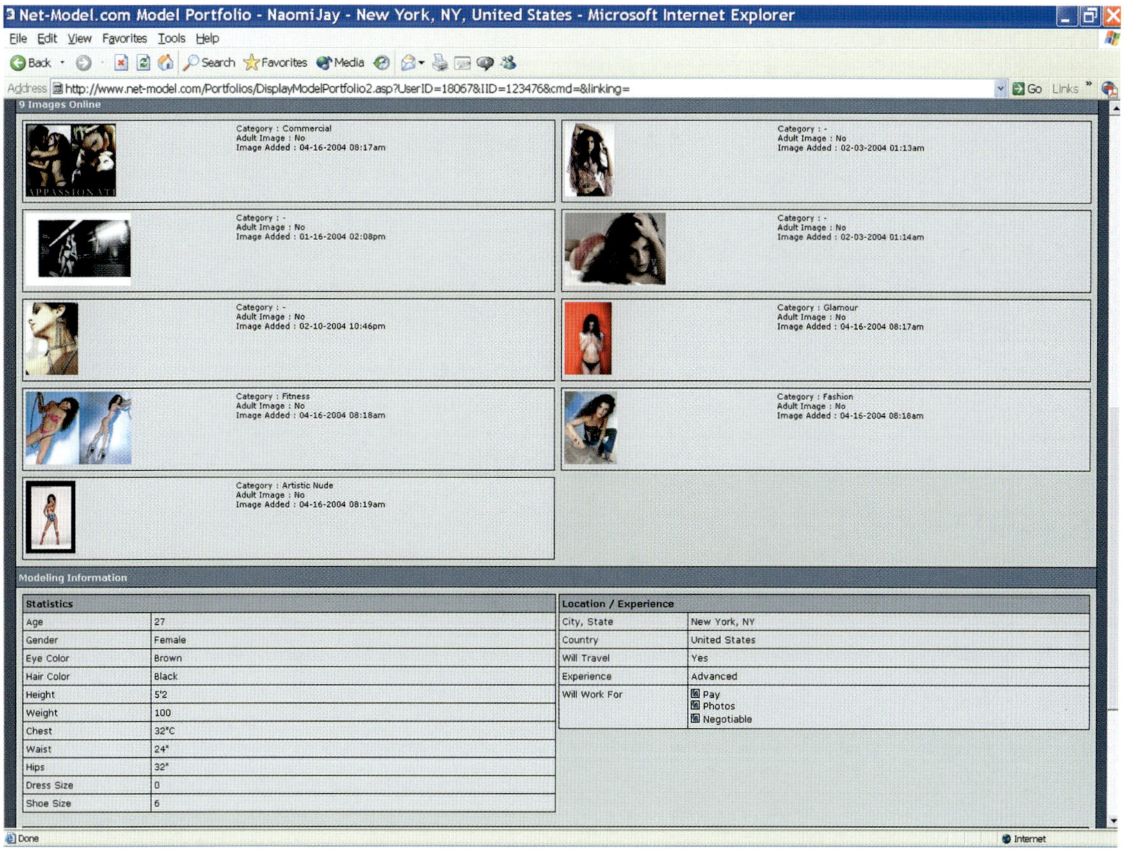

LEFT: Finding models, and models advertising themselves, has been made much easier thanks to the internet. This website—www.net-models.com—is mainly US and UK but covers other countries around the world, and allows models to display portfolios of their work. This enables the photographer to browse for someone who fits the bill and to carry out detailed searches of the online database for people near the location shoot. Photographers can also show off their portfolio of finest images on this particular site.

However, they will need to be technically excellent, require no enhancement, and be shot at 6Mp resolution as a minimum.

Developing a good working relationship with your agency is extremely important. You must not ask them to syndicate work you have already sold independently in any circumstances. Unless the agency knows it has sole distribution rights to your work, it will not make any effort on your behalf and both parties will suffer accordingly.

In general, stock sales usually work best for photographers who shoot a large amount of material in the normal course of their careers and so find the extra sales a pleasant bonus. With persistence, however, it is possible to make it your main activity, particularly in the glamour field.

Model Agencies

In the professional world, just as much can depend on the quality of the model as on that of the photographer. Model agencies are therefore a vital part of the glamour photographer's world. Many photographers prefer to work through an agency if they need a model for a specific job. By doing so, they are guaranteed certain standards and are saved the problems that often arise when a model is unsure of herself and the situation. This is not to say that such photographers will not work with a model who is not attached to an agency. If someone is worth photographing, her status is irrelevant, but sooner or later most successful models are represented by agencies in order to procure regular work.

Samantha Bond runs an agency that specializes in glamour models. As a former model herself, she is acutely aware of the needs not only of her models, but also of clients and photographers. "Glamour models are different from fashion models," she explains, "in that they are generally prettier in the conventional sense and must have a good figure. While they have to be slim (the camera adds 14lb all over), they cannot be bony or flat-chested."

To these qualities, Bond also adds those of dedication and enormous stamina. "Professional models are paid good rates," she says, "and for this they are often expected to work long hours under difficult conditions and still appear fresh and alluring. They must know exactly what they look like and how to project in a certain way on command." With such exacting standards, it is not surprising that few models make the grade.

"Getting a good set of photographs is essential for any model," Bond explains, "and, in order to cut costs all around, we often work with photographers who want to build up their portfolios. Neither the model, nor the photographer, charges a fee for their services, so everyone benefits." This also applies to semi-pro models who advertise on modeling websites. The aspiring photographer can often find would-be models who will work for a set of prints or images on CD. Be aware that there is a boom in would-be models and that most of them are, in fact, deluding themselves. Check out photos of any potential partners in a project before committing yourself, unless you simply need the experience.

Most agencies charge 20 percent of the overall fee for matching model and client. Hourly and daily rates are set, but trips are usually negotiable, since the model is not required to work all the time. Also, it is normal practice for overseas assignments to involve, or be regarded as, perks and the fees tend to reflect this point of view.

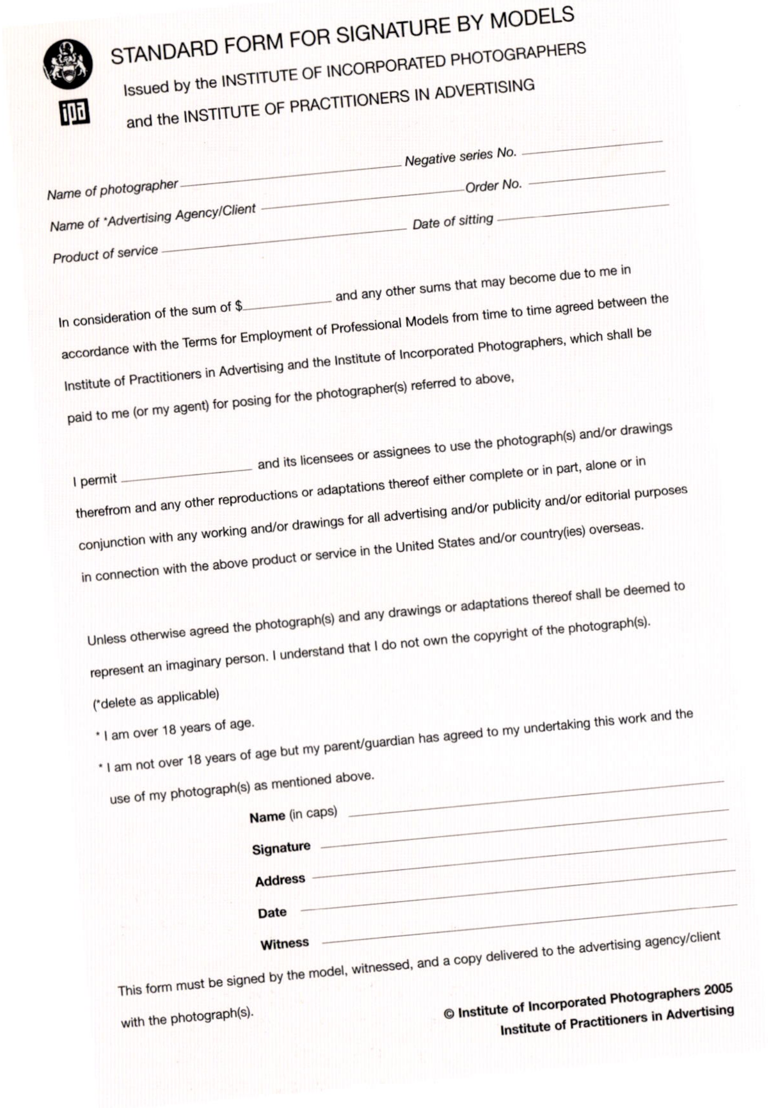

STANDARD FORM FOR SIGNATURE BY MODELS

Issued by the INSTITUTE OF INCORPORATED PHOTOGRAPHERS

and the INSTITUTE OF PRACTITIONERS IN ADVERTISING

Name of photographer ______________________ Negative series No. ______________

Name of *Advertising Agency/Client ______________________ Order No. ______________

Product of service ______________________ Date of sitting ______________

In consideration of the sum of $__________ and any other sums that may become due to me in accordance with the Terms for Employment of Professional Models from time to time agreed between the Institute of Practitioners in Advertising and the Institute of Incorporated Photographers, which shall be paid to me (or my agent) for posing for the photographer(s) referred to above,

I permit ______________ and its licensees or assignees to use the photograph(s) and/or drawings therefrom and any other reproductions or adaptations thereof either complete or in part, alone or in conjunction with any working and/or drawings for all advertising and/or publicity and/or editorial purposes in connection with the above product or service in the United States and/or country(ies) overseas.

Unless otherwise agreed the photograph(s) and any drawings or adaptations thereof shall be deemed to represent an imaginary person. I understand that I do not own the copyright of the photograph(s).

(*delete as applicable)

* I am over 18 years of age.

* I am not over 18 years of age but my parent/guardian has agreed to my undertaking this work and the use of my photograph(s) as mentioned above.

Name (in caps) ______________________

Signature ______________________

Address ______________________

Date ______________________

Witness ______________________

This form must be signed by the model, witnessed, and a copy delivered to the advertising agency/client with the photograph(s).

© Institute of Incorporated Photographers 2005
Institute of Practitioners in Advertising

LEFT: A basic model-release form covering a photoshoot. Typically, you should mention what the shoot is about, where it is, and the date, so that there can be no counterclaim regarding the photos at a later date.

Model Releases

To avoid the risk of misunderstandings, it is important that the model signs a release form, giving you permission to use any photographs you take of her. This should contain her name, address, and age and assign all copyright to the photographs to yourself. One procedure is to sign such a release after the photographs have been taken, since your model should be happy with the way the session went and is content to let you have the results published. If, however, she indicates that she will only allow the photographs to be used in a specific publication, it is vital that you agree this before you take any pictures at all. Occasionally, a model will insist on seeing the photographs before she signs a release, but this is very rare with professionals. You may prefer to get the paperwork done before the shoot begins so that the model understands and signs the form first and you do not waste your time photographing her. Make this clear at the outset to avoid any problems.

Studying the Market

Without an agent or stock agency, it will be an extremely difficult and expensive process to get your work syndicated. However, it is not an impossible one. All over the world, there are magazines and publications looking for good-quality glamour photographs. If your models are beautiful and your work professional enough, you should certainly get your photographs published. Picture editors of magazines, in particular, are always searching for new talent.

If you have a set, or number of sets, of photographs to sell, present them in the best way possible. If you are aiming for a commission, prepare an idea in advance, keeping in mind editorial and artistic policy. Better still, bring some good pictures of the model you intend to use with you. It is vital that your work is of a high enough standard to convince an editor that you are capable of executing your ideas effectively. There is no point in having brilliant concepts but an inadequate portfolio.

Remember, too, that one of the greatest assets any photographer can possess is a good model. Many photographers' careers have been launched on the strength of a successful partnership with a new, exciting model.

LEFT: This spread from a recent glamour book shows that there is potential for getting your photos published around the world. However, unless you happen to be the book author, the fees for inclusion in such works is usually not high.

What Mens Magazines Look For

There are two branches of male-interest magazines that publish glamour photos. The first is the so-called "lads mag," popularized by titles such as *Loaded* and *FHM*. Here, the glamour is softer, more lingerie-based, and does not involve full-frontal nudity. However, the model will need to be outstanding and the lighting and technique innovative and fresh. If you can manage this, you should be able to sell your images. The other magazine market is the "top-shelf" one, populated by *Playboy* and such titles. Here, the images are much more graphic. There are also subdivisions, with the *Playboy*-type titles at the top end of the market demanding first-rate models placed in quality settings. The models must be beautiful and possess real desirability. Farther downmarket the models still need to be highly attractive, but in a girl-next-door style. Innovation of location is the key here and the beginner can find a ready market for good-quality photo sets.

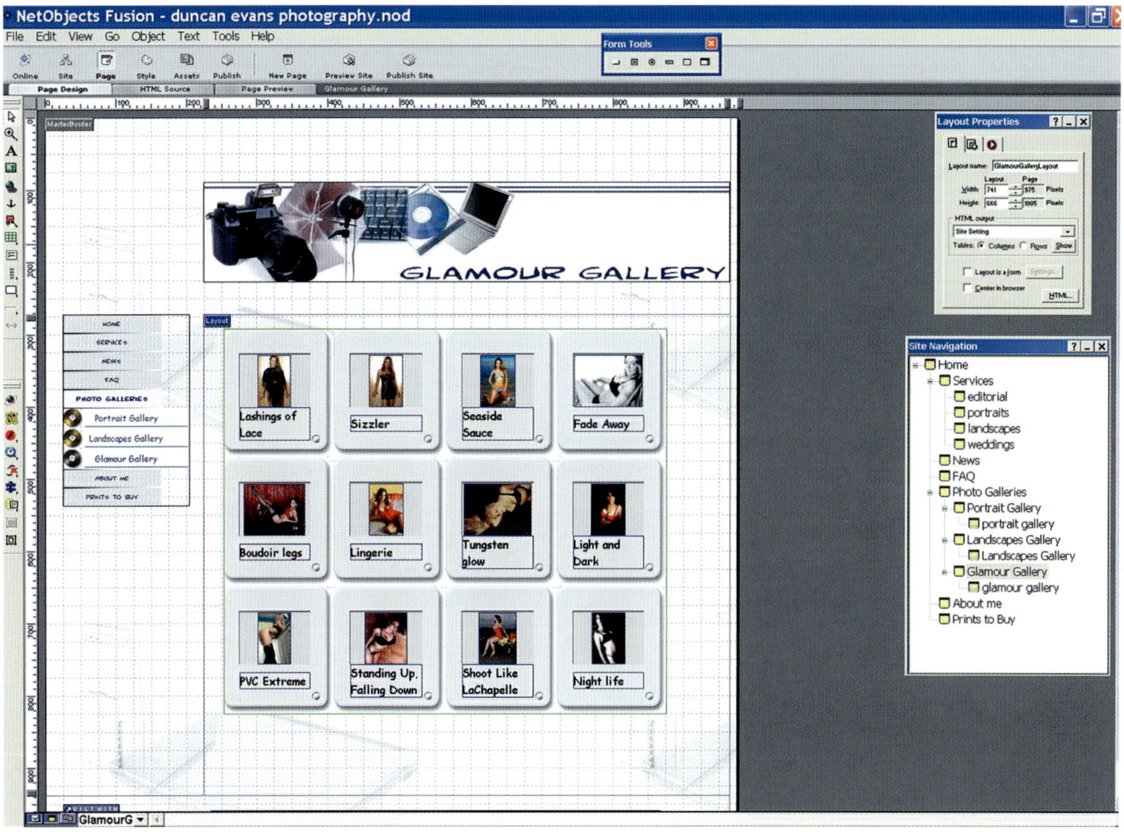

LEFT: Creating your own website is relatively easy thanks to website creation software such as NetObjects Fusion. A website is almost essential for any photographer starting out because it acts as a virtual advertisement for your skills.

Fees

When starting a professional career, gaining experience is more important than anything else. Never overprice yourself or turn down a job because the fee is low. It is only by doing a lot of work—some, indeed, outside the glamour field—that you will be able to establish yourself as a true professional.

Nevertheless, it is important to know what you are worth. If you have an agent, or are registered with a stock agency, they will be able to guide you. However, very few beginners have this advantage. By contacting any of the major photographers associations, such as the American Society of Magazine Photographers in the US and the Association of Fashion, Advertising, and Editorial Photographers in the UK, you can ascertain what is the general scale of fees. Remember, though, that such figures only serve as guidelines. For the most part, photographers sell their services on a free market.

Magazines offer standard rates for uncommissioned photographs, no matter how much it cost you to set up the shot. Commissions are negotiable; the fee will obviously reflect the amount of work and skill involved. If special effects or elaborate sets are called for, the fee will obviously be higher than that for a more straightforward photograph.

The highest fees are found in advertising. The logistics of an advertising assignment can be complex; a one-day shoot can require several days of preparation. While the client may carry a large part of the preproduction burden, the photographer is still expected to contribute heavily. Make sure you agree to your fee in advance and what is expected for it in writing. This rule applies to all assignments.

Copyright

Copyright law varies from country to country. There are also differences in the degree to which the law may be interpreted. You should be aware of the copyright laws of the country in which you are based and of any country to which you may be selling work.

In the US and UK, the owner of the copyright is the photographer in nearly all cases. The main exception is in the case of staff photographers, where the employer retains copyright. You can, of course, surrender your copyright, so examine any contract carefully before you sign it if you object to such a clause. Also, in order to publish or use photos featuring a model commercially, you must have a model-release form so that there can be no claim from a third party over copyright. It is generally accepted that unless you have a signed model-release form, your photos are unusable for commercial purposes. In all cases, establish in writing who holds the copyright for any work done before you take on an assignment.

As a general rule of thumb, you hold copyright for any photographs you take independently at your own expense. These you are free to sell several times over, or to assign permission for their use, unless you make an agreement to the contrary. In commissioned work, the copyright is retained by the person who commissioned you.

Regardless of the legal position, there are certain ethical standards that any professional photographer would be foolish to breach. If a client is led to believe, for instance, that he has an exclusive on a photograph that is subsequently published elsewhere, he will almost certainly refuse to do business with that photographer again. If you want to publish or display any work in which you do not hold the copyright, contact the person who does and ask for permission to use it. Unless there is a conflict of interests, you will usually be given permission, provided you credit the copyright holder. In the event of a dispute, it is essential to seek professional advice.

Index

Page numbers in *italics* refer to photographs/captions

Credits

Quarto would like to thank and acknowledge the following photographers for kindly supplying images for inclusion in this book.

Key: a above; b below; c center; l left; r right

1 & 2 Dan Howell; 4a Duncan Evans; 4b Manfred Baumann; 5 Dan Howell; 6–7 Paul Jones; 8–9ac Martin Grainger; 8–9bc Paul Jones; 9ar Duncan Evans; 9br Dan Howell; 10bl Duncan Evans; 10br Steve Greenlees; 11 Duncan Evans; 12a & c John Kelly; 13al & ar Duncan Evans; 14 John Kelly; 15bl & bc Duncan Evans; 16–17b Duncan Evans; 17br Manfred Baumann; 18bl Duncan Evans; 18–19a Martin Christie; 19bl & br John Kelly; 20a John Kelly; 21bl & bc Duncan Evans; 22a & c John Kelly; 23 Duncan Evans; 24a Paul Jones; 24b Manfred Baumann; 25l Paul Jones; 25r John Kelly; 26 & 27 John Kelly; 28al, ar, & bl John Kelly; 28c Duncan Evans; 28br Paul Jones; 29 John Kelly; 30 Manfred Baumann; 31 Duncan Evans; 32bc Paul Jones; 32bl & r John Kelly; 33 & 34 Duncan Evans; 35 Dan Howell; 36l John Kelly; 36r Dan Howell; 37 Paul Jones; 38 & 39 John Kelly; 40a & 41r Dan Howell; 42bl John Kelly; 43al Duncan Evans; 44l John Pirrie; 44r Manfred Baumann; 45l Paul Jones; 45r Dan Howell; 46 John Kelly; 47l Dan Howell; 47r Manfred Baumann; 48a & c John Kelly; 48b Steve Greenlees; 49 Dan Howell; 50 & 51 John Kelly; 52 Dan Howell; 53a John Pirrie; 53b John Kelly; 54 & 55 Manfred Baumann; 56l John Pirrie; 56r Dan Howell; 57l Martin Grainger; 57r, 58al, cl, & bl John Kelly; 58cr Martin Grainger; 59 John Kelly; 60l Duncan Evans; 60r, 61, & 62bl John Pirrie; 62ac Paul Jones; 62–63c, 63ar, br, & 64 John Kelly; 65 Dan Howell; 66 & 67al Manfred Baumann; 67ar, cl, cr, bl, & br John Kelly; 68ar Martin Grainger; 68cl, bl, 69, & 70l John Kelly; 70r Manfred Baumann; 71 Duncan Evans; 72, 73bl, & br John Kelly; 73a John Pirrie; 74cl, cr, & b John Kelly; 74ar & 75al Dan Howell; 75bl Manfred Baumann; 75br Duncan Evans; 76 John Kelly; 77a Manfred Baumann; 77b John Kelly; 78a Manfred Baumann; 78b, 79, & 80 John Kelly; 81a Duncan Evans; 81bl & br John Kelly; 82a Duncan Evans; 82b & 83 Dan Howell; 84 John Kelly; 85 Dan Howell; 86a & bl John Kelly; 86br Dan Howell; 87a Manfred Baumann; 87c, b, & 88b John Kelly; 88–89c Dan Howell; 89ar John Kelly; 89bl & br Manfred Baumann; 90al & c John Kelly; 90ar Manfred Baumann; 90cr, bl, br, & 91 Dan Howell; 92ar & cr John Kelly; 92cl, bl, & br Manfred Baumann; 93al John Kelly; 93ar Dan Howell; 93bl Manfred Baumann; 94a & c John Kelly; 94b Manfred Baumann; 95 & 96b John Kelly; 96a & 97b Manfred Baumann; 97a John Kelly; 98a Duncan Evans; 98–99bc & 99br John Kelly; 100 Manfred Baumann; 101 & 102 John Kelly; 103 Manfred Baumann; 104a John Kelly; 104b & 105a Manfred Baumann; 105b John Kelly; 106–107al & 107br John Kelly; 107ar Dan Howell; 108a Paul Jones; 108b Kevin Wyllie; 109l Manfred Baumann; 109r John Kelly; 110 & 111r Duncan Evans; 111l Paul Jones; 112 Manfred Baumann; 113a Paul Jones; 113bl & br Duncan Evans; 114l John Kelly; 114ar & br Dan Howell; 115, 116al & bl John Kelly; 116ar & 117 Dan Howell; 118, 120, 121, & 122 Duncan Evans; 123a Dan Howell; 123b & 125a Manfred Baumann; 125b Dan Howell; 126al Duncan Evans; 126ar & bl Manfred Baumann; 127al Dan Howell; 127ac, ar, c, & cr Paul Jones; 127bl & br John Kelly; 128 Dan Howell; 129a John Pirrie; 129b Paul Jones; 130–131a Manfred Baumann; 132–147 John Kelly; 148a Manfred Baumann; 148b Duncan Evans; 149a Dan Howell; 149b Manfred Baumann; 150 & 151 David Kimber/Chas Wilder; 152 John Kelly; 153al Dan Howell; 153ar & br Duncan Evans.

The work of contributing photographers can be viewed at the following websites:

- Manfred Baumann—www.manfredbaumann.com
- Martin Christie—www.martinchristie.tk
- Duncan Evans LRPS—www.duncanevans.co.uk
- Martin Grainger—www.uk-new-media.co.uk
- Steve Greenlees—www.outlooks.co.uk
- Dan Howell—www.danhowell.com
- Paul Jones—www.pauljones.org
- John Pirrie—http://members.lycos.co.uk/dangerpics
- Kevin Wyllie—www.kevinwyllie.com